TENSIONS AND TRANSITIONS
(1869–1990)
The Mediating Imagination
for Ian Gregor

Edited by Michael Irwin,
Mark Kinkead-Weekes
and A. Robert Lee

faber and faber
LONDON · BOSTON

The publishers gratefully
acknowledge the support of
The Kent Society

First published in 1990
by Faber and Faber Limited
3 Queen Square London WC1N 3AU

Photoset by Parker Typesetting Service Leicester
Printed in England by Clays Ltd, St Ives plc

All rights reserved

This collection © Faber and Faber, 1990

A CIP record for this book is
available from the British Library

ISBN 0–571–14396–2

Ian Gregor

Liturgical Merrygoround

for Ian Gregor

All green Sundays
follow after
white and red

All green Sundays
end in
violet

Man's life used to
end in
black and gold

Now for the death
we have
white   gold

any colour you
like   Perhaps
we think more

of the resurrection
of the flesh
perhaps we're saints

(interval for laughter and recreation   coffee and doughnuts)

perhaps we're idiots
Kahil Gibran   Ayn Rand
all that jazz

But under the motley
(thank God)
the same performance

J. M. Cameron

Contents

Notes on Contributors	ix
Introduction	xiii
1 Ford Madox Ford's Opening World: A Story of the Modern Movement by Malcolm Bradbury	1
2 Going Back to Pater and Wilde by Denis Donoghue	27
3 Voices Across the Echoing Straits. Dialogue, Translation and Irony in Arnold and Clough by Miriam Allott	47
4 Seriousness and Triviality: Towards *The Importance of Being Earnest* by Brian Nicholas	65
5 Thresholds and Verges: Hardy Imagines Imagination by Barbara Hardy	82
6 Odd Man Out? Henry James, The Canon and *The Princess Casamassima* by A. Robert Lee	103
7 To the Sulaco Lighthouse by M. M. Mahood	121
8 Late Turner, Hardy's Tess and Lawrence's Knees by Howard Mills	137
9 Present Laughter – Reading Our Contemporaries by Michael Irwin	155
10 Pinter and Politics: Re-entering *No Man's Land* by R. A. Foakes	167
11 Fact and Fiction in the Novel: An Author's Note by David Lodge	185
12 Word and World by Laurence Lerner	203
13 From Ascesis to Conversion: René Girard and the Idea of Vocation in Modernist Writing by Stephen Bann	216
14 Glimpses of 'Gregor' by Mark Kinkead-Weekes	236
15 Ian Gregor: A Bibliography. Compiled by Louis James	253
Index	256

Notes on Contributors

Miriam Allott has held professorships at the universities of Liverpool and London and written extensively on nineteenth-century poetry and fiction. She is editor of the complete poems of Keats and of Arnold for Longman (works first edited in 1969 by her late husband Kenneth Allott). She is currently completing with Nicholas Shrimpton an edition of the poems of Matthew Arnold for Oxford University Press and is also working on a critical biography of Arthur Hugh Clough for Faber & Faber.
Stephen Bann is Professor of Modern Cultural Studies at the University of Kent. He was co-translator of René Girard's *Things Hidden Since the Foundation of the World*, and is planning a volume of essays on the implications of his work. His most recent book is *The True Vine: On Visual Representation and the Western Tradition* (1989).
Malcolm Bradbury is a well-known novelist and critic, and Professor of American Studies at the University of East Anglia. His novels include *Eating People is Wrong* (1959), *The History Man* (1975), *Rates of Exchange* (1983) and *Cuts* (1987). His criticism includes *The Modern American Novel* (1983) and the essay collection *No, Not Bloomsbury* (1983). He has frequently written on Modernism, co-editing the *Pelican Guide to European Literature: Modernism* (1976; rev. edn, 1985) and writing *The Modern World: Ten Great Writers* (1988). He also teaches creative writing and writes much television drama.
Denis Donoghue holds the Henry James Chair of English and American Letters at New York University. His most recent books are *We Irish* (1986), *Reading America* (1987) and *England, Their England* (1988). His new book, *Warrenpoint*, a memoir of his childhood in Northern Ireland, will be published in late 1990 by Knopf. He is currently working on a book to be called *Modernity*.

NOTES ON CONTRIBUTORS

R. A. Foakes, who now teaches at the University of California at Los Angeles, was founding Professor of English at the University of Kent, where he counted himself fortunate to have Ian Gregor as one of his first colleagues and friends. His recent publications include an edition of S. T. Coleridge's *Lectures 1808–1819: On Literature* (Princeton, 1987) and *Illustrations of the English Stage 1580–1642* (London and Stanford, 1985).

Barbara Hardy is a Professor Emeritus of London University, having until recently held the Chair of English Literature at Birkbeck College. Her work has been particularly concerned with nineteenth-century fiction, and includes books on Austen, Dickens, Thackeray and George Eliot. *Forms of Feeling in Victorian Fiction* was published in 1985 and *Narrators and Novelists* in 1987.

Michael Irwin is Professor of English Literature at the University of Kent. He taught previously at universities in Poland and Japan, and at Smith College. His academic publications include *Henry Fielding, the Tentative Realist* (1967) and *Picturing: Description and Illusion in the Nineteenth-Century Novel* (1980). He has also written two novels and translated a number of opera libretti.

Louis James has lectured in various universities in Europe, the United States and the Commonwealth. He is currently Professor of Victorian and Modern English Literature at the University of Kent. He has written books and articles in the fields of nineteenth-century and Commonwealth literature, including *Fiction for the Working Man* (1963, Rev. edition, 1975), *Print and the People* (1976) and *Jean Rhys* (1978).

Mark Kinkead-Weekes came from Edinburgh to be in at the beginning of the University of Kent, and, having been Pro-Vice-Chancellor, is now Professor Emeritus there. He wrote a study of William Golding (with Ian Gregor) in 1967 and one on Samuel Richardson in 1973 (without). He has lately been working on D. H. Lawrence, having edited the Cambridge University Press *Rainbow* and embarked on the volume covering 1912 to 1922 in the forthcoming Cambridge biography.

A. Robert Lee is Senior Lecturer in English and American Literature at the University of Kent. He is the author of *James Baldwin: Climbing to the Light* (1990) and the BAAS (British Association of American Studies) monograph *Black American Literature Since Richard Wright* (1983), and has edited the Everyman

NOTES ON CONTRIBUTORS

Moby-Dick (1975) and twelve essay collections in the Vision Critical Series, among them *Herman Melville: Reassessments* (1984), *Edgar Allan Poe: The Design of Order* (1986), *Scott Fitzgerald: The Promises of Life* (1989) and *William Faulkner: The Yoknapatawpha Fiction* (1990). He has taught frequently in the United States, broadcasts for BBC Radio and reviews for *The Listener*.

Laurence Lerner is Kenan Professor of English at Vanderbilt University, Nashville, Tennessee, and Professorial Fellow of the University of Sussex. His most recent book is *The Frontiers of Literature* (1988), an attempt at the practical application of literary theory, which discusses the nature of literature by exploring its overlap with contiguous forms of writing. He is also an established poet.

David Lodge is Honorary Professor of Modern English Literature at the University of Birmingham, where he taught until 1987. He is the author of several books of criticism, including *Language of Fiction* (1966), *The Modes of Modern Writing* (1977) and *Working with Structuralism* (1981), and eight novels, of which the most recent is *Nice Work* (1988).

M. M. Mahood taught in London, Oxford, Ibadan and Dar es Salaam, before joining Ian Gregor at the University of Kent, where she is now Professor Emeritus. His first book was on seventeenth-century poetry, and Shakespeare remains her prime interest, but she has also published studies of Third World literature and of the literature of colonialism.

Howard Mills is Senior Lecturer in English at the University of Kent. He has written on Shakespeare, Peacock and Lawrence, and has edited Crabbe and Wordsworth. With his colleague David Ellis he published *D. H. Lawrence's Non-Fiction: Art, Thought and Genre* (1988).

Brian Nicholas is Lecturer in French at the University of Sussex. He collaborated with Ian Gregor in *The Moral and the Story* (1962) and shares with him a longstanding interest in Oscar Wilde.

Introduction

The essays that follow are all concerned, in their various ways, with writings that have the built-in tension of an attempt to resolve contrarieties. Some deal with a transition of sensibility, a period in which established modes of vision and expression are displaced by new ones. Others explore the efforts of some particular author to pursue apparently discrepant aims – though here, too, the divergent pressures are as likely to derive from the age as from the individual sensibility. The collection as a whole amply illustrates the peculiar capacity of literature both to display such oppositions within its very strategies and to suggest how they might be accommodated.

Yet the conception that holds these essays pretty closely together was not originally a neat abstraction. Our project was to pursue the interests of a single scholar, Professor Ian Gregor. As will later emerge, the progress of his career, which comprehended and wove together radically contrasting experiences, seemed to us to be paradigmatic of certain valuable traditions in postwar education – traditions that have been damagingly eroded in recent years. But it is also the case that his academic concerns have been peculiarly all of a piece, not – emphatically not – because located within a narrow area, but because there is a marked pattern within their apparent diversity. The pattern seemed to offer intriguing possibilities of further exploration.

We put the idea to prospective contributors in figurative terms:

Within Ian Gregor's literary criticism three metaphors have recurred: a chasm with a bridge over it (an image which lies behind titles where 'and' joins two unlikely nouns, pointing to both disjunction and connection); a fissure or stress-fracture, to peer into which is to see how apparent solidity is sustained or indeed created by opposing pressures;

INTRODUCTION

and a web, in which the weave and the gaps that the weave encloses are seen as mutually defining.

Our potential essayists were invited to pursue the implications of these metaphors, to investigate some of the ways in which literature mediates between opposing energies. None of them refused or demurred; all saw the point of the exercise. Though no chronological limits had been set, the contributions, almost without exception, proved to concern writers who flourished after the publication in 1869 of *Culture and Anarchy*. While the pattern happens to reflect Ian Gregor's own literary preferences, there is surely more to it than that. Arnold perceived the divisions in his own society, and was one of the first notable exponents of the text 'only connect'. But further stresses were to ensue with the disruptive emergence of Modernism, and Modernism itself was to dilate and divide. The capacity of literature to define antimonies and to harmonize them was to be tested almost to breaking-point in the later Victorian period and through the twentieth century. This collection of essays is among other things a commentary on that testing process.

The editors have met with willing cooperation and assistance on all sides, but would like particularly to acknowledge the help of Sian Dixon, Bob Gibson, Roland Hurst, Jim Styles and Sheila Taylor. Nick Wells most kindly took on the compilation of the index, a task which put us greatly in his debt. We would also especially want to thank The Kent Society for its generous support in the making of this book.

Michael Irwin
Mark Kinkead-Weekes
A. Robert Lee

1 Ford Madox Ford's Opening World: A Story of the Modern Movement

Malcolm Bradbury

I

Ian Gregor's interests have frequently led him to look at the great eras of artistic transition – the formidable times in the history of the arts, ideas and society when the veil trembles, old gives way to new, and images of fracture and fissure, gap and chasm, acquire central place in the making of the arts, and in our critical understanding of it. And, as his own writings have displayed, there was no time when such imagery, such antimonies, such radical separations and then tentative rebridgings, seemed more important than in the founding episodes of the Modern Movement – when awareness of historical discontinuity, break with the past, the fading of old ideologies and the forging of new ones, seemed essential activities. This interest has been shared between Ian Gregor and myself, perhaps not surprisingly; we share not only a friendship but a generation in common, and have both done much of our work, be it critical or creative, in the long shadow of Modernism. We have watched that shadow change its shape and vary its angle as the postwar decades have passed and the spirit of what we learned to call the 'Postmodern' world shifted regularly. We have watched the discontinuous continuity Modernism left behind provoke reaction in some and sophisticated elaboration in others. We have seen the critical heritage the Modern Movement brought to literary thought form and re-form, as New Criticism turned into Yet Newer Criticism, Reconstruction into Deconstruction, Modernist canonization into Postmodernist Decanonization. Still the Modern Movement remains an ambiguous inheritance that as writers and critics we have yet to resolve fully.

Just as Modernism has moved steadily further behind us, to be constantly reshaped and revised, so Postmodernism seems, as we reach the closing of the century, to be suffering a similar fate. Looking back from beyond the end of things, somewhere post Postmodernism, we have good reason to gaze again at the beginnings. If literary criticism can do anything for us (I am getting old enough to wonder, now and then), it can surely tell us we have been here – or somewhere like here – before. Transitional thoughts belong to our times, as the geopolitical map of our own world changes fundamentally, and our Western historical clock tells us that the great calendar is taking us toward a New Age. Thoughts of the New Age dominated 100 years ago, in the 1890s, when, as Holbrook Jackson reminds us in his classic *The Eighteen Nineties* (1913), at a time during which the nature of the deep transition in Western culture that the 1890s embraced was becoming all too clear, the word 'new' was everywhere: 'The range of the adjective gradually spread until it embraced the ideas of the whole period, and we find innumerable references to the "New Spirit," the "New Humour," the "New Realism," the "New Hedonism," the "New Drama," the "New Unionism," the "New Party," and the "New Woman."' Jackson, John Stokes reminds us in his valuable *In the Nineties* (Harvester Wheatsheaf, 1989), wrote from the retrospect of his own historical standpoint, seeing the 1890s as 'an "age of transition" that prepared the way for his own contemporary Edwardian ['Georgian' might have been better] milieu, with its penchant for vitalist or Nietzschean philosophies.' The Modern was being rewritten from its beginnings, and Jackson was a key recorder. But there were other major figures who performed a similar task, both of stimulation and of retrospect, and a current anniversary reminds us of what to my mind was among the most important and still least honoured of them – the 1890s francophile Pre-Raphaelite and writers' writer Ford Madox Hueffer who, by some strange *progression d'effet*, and having survived the Great War that was one product of the modernizing enterprise, emerged as the English Tory gentleman and Parisian modernist Ford Madox Ford.

It is just over fifty years since Ford Madox Hueffer/Ford died, more or less at the end of the episode of Modernism. Not only did he do so much to shape its direction and forge its practice; he was also one of Modernism's great sources of retrospect and reminiscence. 'Fordie' was an inveterate reminiscer, a constant revisitor of literary occasions, and he was famous for it. He was also famously unreliable, apt to start his sentences with, 'When I was talking to the Kaiser . . .', and ready, if you pressed him, to recall his meeting with Lord Byron, even though the good lord had died half a century before his birth. Of his more than eighty books, a good many are reminiscences, some specific, like the remembrances of his most admired writers, Henry James and Conrad, and some general, with titles like *Ancient Lights* (1911), *Thus To Revisit* (1921), *Return to Yesterday* (1931) and *It Was the Nightingale* (1933). These books offer clear proof of how a tale can constantly improve in the retelling, and Hueffer/Ford is more an elegant storyteller of our modern literary history than an accurate source of perfect truth. He was a specialist in meta-reminiscence, and many of his novels are constructed according to principles of semi-oral recollection and recall. Over his lifetime, Hueffer/Ford composed an elaborate narrative of the coming of the Modern, one which has helped structure our own elaborate legend of the Anglo-Irish-American Modern Movement and its evolution. And one aspect of his often-told story seems to me of special interest: the fact that he constructed much of it over the bridge of a double identity, as postwar Ford, the last Tory gentleman who was none the less settled in expatriate Paris or the even more expatriate American Midwest, looked back on prewar, Pre-Raphaelite Hueffer, gazing across some strange and cataclysmic bridge of culture, which was also a strange passage of identity and self.

It was just over seventy years ago, in 1919, that Germanic Ford Madox Hueffer became very English Ford Madox Ford. Domestic reasons had something to do with it, as well as the fact that during the war Germanic names became unpopular in Britain and many were changed (Battenburg to Mountbatten). Yet it was not until a year after the war was over and Hueffer began to reconstruct his life as a writer, after having served at the front and been wounded, that he made the change. We should recall how very important a writer's name is to his identity and the making of his text; a writer's name, quite literally, speaks volumes, authors and authorizes the work. The change is even more remarkable when it comes late in a career, and by 1919 Hueffer/Ford had produced a very large proportion of his work – including the book he was proudest of, *The Good*

Soldier – and was uncertain whether there would be more. Ford considered the experience of war had made him a different person – a view that was, we recall, shared by many other writers, including D. H. Lawrence. Yet the new identity was itself something of a paradox. It turned the author, he seems to tell us, from a prewar cosmopolitan into a Tory Christian gentleman, like Christopher Tietjens (we might note the complex displacement whereby Ford Madox Ford writes a novel about a traditional Englishman with a Germanic name). Yet the Tory Christian gentleman was deeply dismayed by a postwar Britain where writers were demobilized last, along with window cleaners, and where London's Regent Street was being pulled down. In fact, like many of his literary friends and contemporaries, he promptly departed London to become a literary expatriate in postwar Paris, which Pound called 'the laboratory of ideas', and became an active figure in the experimental scene there. Though it was not what he seemed to be saying about himself, postwar Ford was rather more of a cosmopolitan than had been prewar Hueffer. Perhaps the true point of his declaration was that it sought to announce that an era of culture, a phase of creative identity, had closed, an entire episode in the arts was over and done.

This raises an interesting question about our own interpretation of the modern arts. It is reasonable to think that the cycle of the Modern Movement runs roughly for fifty years, from the trembling of the veil and the sense of the New that came at the end of the 1880s, through to around 1939 – the span, of course, of Hueffer/Ford's writing lifetime. It then divides into a prewar and a postwar phase; at the precise centre, twenty-five years on from 1889, twenty-five years before 1939, the cataclysm of August 1914, the Great War, occurs. As Hueffer's friend Henry James put it in a letter, the 'plunge of civilization into this abyss of blood and darkness ... so gives away the whole long age during which we have supposed the world to be, with whatever abatement, gradually bettering, that to have to take it all now for what the treacherous years were all the while really making for and *meaning* is too tragic for any words'. There was thus the prewar season of high experiment and *aube de siècle* joy, as the world changed, as Victorianism collapsed into Edwardianism, Edwardianism into Georgianism, Georgianism into Modernism.

Then, the war over, there came what D. H. Lawrence called, in *Lady Chatterley's Lover*, the 'tragic age' that we refused to take tragically. Here we find the *anni mirabiles*, the peak of Modernism, somewhere between 1922 (*Ulysses*, *The Waste Land* and much else) and 1926. Of the key books published then, many were written across the war – begun before it or during it, completed and published after it. They include Thomas Mann's *The Magic Mountain*, Kafka's *The Trial*, begun in August 1914, *Ulysses* itself, Forster's *A Passage to India*, Proust's *A la recherche du temps perdu*, the transitional phase of Pirandello's drama, Pound's *Hugh Selwyn Mauberley*, the poems of *Prufrock* and many more. They also include the transition of Hueffer/Ford's work, from *The Good Soldier* to the *Parade's End* sequence of novels. Many of these works reveal a double identity; they show us both the prewar Modernist excitements and the postwar confusions and miseries, the Futurist promise and the fragments that we shore against our ruins. They both separate and bridge the two eras of Modernism, just like Hueffer/Ford's own change of identity. It seems that, in the explosion of war, when there were no more social but many military parades, when an old cultural order finally dissolved and a language fell out of use, when amnesia and disconnection set in, when the space between past and present, pre and post, seemed to grow wide, more than one Hueffer turned into a Ford.

II

'It was – truly – like an opening world . . .,' Ford recalled in 1921, as he attempted to bridge the gap by reminiscence in *Thus To Revisit*, 'for, if you have worried your poor dear brain for at least a quarter of a century over the hopelessness of finding, in Anglo-Saxondom, any traces of the operation of conscious art – it was amazing to find these young creatures not only evolving theories of writing and the plastic arts, but receiving in addition an immense amount of what is called "public support".'[1] The 'opening world' Ford was recalling was, of course, that key patch of London years between 1908 and 1914, when, with an ever-accelerating motion, an era of movements, groupings, little magazines, manifestoes, art exhibitions and declarations of artistic rebellion and revolution upturned the conventional artistic order. The 'young creatures' included Pound, Eliot, Wyndham

Lewis, D. H. Lawrence and T. E. Hulme, all of whom Hueffer supported. There can be no doubt that in the London of the immediately prewar years an era of fundamental artistic change occurred, in which we may fairly look for the seedbed of much of Modernism. The experimental spirit of the 1890s revived, and London became an avant-garde wonderland. Once more it drew in all the artistic news, from Paris and Rome, Munich and Moscow, and the transformation within the national arts merged with the greater transformations taking place outside them. The new British writers found themselves in tune with the expatriates who flooded in from elsewhere. There were Poles like Conrad and Gaudier-Brzeska, Irish like Yeats, Shaw and Joyce, Americans like James, Pound, Eliot and 'H. D.' There were some who were appropriately stateless, like Wyndham Lewis, who was born on a ship at sea. And there was Ford Madox Hueffer, born of a German father and a Pre-Raphaelite English mother, with French family connections – one reason why Hueffer found himself reading his literary heritage from Flaubert and Maupassant, speaking all the time of the *ficelle* and the *mot juste*, and in due time writing the finest French novel in the English language.

There can be no doubt that this was a major phase in the development of Anglo-Irish-American experimentalism, bohemianism, cosmopolitanism and Modernism, and the surprise was that it occurred in philistine Britain (all artists knew that, by definition, Britain was philistine). No wonder it was constantly recollected and revisited, first by the participants, then by the critics looking for the heartland of modern literary change. 'It was an age of noise, and every new effort had to be announced with a blare of trumpets,' reminisced another reminiscer, R. A. Scott-James, looking back from the grimmer mood of 1930:

It was a sort of *mi-careme* festival of big drums and little tin whistles and fancy dress. A new show of Post-Impressionist pictures had much the same character and purpose as the marches of flustered suffragettes on Whitehall . . . Marinetti was attracting attention with his violent denunciations of *Passe-isme* and his rhapsodic proclamations of *Futurisme*, and this – in the new age of motor-cars – inevitably became associated with 'Automobilisme.' To which, understandably enough, the vorticist Wyndham Lewis made the retort that it was the English and not the Italians who had introduced the Machine Age . . .[2]

It was the age of isms, and in a short patch of time all the artforms seemed to change, as indeed did social rules and practice. Roger Fry exhibited French painters like Picasso and Braque at the Grafton Gallery in 1910, and Marinetti toured Europe, including Britain, just after, declaiming the radical and outrageous manifestoes of Futurism, calling for the annihilation of the past and the creation of the future. In the lineage of European Modernism this was the period that ran from Post-Impressionism to Expressionism, from Cubism to Futurism, and from Worringer's identification of 'abstraction' as the characterizing feature of the modern arts to Marinetti's, Pound's and Lewis's more vehement and kinetic idea of the vortex of energy hidden in the modern forms. It was also the period that ran from a rebellious warfare of avant-garde putsches, movements, cadres and campaigns to a mechanized battlefield where, with tanks, planes and modern explosives, the young men of Europe enacted the revolt of the modern machine for real. It was an age of dying certainties and new relativities, of the collapse of Romanticism and sentimental Victorianism and the rise of the uncertainty principle and quantum theory, of, said Henry Adams, the closure of the era of the Virgin and the birth of the era of the Dynamo, which introduced the modern multiverse. It was the time of the dying of the classes and the revolt of the masses. It was a time of acceleration when, filled with Nietzschean expectations of historical transformation, the Moderns, who had been around for some time, became the Modernists. Everywhere, from France to Russia, from Scandinavia to Italy, new movements were being declared, and their often hard and aggressive names – Post-Impressionism and Expressionism, Acmeism, Constructivism and Futurism, and, in Britain, Imagism and Vorticism – implied their radical claim on contemporary history. In their different ways they called for energy, for explosion, for destruction, for recommencement; they offered to blast down the past in the hope of blessing the future.

Like the war that followed it, Ford's 'opening world' was thus a great Europe-wide event. 'Europe was full of titanic stirrings and snortings – a new art coming to flower to celebrate or to announce a "new age",' wrote Wyndham Lewis in 1937 in his book of reminiscences, very appropriately titled *Blasting and Bombardiering*; Lewis had started the magazine *Blast* and then fought in the war, and seen the connection between the two. And, like Ford, Lewis looked back on nothing less than a Modernist wonderland, a unique and experimental pastoral that was as yet untainted by the real future. What was happening between 1908 and 1914, he claims, was nothing less than that a great new historic school was in the process of formation, more significant than the Romantic revolution, transforming the philosophical rudiments of life, and heralding great social changes: 'Then down came the lid – the day was lost, for art, at Sarajevo.' In retrospect, Lewis says, it will appear 'an island of incomparable bliss, dwelt by strange shapes labelled "Pound," "Joyce," "Weaver," "Hulme,"' and, 'As people look back at them, out of a very humdrum, cautious, disillusioned society . . . the critics of that future will rub their eyes. They will look, to them, so hopelessly *avant garde*!, so almost madly up and coming! What energy! – what impossibly spartan standards, men will exclaim! . . . *We are the first men of a Future that has not materialized!*'[3]

III

But of all the strange shapes in this strange new world, there can be no doubt that one of the most important and indeed one of the strangest was the one that was then labelled 'Hueffer'. Lewis himself reports him as odd and chubby, 'a flabby lemon and pink giant, who hung his mouth open as though he were an animal at the Zoo inviting buns – especially when ladies were present'. The son of the German-born music critic Dr Francis Hueffer and of the daughter of the painter Ford Madox Brown, he was a movement man. He had been born into Pre-Raphaelitism and seen that tendency move on through Arts and Crafts to 1890s Aestheticism and Decadence, the first stage, we might say, of Modernism. He wrote fairy stories, publishing his first book at the age of seventeen, and by the turn of the century he was collaborating with the still little-known Joseph Conrad on novels. They jointly wrote *The Inheritors* (1901) and *Romance* (1903), and jointly evolved an Impressionist theory of fiction developed from Flaubert and Maupassant, a theory of rendering and what Hueffer liked to call *constatation*, to which he remained faithful thereafter. Impressionism and Naturalism were the dominant tendencies of the 1890s, and Hueffer/Ford always remained something of an 1890s man. 'We accepted the name impressionists because we saw that life did not narrate but made impressions on our brains,' Ford recalled in his *Joseph Conrad: A Personal Remembrance* (1924). 'We in turn, if we wish to produce an effect of life, must not narrate but render impressions.' The novels he went on to write were historical and social novels, frequently with a Condition of England theme, yet they always pursued Flaubertian perfection of form. Perhaps somewhat surprisingly, he even applied Impressionist methods to the historical romance in his *Fifth Queen* trilogy, an important venture that he completed in 1908, just as his 'opening world' began.

Virginia Woolf later claimed that it was in or about December 1910 that human character and therefore the novel form changed (that was when Edwardianism ended and Georgianism began), but there is much more to be said for picking on the year 1908. In 1908, in painting, to which Hueffer was attentive, the Impressionism he so much admired was being displaced by Post-Impressionism and Fauvisme, Picasso had completed *Les Demoiselles d'Avignon*, Cubism was declared in Paris and Worringer identified 'abstraction' as the aesthetic centre of art. In 1908 Hueffer was thirty-five and had about twenty-five books behind him, and he was seeking some new venture that would allow him, he said, to 'meddle in English literary affairs'. The venture took the form of the *English Review*, the monthly magazine that he went on to edit for a dozen or so issues from December 1908 to early 1910. The *English Review* has been described as the first Modernist 'little magazine' in Britain, and celebrated so elaborately that it is salutary to go back and look at the actual volumes to capture its location and its perspective. For one thing, it was not little, but a solid-looking monthly, devoted, said the first editorial, 'to the arts, to letters and ideas'. Hueffer said he wanted to found 'an *aube de siècle* Yellow Book', showing his 1890s spirit, but it was a fat, unillustrated volume in a drab blue cover. He also said he 'wanted it to form the nucleus of some sort of movement', but from the start it was intended as a magazine for liberal politics and current affairs, as well as a literary periodical; after he left it that is what it largely became. And though he wanted a literary journal, he admitted that 'to imagine that a magazine devoted to imaginative literature and technical criticism alone would find more than a hundred readers was a delusion that I in no way had'.

In fact the *English Review* was a mongrel construct appropriate to its time, a cross between the old-fashioned 'great review' and the evolving modern 'little magazine' with innovative literary interests. Hueffer persuaded an unnamed political friend into providing £5,000 to finance it; when he dropped out, the role was taken on by Arthur Marwood, the Yorkshire Tory who was later to become the original of Christopher Tiejtens, the suffering hero of *Parade's End*. Like E. M. Forster's *Howards End* (1910) and several of Hueffer's own novels, the *English Review* was a Condition of England attempt to bridge the prose and the passion, to bring the arts into relation to affairs. As in Forster's novel, the attempt did not lead to an entirely happy ending, not only because politics and the arts, materialism and aestheticism, were increasingly splitting apart, but also because Hueffer was a less than ideal businessman himself, and the paper's financial affairs soon fell into disarray. Yes, Hueffer wanted a movement: 'A movement – *any* movement – leavens a whole Nation with astonishing rapidity,' he wrote in *Thus To Revisit*; 'its ideas pour through the daily, the weekly and the monthly press with the rapidity of water pouring through interstices until at last they reach the Quarterlies and disturb even the Academicians asleep over their paper-baskets . . .'.[4] But much as he loved 'movements', having grown up with so many of them, the *English Review* never became the paper of a single tendency. Hueffer retained the spirit of artistic radicalism that came out of the brilliant transitions of the 1890s, and he carried these forward. So the magazine opened its doors wide in a spirit of pluralistic literary liberalism. Hueffer wrote to his prospective contributors: 'The only qualification for admission to the pages of the Review will be – in the view of the Editors – either distinction of individuality or force of conviction, either literary gifts or earnestness of purpose, whatever the purpose may be . . .'. And his chief explanation for starting the magazine was that he wanted to get a long poem by Thomas Hardy, 'A Sunday Morning Tragedy', which had been rejected by other editors for indelicacy, into print. That poem, not especially radical but reminding us of Hardy's own trials in the 1890s, forms the first item in the first issue.

So why did the *English Review* become so exemplary, and why should Ezra Pound declare in his letters that 'the man who did the *work* for English writing was Ford Madox Hueffer (now Ford)'?[5] When Pound was in Rapallo in Mussolini's Italy, where Ford occasionally visited him, he constantly reverted to his influence and his magazine: 'the EVENT of 1909–1910 was Ford Madox (Hueffer) Ford's ENGLISH REVIEW, and no greater condemnation of the utter filth of the whole social system of that time can be dug up than the fact of that review's passing out of his hands'.[6] Given Hueffer's poor head for business, this is extreme, but not unfair. The strength, as Pound shrewdly saw, lay in Hueffer's critical attitude, his taste for artistic innovation and his capacity to tolerate and relate a wide variety of literary generations and tendencies, taking a few people from each camp. The *English Review* became a compendium of literary development at an exciting time, even though, as Hueffer explained, 'of all the writers who contributed to the early numbers scarcely one failed to write and say that *The English Review* was ruined by the inclusion of every other contributor'.

Hueffer was certainly a very open and hospitable editor. He ran the magazine flamboyantly, editing it from rooms above a fishmonger's shop at 84 Holland Park Avenue, where he entertained grandly and gathered generations of literary troops around him. He saw himself as a literary manager, belonging to a generation that was already dying, but alert to all the various generations of literary change around him. He describes the scene as he saw it in *Return to Yesterday*:

... the old literary gang of the *Athenaeum–Spectator–Heavy Artillery* order were slowly decaying. Young lions were not only roaring but making carnage of their predecessors. Mr Wells was then growing a formidable mane, Arnold Bennett if not widely known was at least known to and admired by me ... Experimenting in forms kept Conrad still young. Henry James was still 'young James' for my uncle William Rossetti and hardly known by the general public. George Meredith and Thomas Hardy had come into their own only very little before, Mr George Moore was being forgotten as he was always being forgotten, Mr Yeats was known as having written 'The Isle of Innisfree.' It seemed to me that if that nucleus of writers could be got together with what of undiscovered talent the country might hold, a Movement might well be started. I had one or two things I wanted to say. They were mostly about the technical side of novel writing. But mostly I desired to give the writers of whom I have spoken as it were a rostrum.[7]

Hueffer thus freely united Naturalists and Impressionists, the writers of the 1870s, the 1880s, the 1890s and the new century, seeming to like them all. So his first issue contained Thomas Hardy, James's story 'The Jolly Corner', Conrad's reminiscences, a tale by Tolstoi and part of Wells's novel *Tono-Bungay*. Future issues soon saw the serialization of Conrad's *Under Western Eyes* and Wells's *New Machiavelli*, and contributions from, among others, Norman Douglas, Arnold Bennett, Robert Bridges, E. M. Forster, Bernard Shaw and John Galsworthy, whom Hueffer found one day sitting in the editor's chair, appointed by the publishers to succeed him; when Galsworthy discovered that Hueffer did not know about this, he gracefully withdrew. Along with this ran Hueffer's editorials, castigating the British for their lack of a critical attitude and their disregard of the serious artist, and developing the growingly serious debate about the future of the novel. As Frank Kermode has said, the Condition of England question at this time was also becoming the Condition of the Novel question, and Hueffer ensured that the new spirit in fiction was thoroughly debated.

Even so, what transfigured the *English Review* was that the magazine coincided with time of new openings and the emergence of a new generation, those whom Hueffer called 'Les Jeunes'. As he remembered it:

Les Jeunes, as they chronologically presented themselves to us, were Mr Pound, Mr D. H. Lawrence, Mr Norman Douglas, Mr [F. S.] Flint, 'H. D.,' Mr Richard Aldington, Mr T. S. Eliot ... in our Editorial Salons they found chaises longues and sofa on which to stretch themselves while they discussed the fate of already fermenting Europe. So, for three or four years, culminating in the London season of 1914, they made a great deal of noise in a city that was preparing to reverberate with the echoes of blasts still greater ... They stood for the Non-Representational in the Arts; for *Vers Libre*; for symbols in Prose, *tapage* in Life, and death to Impressionism ...[8]

Hueffer's own theories were hardly theirs; he had a longer experience of the New. Still a declared Impressionist, he commented:

The Impressionists – and it was the Impressionists that the Vorticists, Cubists, Imagistes and the rest were seeking to wipe out – the Impressionists in the plastic or written arts had been the leaders of the Movement that came immediately before these young fellows. And the main canon of the doctrine of Impressionism had been this: The artist must aim at the absolute suppression of himself in his rendering of his Subject.[9]

Yet both his hospitality to and his judgement about the new became legendary. May Sinclair brought in the young Ezra Pound, recently arrived from Venice, and his publication of *A Lume Spento*, introducing, she said, 'the greatest writer to the greatest editor' of the time. Soon the *English Review* rang its alarm with Pound's impersonation of Bertrand de Born, 'Sestina: Altaforte', so that in the issue for May 1909 we find wedged between poems by Eden Philpotts and an article in French on peace and war in Europe the formidable opening:

> Damn it all! all this our South stinks peace,
> You whoreson dog, Papiols, come! Let's to music!

Wyndham Lewis walked in, left a manuscript on the desk and went away again. Jessie Chambers sent in work by the unknown D. H. Lawrence, and four of his poems appeared under the title of 'A Still Afternoon', to be followed later by several stories. As Lawrence wrote to an admirer in 1912: 'Ford Madox Hueffer discovered I was a genius – don't be alarmed, Hueffer would discover *anything* if he wanted to – published some verse and a story or two, and sent me to Wm. Heinemann with *The White Peacock* . . .'[10] It was, truly, an opening world.

The truth is that Hueffer managed to put a variety of movements together, just when, collectively, these different tendencies and generations offered the possibility for creating a new spirit and future for the arts. Hueffer championed the new because it was new, and it helped to make him new. Though a declared Impressionist, he supported those who cried 'Death to Impressionism'. Though he had, he said, 'total contempt' for the Novel with a Purpose ('A novel should render, not draw morals'), he championed the Naturalists, who often had purpose but not much else ('it is only in the pages of the naturalistic novel that we can hope nowadays to get any experience of modern life'). 'The critical attitude', 'the serious artist', 'the spirit of modern life', these were his watchwords. The *English Review* indeed coincided with an era of massive change in the arts, coming from within and without, and from young and old. Moreover, Les Jeunes were not necessarily in artistic advance of the older writers. Late James and middle Conrad, both heroes to Hueffer, contested the modern with early Joyce and Lawrence. The middle Yeats often outran in experiment the youthful Pound, and led the way beyond Decadence into modernist Symbolism. The result was a volatile mixture, in which each generation affected the other. Older writers, like Arnold Bennett, looking at the Post-Impressionist paintings at the Grafton Gallery Exhibition in 1910, thought they might have to begin again.

And some did, not the least of them Hueffer himself. For not only had he encouraged and developed the younger writers; they had encouraged and developed him. So aware of their impact was he that, in a magazine called the *Thrush*, he actually announced his farewell to literature – in order, he said, to leave the field to the Pounds, the Eliots and the Lewises, writers of revolutionary force 'whose claim or whose need for recognition and what recognitions bring were greater than my own'. He confessed that the effect of the new authors was to disclose to him his own waywardness as a writer, his failure to extend himself or put into fiction all he knew about writing. He said this in the dedicatory letter to *The Good Soldier*, a book which of course proves his farewell was not entirely permanent. For, on his fortieth birthday, in 1913, he gave himself a last chance. 'I have always been mad about writing – about the way writing should be done and partly alone, partly with the companionship of Conrad, I had even at that date made exhaustive studies into how words should be handled and novels constructed.' He set to work on what he called his last book. Following the model of the late James, he largely dictated the story, which covered the Edwardian and *belle époque* social worlds from the turn of the century to its peak in 1913. He wanted to call the book *The Saddest Story*, but when it appeared the world it was about was over and the novel appeared under a wartime title, *The Good Soldier*. By now Hueffer was a good soldier himself, for though overage he had joined the Welch Regiment. And soon it seemed that if his book had the wrong title, so did its author. It was, he said, his best novel of the prewar period; he added that everything that came after it was written by a different man. And so it was. *The Good Soldier* of 1915 was written by Ford Madox Hueffer; the books that followed were written by Ford Madox Ford.

IV

Some of the best comments I know on *The Good Soldier* are found in Frank Kermode's book *Essays on Fiction: 1971–1982* (1983). Kermode starts with the famous opening sentence, 'This is the saddest story I have ever heard', and points out how deceptive it is. As he says:

> [this] seems to tell you that what is to follow is a story, that it is very sad, and that it is going to be told by a narrator who was privileged to hear it. Later we discover that the story involves the suicide of two of the four main personages, the sudden death of another, and the hopeless insanity of a young girl, so *saddest* is a bit lame, perhaps, and certainly misleading. We also discover that the narrator is the husband of one of the suicides and the keeper of the mad girl. It is not exactly some *anecdote* he's been told, and so *heard* is strikingly peculiar.[11]

We can go on; so is *story*, because this is not as yet a story but the, as it were, disordered or potential material for one which the narrator, Dowell, will have both to discover and to order. Since the material will find its meaning and shape through the process of its telling, it will not *be* a story until we finish it. Unless, that is, we take the story to be an oral form, because Dowell has two tasks – to unravel the shape and significance of a series of events which he himself does not properly 'know', and to narrate this to the reader's surrogate, the 'silent listener' who is within as well as outside the narrative. We might therefore be tempted to recast the opening sentence, of which Hueffer/Ford was so proud, to read, or sound like, 'I want to recount to you a story that is sadder than all the other sad stories I have heard.' But is *The Good Soldier* really a sad story, a form of lament or tragedy? To many of its listener-readers it has seemed first and foremost a savage social satire or perhaps a sociopolitical allegory, about the hypocrisies, deceptions, displacements and secrets of the world of the *belle époque* and all that is hidden beneath a surface world of duty, honour, responsibility, valour, integrity and class. Among those deceived by this world and its doings we must put high on the list the narrator Dowell himself, who is not so much the interpreter but the victim of the story he is telling.

The Good Soldier is constructed out of a set of complex displacements, in its subject as well as in its form. There is the central sexual displacement: the two central couples, the Ashburnhams and the Dowells, both have white marriages on the pretext of heart disease. Mrs Ashburnham is a Catholic who will not bear Protestant children to her husband, and Mrs Dowell is a 'cold-hearted sensualist' who has married the narrator in order to conceal and perpetuate an illicit affair. Just as she successfully pretends to a heart condition in order to avoid marital lovemaking, Ashburnham pretends to one in order to meet his mistresses at a German spa, a 'polygamous' arrangement to which his wife consents in order to protect her sexual sanctity. Married love is thus conducted through surrogates and secret liaisons; desire itself is constantly slipping, in a polygamous chain. Only Dowell, the narrator as cuckold, is unaware of the deceptions; the story itself, as it were, deceives him, though as he tells it, he deceives us. This produces a moral displacement: we could feel moral outrage at the events, or blame them on a corrupt society, but our narrator is less concerned with judgement than with establishing the progressive sadness of the story. It is also a novel of displaced spaces: the operations of the social world are described as 'secret', 'subtle', 'subterranean', while those of the sexual world are more abstruse still. Bedrooms, where secrets occur, are rarely entered by the narrative, as it were, and Dowell is initially mystified by how it is possible for the lovers to spend any active time in them, busy as they are in the social space. As Guido Fink has brilliantly said, sexual activity in the book seems the echo of an echo; now you see it, now you don't. Utterance is displaced: when Leonora wants to say, 'Your wife is a harlot who is going to be my husband's mistress,' she says, 'Don't you know I am an Irish Catholic?' With this goes a chronological displacement: the events are largely told from an (ambiguous) position subsequent to the main events, so the main task is, again, reminiscence and reconstruction. The reconstruction is done out of chronological order, and not even in an order that makes them cumulative in the normal narrative sense ('It suddenly comes to me that I had forgotten to say how Edward met his death,' we are told after what has been described as 'the end of the story', though obviously it isn't). Hueffer believed in 'time-shift' as one of his main modern effects, but the story is in fact constructed according to an elaborate calendar, with most of the key events occurring on 4 August in a variety of years from the turn of the century up to 1913. This is coded with an important post-narrative implication, since it could hardly be missed by the reader that on the following 4 August Europe went to war and the social world of the novel came to its end; this is why we can justify seeing the novel as an allegory of the prewar world, which it partly is.

Above all, this disorderly narrative chronology means that the narrator/novelist's method has a fundamental air of arbitrariness. A reason is given for this:

I have, I am aware, told this story in a very rambling way so that it may be difficult for anyone to find their path through what may be a sort of maze [it is]. I cannot help it. I have stuck to my idea of being in a country cottage with a silent listener, hearing between the gusts of the wind and amidst the noises of the distant sea, the story as it comes. And, when one discusses an affair – a long, sad affair – one goes back, one goes forward. One remembers points that one has forgotten and one explains them all the more minutely since one recognizes that one has forgotten to mention them in their proper places and that one may have given, by omitting them, a false impression.

The word 'impression' is crucial to the novel. It occurs, for example, something like ten times in the opening paragraphs of part 3, Chapter IV, in various recurrent formulations: 'all-round impression', 'due impression', 'first impression', as well as 'false impression'. The narrator is trying to give us not a correct impression but a structure of impressions, while at the same time we come to know, we get the impression, that his own impressions, his first impressions, of other people are almost always erroneous. Beyond all this there are various other meta-narrative displacements. There is a suggestive implication that Ashburnham is actually a displaced version of Dowell ('I have only followed faintly, and in my unconscious desires, Edward Ashburnham'). And finally there is an epistemological displacement, a question mark over knowing itself. Dowell at some times seems to know too little, but at other times too much, and indeed he is constantly constructing what from his standpoint must be the unknowable. But then he is also doing for us the novelist's work, and he has to know the story for us, even when he doesn't, since like all first-person narrators he is not only Dowell but his constructor and creator, Hueffer himself. And he is doing it for a silent listener who is not a silent listener at all, but a sceptical reader of text. Even we, the readers, are displaced.

Dowell is what is usually called an unreliable narrator, but in a far more devious and deviant sense than is generally meant by that term. The result is a very modern kind of narration, but not entirely new. As Kermode reminds us, the kind goes back to James's *What Maisie Knew*, the truly *new* novel of the 1890s, the importance of which Hueffer clearly saw. This is the kind of novel Barthes would call *scriptible*, where the story is an 'affair', the telling is a 'treatment' and the method displays James's 'baffled relationship between the subject-matter and its emergence'. For Hueffer, it was James's 'complexity of treatment', his 'distorted point-of-view', that made him the master. But where James likes to create the story for an interpreting consciousness – Maisie trying to know, Strether learning to see and so *live* – Ford turns knowledge itself into an ambiguity. The narrator seems consciously to *defer* the story; much of the action takes place, as we have seen, offstage or in secret, and must be retrieved by ambiguous difficulty, because the method is once more that of meta-reminiscence. Behind all this is a dark and disillusioned version of the Condition of England novel. On the one hand there is the image of a society redeemed by the 'good soldier' who accepts responsibility for others. On the other, there is the vision of society lost by what it persistently suppresses, the secret, polygamous sexual world behind the social façade, the offstage space which Dowell is forced to penetrate. The result is a devastating irony which Ford attempts to control by a new type of narrative – a 'hard' and 'flawless' object in the modern way, like a 'polished helmet', he said. The method perpetuates some of the forms of the progressive, redemptive social novel, granting the outward face of society its substance and significance. But it is also a novel of what has been displaced offstage, and uses an oblique method of association, random juxtaposition and obscure interpretation with which to question it. It is a book that sums up the uneasy postwar pastoral, but also the book in which it ceases. The reconciliatory methods of Condition of England fiction give way to a universe dominated by deceptions, secrets, doubles, madness, suicide. And, as Hueffer implies with his emphasis on 4 August, what will finally complete the process is war itself. And this is what the book prefigures; but it also prefigures something else, Ford's own novel of that war, *Parade's End*.

V

It has been widely agreed that the experience of the First World War radically changed the spirit of modern writing, transforming all the familiar constituents of literary art – language, form and style, and historical, social and human representation. The wound of war struck deep into the materials of expression, decentring its language, derealizing its realities, divesting its cultural substance, dehumanizing its human subjects. To many critics this change marks the move into a fully Modernist sensibility. So, in his reading of modern American literature, *American Literature 1919–1932* (1971), John McCormick fairly typically argues that the war 'smashed all the Stendhalian mirrors', forcing a general shift away from representation of society towards the shattered representation of self. Frederick J. Hoffman, in his *The Mortal No: Death and the Modern Imagination* (1964), sees in the war novel the rise of a new 'abstract factuality', in which new rhetorical ambiguities and ironies resemble 'the fragments of body and machine strewn about the landscape'. Techniques of spatialization, expressionist devices, a hard, indifferent method of writing and mechanization of the human figure are the result. Paul Fussell in *The Great War and Modern Memory* (1975) also looks at this linguistic dislocation in memoirs as well as fictions. But perhaps the most famous statement of all is Walter Benjamin's: 'men returned from the battlefield grown silent – not richer but poorer in communicable experience,' he notes, and this brought a new and reduced mode of expression which recognized what had happened: 'A generation that had gone to school on a horse-drawn streetcar now stood under the open sky in a countryside in which nothing remained unchanged but the clouds, and beneath these clouds, in a field of force of destructive torrents and explosions, was the tiny, fragile human body.'[12]

Yet, as the critics also acknowledge, there had been a shattering of forms already, a 'turn of the novel' that writers like James, Conrad and Hueffer already represented. And much of this evolution was manifest in the arguments of the prewar years, most obviously in the movements of Futurism and Vorticism. Each in their different ways celebrated the explosive energy at the centre of works of art that were essentially conceived as abstract machines. When the Vorticists from the Rebel Art Centre published their manifesto-magazine just before war began, they called it *Blast*. Among its contents, its lists of 'blasts' and 'blesses', was part of Hueffer's *The Good Soldier*. Its manifesto statements took as a main theme the dehumanization of art and culture; here Wyndham Lewis declared that 'Dehumanization is the chief diagnostic of the Modern World.' The whole explosive campaign led to a spirit of new artistic 'hardness' among writers, painters and sculptors, a good number of whom went to the front. This new 'classicism', 'abstraction' and what Wyndham Lewis called 'the method of the great without' thus came to coincide fairly exactly with the retreat from Georgian pastoralism among the war poets, as their verse shifted from heroic romanticism to a shocked expressionistic cry or a bitter hard irony. And it was no surprise that the new spirit in postwar poetry therefore took to forms of fragmentation and dispossession – with such works as Pound's *Mauberley*, a disjunctive epic of a civilization failed, an 'old bitch gone in the teeth', through which dead soldiers march, deprived of their classic justifications for self-sacrifice, or Eliot's *Waste Land*, that image-cluster from a ruined postwar landscape, fragments shored against the ruins. Yet much of this poetry is cast according to the prewar Imagist rules of hard representation, anti-romanticism, impersonality and super-positioning; the difference is in underlying attitude. The spatial and fragmentary forms moulded just before 1914 came to serve the expression of war and the world left by it. Modernism was played twice, once just before the war and again after it, with qualitative differences. The new spatial preoccupations of the 1920s – the turn to a lost generation vision and to *Waste Land* cynicism, to harder, more Expressionist styles, to a sense of existential exposure and victimization, to a vision of human life as decultured, nakedly split between mechanism and passion –

are all responses to a central human experience which had numbed sensibility, intensified the destructive element, opened a gap between historical expectation and human purposes, and devalued human life. But much of this is an anguished development of formal preoccupations begun well before 1914.

Like many writers in Britain before the War, Hueffer, as *The Good Soldier* shows, had already displayed both a growing disillusion with the nature of his culture and an increased devotion to harder techniques. War drove that process very much further. In 1915 Hueffer published not only *The Good Soldier* but two important propaganda books on behalf of the war effort. They are attacks on German imperialist materialism, but they also challenge the related progress of mass materialism and bureaucratic statism in Britain. In the same year, Hueffer got himself a commission in the Welch Regiment and served for a time on the Western Front. He was wounded, suffered a three-week loss of memory and was invalided home in 1917, an experience that produced, he said, a profound moral change. In 1919, when he changed his name, he saw himself afresh as a disappointed Tory patriot, dismayed by the new England he had been fighting for, which was now, he felt, sinking into commercialism, bureaucracy and statism. Upset not only by Regent Street but by the loss of friends and the rise of a new literary generation that seemed largely female, he left London for avant-garde Paris, the postwar substitute. Here he became editor of the *transatlantic review*, which printed Joyce, Pound, Stein and Hemingway, and established himself as a central figure in the Anglo-American expatriate community and the spirit of postwar Modernism.

He also now began what is surely the most significant British novel to deal with the Great War – the *Parade's End* sequence, which certainly consists of *Some Do Not . . .* (1924), *No More Parades* (1925) and *A Man Could Stand Up* (1926), and may include *Last Post* (1928), though Ford was uncertain about its role in the sequence. He naturally reminisced about the making of this book, too, in his volume of postwar recollections, *It Was the Nightingale* (1934). Famously he claimed that it was the death of Proust in 1922 that 'made it certain I should again take up a serious pen' – though Proust's vast *roman fleuve* is not what we would naturally compare *Parade's End* with, save for the fact that there is a common commitment to an art of indirect sequences, time-shifts and Modernist mannerism. But Proust perhaps explains the sense of large scope that Ford brought to his task, which he describes thus:

> The work that at that time – and now – I wanted to see done was something on an immense scale, a little cloudy in immediate attack, but with the salient points and the final impression extraordinarily clear. I wanted the Novelist in fact to appear in his really proud position as historian of his own time ... The 'subject' was the world as it culminated in the war.[13]

Ford then gives us an elaborate description of the development of the idea – his decision to deal not with a mass process of history but to centre the story on a single character, Tietjens, the 'mealsack elephant', 'the last Tory', a 'poor fellow whose body is tied in one place, but whose mind and personality brood eternally over another distant locality', a romantic English figure caught on the point of extinction, and several other aspects of the creative impulse. He also acknowledges that though the method was of Impressionistic rendering, his vast historical work would also be what he despised, the Novel with a Purpose: 'I sinned against my gods to the extent of saying that I was going ... to write a work that should have for its purpose the obviating of all future wars.'[14]

Parade's End shows us that the Condition of England novel itself, when found at the end of its tether, could take on Modernist form. W. H. Auden once said that the sequence 'makes it quite clear that World War I was a retribution visited upon Western Europe for the sins and omissions of its ruling class, for which not only they, but also the innocent conscripted millions on both sides, must suffer'. This is a very plain reading, but there is no doubt that it is a work of very large historical intentions, covering an extended historical time-span and a Spenglerian cycle of decline, from honourable feudalism to modern class war and the coming of a hard new materialism. Tietjens, the last 'Christian gentleman', sees the end of the world of parades, and is the sacrificial victim both of the work and the late Protestant secular age. From the beginning it is clear that his world has already collapsed, before the war, amid the new dispositions of power, new mercantile standards and the changed sexual mores and gender roles of Georgian Britain. War extends the process, both multiplying the official class, the social hypocrisies, the 'swine in the corridors of Whitehall', indifferent to the consequences of their policies, and bringing on its battlefields the chaos of consciousness that is hence inevitable. The battlefield is Tietjens's purgatory, but it is always intruded upon by 'money, women, testamentary bothers', as the social war and the sex war move to the front, where Tietjens learns an instinct for popular democracy and where his bitch-wife, Sylvia, appears in her destructive pursuit of him. Through victimization, he is brought to a new postwar reality, but it is a lowered state in a debased world, in which society and war alike have conspired to take away the chivalric values by which he has sought to live.

One effect of life at the front, Ford comments in *It Was the Nightingale*, was to take away all confidence in substance: 'A social system had crumbled . . . Nay, it had been revealed to you that beneath Ordered Life itself was stretched, the merest film with, beneath it, the abysses of Chaos. One had come from the frail shelters of the Line to a world that was more frail than any canvas hut.'[15] And it is this – the sense of the frailty of reality, the mental and social disorientation – that now justifies Ford's postwar use of Impressionist methods, with their time-shifts and their movements through consciousness. The tactics of displacement now have a complete historical justification. The method provides for the hard-edged realism of the famous opening: 'The two young men – they were of the English public official class – sat in the perfectly appointed railway carriage. The leather straps to the windows were of virgin newness; the mirrors beneath the new luggage racks immaculate as if they had reflected very little . . .' It can also penetrate beneath and beyond the material surfaces to show this world of 1912 as one of breaking principles, muddled history, colliding forces, and, by time-shift, take us through Tietjens's consciousness to the battlefield world where all order, inward and outward, has collapsed. As Tietjens seeks to maintain order and value, hold on to 'the skeleton map of a country', he grasps at a temporally shifting, physically dissolving and ever more chaotic world. Impressionism now allows Ford to merge historical and social realism with a fiction of shifting consciousness, and acquires a direct historical meaning, most obviously apparent in the battlefield sections of the sequence. Indeed, in his fable of Tietjens entering, as the last Christian gentleman, a collapsing history, a world of ever-reducing substance and solidity, Ford led the way for many writers of the 1920s and 1930s who found their times accessible to fiction only if treated with his irony, his high technicality, his narrative deceptions and his pained Modernist indifference.

VI

Ford died fifty-one years ago, in Deauville, as he revisited his beloved France. His death, in 1939, fell between the publication of *Finnegans Wake*, the vast polyglot 'work in progress' which Ford himself had helped title, and the outbreak of a second world war which his own Novel with a Purpose had been quite incapable of halting; so much, he would doubtless have concluded, for Novels with a Purpose. It was a time of endings, of significant literary deaths – Yeats, Freud, Ford, Fitzgerald, Woolf and Joyce himself all died within a year or so of each other. *Finnegans Wake*, with its vast and babelian intentions, the Modernist novel of Here Comes Everybody, has often been seen as the last great monument of the Modern Movement, and much that underpinned that movement surely died in the experience of the Second World War, as the conflict came to involve other crucial modern isms – Bolshevism, Fascism, Nazism, Totalitarianism. When the new writers of the *next* postwar world gathered together, they felt themselves to be the citizens of another age of forms, though Ford left his impact: Evelyn Waugh's *Sword of Honour* trilogy is in many respects a replay of *Parade's End*, though less dependent on Impressionist method. The new writers found themselves faced with a changed task, of confronting an era of shattered ideologies in an age of anxiety and absurdism. Much in Modernism became an ever more distant memory, a site for extraordinary choices and opportunities that opened some options but closed others for good. Modernism's heritage left a discontinuous continuity, conveyed in the ambiguous term Postmodernism. For some it led to a new experimentalism, especially in the United States; for others like Philip Larkin it represented a false tradition best left to foreigners and Americans.

FORD MADOX FORD'S OPENING WORLD

It took time for those of us in the postwar generation to understand the radical significance of the Modern Movement, and understand how massive and inclusive was its break with the past, to give it a sufficient history and a serious aesthetic explanation. But Modernism's long shadow continued to fall; it even came back again, shorn of its social, ideological and historical origins, as chic. Bauhaus became Our House, Pablo Picasso somehow turned into Paloma Picasso, Guernica became Gucci and radical outrage ceased to seem an epistemological breakthrough and became a punk fashion style. In the United States, which by now seemed its natural home, it begat, ambiguously, Postmodernism, which both affirms and denies the surviving relevance of the tendency. Yet, as the century ends, what was originated in the radical arts in the time of new ideologies now has a vivid relevance, as we try to read the new tremblings of the veil and reach out towards the newest arts of our late modern chaos. My argument here has been that looking at Hueffer/Ford helps us to see the Modern Movement as a continuity running for about fifty years, with a major cataclysm at its centre. Yet many of the postwar forms are bred from prewar aesthetics, and the new novels of the 1920s were partly born of novelties that started some two decades before hostilities began. Modernism itself was a discontinuous continuity, and, as the ideologies that were forged around the beginning of our century flag, the world map changes radically and our mental and artistic maps reshape along with this, we would do well to look back over the last great period of radical artistic change. From our point of view still, Hueffer/Ford was perfectly right: the world of early Modernist discovery, in which he was central, was – truly – like an opening world, though it came to close. Perhaps, in our own strangely opening world, we will find plenty here from which to learn.

NOTES

1. Ford Madox Ford, *Thus To Revisit* (London, Chapman and Hall, 1921), pp. 136–7.
2. R. A. Scott-James, 'Modern Accents in English Literature', *Bookman* (New York), 74, September 1931.
3. Wyndham Lewis, *Blasting and Bombardiering*, (London, Eyre and Spottiswoode, 1937), pp. 254–62.

4 Ford, *Thus To Revisit*, pp. 59–64.
5 Ezra Pound, *The Letters of Ezra Pound, 1907–1941*, edited by D. D. Paige (London, Faber and Faber, 1951), p. 389.
6 Ezra Pound, 'This Hulme Business', *Townsman*, 2, V, January 1939.
7 Ford Madox Ford, *Return to Yesterday: Reminiscences 1894–1914* (London, Gollancz, 1931), p. 377.
8 Ford, *Thus To Revisit*, pp. 59–64.
9 *Ibid*, p.138.
10 D. H. Lawrence, *Letters of D. H. Lawrence*, edited by Aldous Huxley (London, Heinemann, 1932), p. 72.
11 Frank Kermode, *Essays on Fiction: 1971–1982* (London, Routledge, 1983), p. 98.
12 Walter Benjamin, *Illuminations*, translated by Harry Zohn (London, Jonathan Cape, 1970), p. 84.
13 Ford Madox Ford, *It Was the Nightingale* (London, Heinemann, 1934), pp. 180, 195. (First published in the USA in 1933.)
14 *Ibid.*, p. 205.
15 *Ibid.*, pp. 48–9.

2 Going Back to Pater and Wilde

Denis Donoghue

I

On the first page of his *Studies in the History of the Renaissance* (1873) and before saying as much as a word about Renaissance art, Pater dissociated himself from Ruskin and Arnold, without naming either of them. He prevented any comparison of his work with Ruskin's by dismissing as fruitless any attempt 'to define beauty in the abstract', to 'express it in the most general terms', or 'find a universal formula for it'. From Arnold, Pater removed himself in this formidably insouciant passage: '"To see the object as in itself it really is", has been justly said to be the aim of all true criticism whatever; and in aesthetic criticism the first step towards seeing one's object as it really is, is to know one's own impression as it really is, to discriminate it, to realise it distinctly.'[1]

The quoted phrase about seeing 'the object as in itself it really is' comes from Arnold's lecture 'On Translating Homer' (1862). The 'first step' to which Pater alludes is the only one he intends taking: he doesn't believe in the programme which Arnold assigns to every branch of knowledge. Notionally, there may be a thing 'in itself', but Pater doesn't believe that we can get behind the impression it has made on our minds or come to know it independently. He is a relativist, so he cannot deduce his morality, as Arnold does, from the determination to pay attention to objects and to respect their objectivity. Just as serious as Arnold, Pater is a moralist: how we look at objects is an instance of our way of being present in the world. But the only evidence we have that there is an object to be seen is that we have apparently irresistible knowledge of the impressions the experience of looking at it has produced. Pater's moral sense depends upon his epistemology, but the objects of knowledge are his impressions, not the things that appear to have caused them. Otherwise put, his morality is the gravity with which he tries to know those impressions. Arnold's morality depends upon the care he takes to convince himself that an object is truly independent of the mind that pays attention to it.

Later in *Studies in the History of the Renaissance* Pater makes a distinction between dramatic and visionary painters in terms which he might have applied to the difference between Arnold and himself:

Giotto, the tried companion of Dante, Masaccio, Ghirlandaio even, do but transcribe, with more or less refining, the outward image; they are dramatic, not visionary painters; they are almost impassive spectators of the action before them. But the genius of which Botticelli is the type usurps the data before it as the exponent of ideas, moods, visions of its own; in this interest it plays fast and loose with those data, rejecting some and isolating others, and always combining them anew.[2]

It was left to Wilde at once to mock Arnold's morality and to outPater Pater's relativism by saying, in 'The Critic as Artist', that 'The primary aim of the critic is to see the object as in itself it really is not.'[3]

I have glanced at that episode, familiar as it is, because it continues to exemplify a crucial antagonism in modern literature. Not that Pater and Wilde are indistinguishably on the same side, or that Arnold is merely a sturdy, unambiguous Victorian. Arnold had his buried as much as his palpably visible life. Pater took care to distinguish his Epicureanism from Wilde's when, reviewing *The Picture of Dorian Gray*, he said that Wilde's form of Epicureanism was incomplete, upon a major consideration:

A true Epicureanism aims at a complete though harmonious development of man's entire organism. To lose the moral sense therefore, for instance, the sense of sin and righteousness, as Mr. Wilde's heroes are bent on doing as speedily, as completely as they can, is to lose, or lower, organisation, to become less complex, to pass from a higher to a lower degree of development.[4]

Still, the antagonism is clear: there are indeed two sides. If we continue to distinguish, with whatever misgiving, between an objective and a subjective emphasis, Arnold is indeed on one side, while Pater and Wilde testify to the other.

II

The antagonism is even sharper in Yeats's account of it in 'The Tragic Generation'. He has been speaking of the islands of Phaedria and Acrasia in Spenser's description of them:

In those islands certain qualities of beauty, certain forms of sensuous loveliness were separated from all the general purposes of life ... I think that the movement of our thought has more and more so separated certain images and regions of the mind, and that these images grow in beauty as they grow in sterility. Shakespeare leaned, as it were, even as craftsman, upon the general fate of men and nations, had about him the excitement of the playhouse; and all poets, including Spenser in all but a few pages, until our age came, and when it came almost all, have had some propaganda or traditional doctrine to give companionship with their fellows. Had not Matthew Arnold his faith in what he described as the best thought of his generation, Browning his psychological curiosity, Tennyson, as before him Shelley and Wordsworth, moral values that were not aesthetic values? But Coleridge of the 'Ancient Mariner' and 'Kubla Khan', and Rossetti in all his writings, made what Arnold has called that 'morbid effort', that search for 'perfection of thought and feeling, and to unite this to perfection of form', sought this new, pure beauty, and suffered in their lives because of it.[5]

The suffering is the 'dissipation and despair' which Ille, in Yeats's 'Ego Dominus Tuus', ascribes to the artist who has 'awakened from the common dream'. The common dream is immersion in the generally proposed purposes of life, the ordinary sense of reality which the novel of realism enforces and appeases.

In 'At Stratford-on-Avon' Yeats tries, like Pater before him in 'Shakespeare's English Kings', to rescue Shakespeare from the general assumption that he endorsed Henry V and the rough, successful heroes at the expense of the defeated ones. John Butler Yeats's letters to Edward Dowden and Pater's essay persuaded Yeats that Shakespeare's deepest sympathy went out to the defeated Richard II, 'that unripened Hamlet', and not to Henry V, 'that ripened Fortinbras'. Ostensibly, Yeats's essay is about Shakespeare, but it is really a plea for Yeats's contemporaries, who seemed in May 1901, when the essay was written, to have been defeated chiefly because they had the finer claim upon one's sympathy and stood in need of it; he was thinking, as always, of Pater, Wilde, Lionel Johnson, Dowson, Symons, and indeed of himself.

III

Henry James's 'The Next Time' is a variation on much the same theme – the antagonism between the stupid, broad-backed public and the writer, who may to his disadvantage be a true artist. Ray Limbert tries, year by year, to write a popular novel, coarse enough to please the commonest reader, and he fails because his imagination will not permit him to bend low enough to succeed. In the end, and without realizing what he is doing, he turns away from the broad back and consults his imagination, which on this occasion amounts to an aesthetic sense all-demanding. The narrator reports of Limbert at the end:

The great thing was that he was immensely interested and was pleased with the omens. I got a strange stirring sense that he had not consulted the usual ones and indeed that he had floated away into a grand indifference, into a reckless consciousness of art. The voice of the market had suddenly grown faint and far: he had come back at the last, as people so often do, to one of the moods, the sincerities of his prime. Was he really, with a blurred sense of the urgent, doing something now only for himself? We wondered and waited – we felt he was a little confused. What had happened, I was afterwards satisfied, was that he had quite forgotten whether he generally sold or not. He had merely waked up one morning again in the country of the blue and had stayed there with a good conscience and a great idea. He stayed till death knocked at the gate . . .[6]

The novel on which Limbert is working is aptly called *Derogation*; it remains a fragment. The country of the blue is the sky filled with stars, or whatever country a great imagination left to its own devices would invent. 'The Next Time' is James's fantasy; not an unmediated vision but a vision in which the mediations – language, grammar, syntax, diction – don't count as impediments merely but as the occasions of one possibility after another. Limbert has turned away, at the end, from Grub Streets new and old, as James turned away from the broad-backed world which Wells so lucratively beguiled.

IV

I shall give another variation, and then have done with instances:

A girl stood before him in midstream, alone and still, gazing out to sea. She seemed like one whom magic had changed into the likeness of a strange and beautiful seabird. Her long slender bare legs were delicate as a crane's and pure save where an emerald trail of sea-weed had fashioned itself as a sign upon the flesh. Her thighs, fuller and softhued as ivory, were bared almost to the hips where the white fringes of her drawers were like featherings of soft white down. Her slateblue skirts were kilted boldly about her waist and dovetailed behind her. Her bosom was as a bird's soft and slight, slight and soft as the breast of some darkplumaged dove. But her long fair hair was girlish: and girlish, and touched with the wonder of mortal beauty, her face.[7]

The sensibility on show in that passage, Stephen Dedalus's in *A Portrait of the Artist as a Young Man*, has been developed and appeased by 'poetry', not by prose – unless it be by the prose of Yeats's early stories, as in 'The Tables of the Law'. The data – the girl on the strand, her legs, her thighs – have been sufficiently usurped, rather than transcribed, so that their destiny is to become impressions in Stephen's mind and to dissolve there into the only language that corresponds to them, the alternations and repetitions of *fin-de-siècle* verse: 'as a bird's soft and slight, slight and soft as the breast of some darkplumaged dove'. It is not necessary to underline the point to the extent of saying that Stephen sees the girl as in herself she really is not; it is enough to say that his impression of her is the thing to be expressed, her presence on the strand being a matter chiefly for his pleasure rather than for the moral response of description. In the last sentence of the passage, the call of description is barely answered: the repetition of 'girlish' and the suspension of a caressing phrase – 'and touched with the wonder of mortal beauty' – between the repeated adjective and its necessary noun exemplify what Yeats meant by the search for 'this new, pure beauty'.

V

The history of that search is now well established, mainly by the work of Mario Praz and other scholars: one thinks of Praz's *The Romantic Agony*, Arthur Symons's *The Symbolist Movement in*

Literature, Edmund Wilson's *Axel's Castle*, Frank Kermode's *Romantic Image*, Ian Fletcher's essays on Pater, Johnson, Symons and Yeats, the anthology *Strangeness and Beauty*, edited by Eric Warner and Graham Hough, Patricia Clements's *Baudelaire and the English Tradition* and Linda Dowling's *Language and Decadence in the Victorian Fin de Siècle*. It is the history of Aestheticism, so long as the subject is thought to be decent, and of Decadence thereafter. Perhaps it is sufficiently indicated by referring to Poe, Gautier, Baudelaire, Swinburne, Pater, Huysmans, Mallarmé, Wilde, Yeats and Symons. Under these names, or other names that might be added, we are referring to a loose assemblage of preoccupations rather than a movement or a project. Anyone's list of such preoccupations would include these: a sense of crisis – historical, economic, political or linguistic; a corresponding sense of spiritual privilege in those few who are sensitive to this disturbance; a rhetorical division between existence, broad-backed and repellent on the whole, and essence, a notion but a pure one, responsive to the imagination that desires purer conditions than those at large; a sense of modernity as constituted not by an implied continuity but by a necessarily fragmented and intermittent vision; an aesthetic of glimpses. Symons remarks, in one of his essays on the dance, that 'nothing is stated, there is no intrusion of words used for the irrelevant purpose of describing; a world rises before one, the picture lasts only long enough to have been there; and the dancer, with her gesture, all pure symbol, evokes, from her mere beautiful motion, idea, sensation, all that one need ever know of event'.[8]

The list of preoccupations is clearly incomplete. Even in a cursory account of the motives common to Aestheticism and Decadence, one should add: a fondling attention to lateness – 'this late day', as Pater says; a cult of Late Latin as correlative to Modernity; a brooding fascination with the decline and fall of the Roman Empire as prefiguring the same fate inevitably attending the British one; a sense of frail and desperate epiphanies. One should also allude to a definition of the style of decadence, which, according to Linda Dowling, began with Désiré Nisard's *Etudes de moeurs et de critique sur les poètes latins de la décadence* (1834), was developed by Paul Bourget and by Nietzsche (*Der Fall Wagner*) and was made available to English readers by Havelock Ellis in an essay on Bourget. 'A style of decadence,' according to Ellis, 'is one in which the unity of the book is decomposed to give place to the independence of the page, in which the page is decomposed to give place to the independence of the phrase, and the phrase to give place to the independence of the word.'[9] Such a word – Stephen Dedalus's cherished and repeated 'girlish' – finds its place not in the world but in a Mallarméan book.

I have merely mentioned Nietzsche, being unable to do more than mention him. He comes into the story because of his insistence, as early as his first book, *The Birth of Tragedy*, that 'only as an aesthetic phenomenon are life and the world justified eternally'. I am not sure I know what he means; unless it is that life and the world are justified because they indisputably contain instances of beauty which do not require any moral consideration. The fact that life and the world contain these things encourages every artist, every Apollo, to overcome the sickness and horror of life by creating works of art commensurate to whatever the artist has to face. We have Art so that we may escape from Truth, or at least answer it back.

But Nietzsche is an obstacle, a portent, a scandal – in any case, a monster not to be reduced or otherwise got around. Only a little more feasible is one's necessary attention, in such scattered notes as these, to Kierkegaard, although Kierkegaard brings together in *Either/Or*, and in reasonably equable form, nearly every attribute we need to acknowledge in Aestheticism. Adorno has noted, in his book on Kierkegaard, that Aestheticism has both its hour and its place – the early history of the metropolis: 'It is there, like artificial street lighting, in the twilight of incipient despair, that this strange, dangerous, and imperious form emits its beam to eternalize, garishly, life as it slips away.'[10]

Aestheticism has also, according to Kierkegaard, its privileged category of attention, the 'interesting', a turning-point, a border category between aesthetics and ethics. As for its meaning, Kierkegaard uses the concept of the aesthetic, as Adorno remarks, in three senses. The first is the common one, the realm of works of art and the theory of their production. The second is somewhat more pointed: the aesthetic in a man is that by which he is immediately what he is, as distinct from the ethical, whereby he becomes what he becomes. Stephen Dedalus's version of this distinction, in a conversation with his student colleague Lynch, describes 'the aesthetic image' as 'first luminously apprehended as selfbounded and selfcontained upon the immeasurable background of space or time which is not it'. The fact that Stephen has Aquinas rather than Kierkegaard to thank for this perception is beside the present point. Kierkegaard's third meaning, found only in his *Concluding Unscientific Postscript*, refers to the form of subjective communication: 'The subjective thinker is an existing individual essentially interested in his own thinking, existing as he does in his thought. His thinking has therefore a different type of reflection, namely the reflection of inwardness, of possession, by virtue of which it belongs to the thinking subject and to no one else.'[11]

It follows that aesthetic man is a slave to the moment, and can escape this prison only by becoming ethical man. Hence Kierkegaard's ideal trajectory: from aesthetic to ethical man, from poetic to religious experience, from the aesthetic moment to a 'leap' beyond it.

If we remove from Kierkegaard's sense of aesthetic man the *angst* that suffuses it, we come to certain modern instances of Aestheticism according to which 'the aesthetic' is an entirely tolerable mode of being. According to Borges, for instance – I am referring to 'The Wall and the Books', a brief chapter of *Labyrinths* – we could infer 'that all forms have their virtue in themselves and not in any conjectural "content"':

This would accord with the thesis of Benedetto Croce; already Pater in 1877 had affirmed that all arts aspire to the state of music, which is pure form. Music, states of happiness, mythology, faces belaboured by time, certain twilights and certain places try to tell us something, or have said something we should have missed, or are about to say something: this imminence of a revelation which does not occur is, perhaps, the aesthetic phenomenon.[12]

The value of the several states which Borges lists is an intrinsic pleasure. While the moment of such pleasure lasts, we do not inquire about its origin or meaning. In some of the states, the pleasure has as its essential quality the fact that it cannot be acted upon: we do not act upon a message that has not been received, a revelation that has not taken place. The aesthetic quality seems to depend upon being in the vicinity, but only the vicinity, of communications which would require us to act in one way or another if they were to reach us. The only questionable item in the list is 'faces belaboured by time'. But these are, I assume, so weathered that they may cheerfully remain where they are; they are in the vicinity of their other selves, more stirring or peremptory beings who indeed have lived by action or otherwise extrinsically.

VI

Pater died on 30 July 1894, Wilde on 30 November 1900. It was widely thought that the diverse but related sentiments associated in the public mind with each of them might now be regarded as superseded. Henry James, reliable on these and more subtle adjudications, thought Wilde a disgrace and Pater a figure safely to be patronized. In a letter of 13 December 1894 to Gosse, James referred to 'faint, pale, embarrassed, exquisite Pater', and went through the motions of thinking that Pater had done well to put himself entirely into his published work and leave not a trace behind for newspapers to flap their wings on. When A. C. Benson's book on Pater appeared, James noted – in a letter of 31 May 1906 to Benson – that Pater had become a figure, 'a figure in the sense in which there are so few'. But it is clear that by 1906 Pater's reputation was at once secure and innocuous: he was no longer a menace, as he appeared to George Eliot and others when *Studies in the History of the Renaissance* was first published, with its sinister Preface and Conclusion. It is safe to say that between 1906 and 1930 – when T. S. Eliot published his 'Arnold and Pater' – no suspicion of being still in league with corruption attached itself to Pater. He had been sequestered in the history of an unepoch-making epoch.

So the first oddity in Eliot's essay is that he should have represented Arnold and Pater as if on an equal and equally dubious footing. It was Arnold who did the damage of separating religion from thought, not foreseeing that the divorce would issue in *Marius the Epicurean* and *De Profundis*. Eliot presses the contentious issue by quoting throughout from the first edition of *Studies in the History of the Renaissance*, ignoring the fact that in later editions Pater toned down several offensive phrases: 'some abstract morality' was altered to 'some abstract theory', but Eliot quoted the first version. Pater is presented as a 'new variation' upon Arnold, but Eliot refuses to call this variation that of the 'aesthete'. Pater, according to Eliot, is like Arnold, Carlyle and Ruskin in being a moralist. In evidence, Eliot quotes from Pater's essay on Wordsworth: 'To treat life in the spirit of art, is to make life a thing in which means and ends are identified: to encourage such treatment, the true moral significance of art and poetry.'

The quotation, from *Appreciations*, is accurate. But Eliot should also have quoted, from the same essay, Pater's assertion that 'the office of the poet is not that of the moralist'. Or the passage, again from the essay on Wordsworth, in which Pater says that poetry and art, 'by their very sterility, are a type of beholding for the mere joy of beholding'. In fact, Pater's essay on Wordsworth doesn't say anything that should have distressed Eliot; it merely says that the work of such a poet as Wordsworth invites us 'to withdraw the thoughts for a little while from the mere machinery of life, to fix them, with appropriate emotions, on the spectacle of those great facts in man's existence which no machinery affects'. It is not certain that there are any such facts, but it is crucial to Pater, as to Yeats, to believe that there are, and that they are available to an antithetical consciousness.

The second oddity of Eliot's essay is that it brings Arnold's criteria to tell against Pater. When we read Pater on Leonardo or Giorgione, Eliot says, 'we feel that there is the same preoccupation, coming between him and the object as it really is'. Being primarily a moralist, Pater 'was incapable of seeing any work of art simply as it is'.

There are further questionable sentences in Eliot's essay, but it is unnecessary to pester the issues they raise. The only point to be made is that by 1930 Pater was again under scrutiny as a dangerous writer. In 1922, when Yeats wrote 'The Tragic Generation', he wondered whether or not *Marius the Epicurean*, 'the only great prose in modern fiction', had not 'caused the disaster of my friends': 'It taught us to walk upon a rope tightly stretched through serene air, and we were left to keep our feet upon a swaying rope in a storm.'[13]

It is not clear what happened to the air between 1885 and, say, 1900, when Wilde died and, according to Yeats, everybody got down off his stilts, knowing that Victorianism, as Yeats called it, had been defeated. In 1930 Eliot sharpened Yeats's notion. Pater's view of art, Eliot said:

> impressed itself upon a number of writers in the 'nineties, and propagated some confusion between life and art which is not wholly irresponsible for some untidy lives. The theory (if it can be called a theory) of 'art for art's sake' is still valid in so far as it can be taken as an exhortation to the artist to stick to his job; it never was and never can be valid for the spectator, reader or auditor.[14]

The force of that last assertion is hard to justify, or even to explain. It is easy to say that Eliot, in 1930 a recent convert to the Anglican communion, felt impelled to insist that only religion, and specifically Christianity, had the right to claim totality of experience, the supreme perspective made available by divine revelation. That art should be represented as having just as good a claim to totality seemed to Eliot a scandal. Having refused to call Pater an aesthete, and having asserted that the author of *The Renaissance* and *Marius the Epicurean* was a moralist, Eliot had to insist that every view of art, in Pater, was really a view of life. Every general sentence ostensibly about art was really 'a theory of ethics; it is concerned not with art but with life'. Quoting Pater's famous sentence about art coming to you 'professing frankly to give nothing but the highest quality to your moments as they pass, and simply for those moments' sake', Eliot said that this is 'of course demonstrably untrue, or else being true of everything else besides art is meaningless; but it is a serious statement of morals'.

In fact, Eliot's denunciation of this statement is extravagant. Pater's doctrine (if it is that) of 'art for art's sake' is merely a claim that there are some things in life, and some experiences, which are best approached as intrinsic rather than extrinsic values. If you are listening to a symphony, you do well not to be thinking of anything else, even sin, expiation, redemption and God. Indeed, I wish the doctrine could be resuscitated. We are in need of it, now that we are admonished to read every book and look at every painting as a disguised political allegory, and to attend to it in no other respect.

VII

Eliot's debt to Pater was such that he could not bear to acknowledge it. In essays, he separated himself from Pater and tried to dismiss him, but his early poems are in many indelible respects Paterian. I am thinking of the modernity of Eliot's 'moments', as in the 'Preludes', and the sense of 'this late day' in many poems, beginning with 'The Love Song of J. Alfred Prufrock'. Eliot failed to detect Pater, as he detected Arnold, in himself. Now that we no longer think Eliot's quarrels must be our quarrels, we see that Pater is everywhere; not only in Wilde, Yeats, Johnson and Dowson, but in Eliot, Joyce, Virginia Woolf, Borges, Wallace Stevens, Nabokov and Ashbery. That list, too, is far from complete. If we continue to talk about Modernism, as presumably we do and must, then we start with Pater as the chief though not the only begetter.

VIII

Eliot would have found more formidable objects of attack in Wilde than in Pater, but Wilde's vivacities did not stay in place long enough to be assaulted; besides, there was the risk of appearing absurd, attacking some conceit or other. Yeats chose to think that Wilde was serious, and that his aesthetic notions could be useful even when the conditions for using them had changed. Richard Ellmann has observed that the notions in themselves were not original – Wilde had received them mainly from Flaubert, Gautier and the French Symbolists – but that Wilde had made them seem useful, less exotic: 'At the moment when Yeats felt compelled to build his own aesthetic, it was propitious to hear Wilde argue "the truth of masks", and insist that men direct their conduct not by moral tenets but by images furnished through art, that what we behold in nature, as what we make of ourselves, can be imaginatively determined.'[15]

Yeats also found Wilde's theories opportune when he wanted to dislodge 'sincerity' in favour of 'multiplied personalities', speaking through a mask in every respect the opposite of his merely given or primary character. Wilde's idea of the mask was simply the translation of the general theory of the imagination into theatrical terms, but Yeats used it to endorse the possibility of self-creation, self-invention. Without it, he might have had to go to Milton's Satan for such a boon. The boon once acquired, he could engage in an aesthetic of conflict, and think of consciousness as, at its best, tragic, a *geste* of self and anti-self, death only the notional end to such a conflict. He made use of Wilde's doublings without calling them doubles.

I can't believe that we have yet assimilated Yeats's sense of Wilde, or come to terms with the difficult presentation of him in *A Vision*. In some ways, Ellmann's biography of Wilde has made that job more difficult, because of the eloquence with which Wilde is made to exemplify the fate of an artist brought down by Victorian hypocrisy. The fact that the police took no interest in Wilde's activities till he insisted on going to law is not allowed to count. So we are asked to think of Wilde as chiefly a scapegoat, a victim. It is necessary to remind ourselves that, as Ian Gregor's essay on *The Importance of Being Earnest* has shown, Wilde is chiefly to be valued for having brought to perfection a certain form of comedy.

IX

Of the whole 'mood' – if it is not more than that – of nineteenth-century literature that includes Symbolism, Aestheticism and Decadence, it is worth repeating what Thomas Mann said fifty years ago: that Aestheticism was 'the first manifestation of the European mind's rebellion against the whole morality of the bourgeois age'. In Nietzsche, Aestheticism – his raging denial of intellect, as Mann puts it, in favour of the beauty, strength and wickedness of life – was 'the self-lashing of a man who suffered profoundly from life'.[16] Mann's reading of Nietzsche is controversial: there are readers who repudiate any suggestion of a 'denial of intellect' in Nietzsche. I cannot enter upon that dispute here, but Mann's general sense of the provenance of Aestheticism as a rejection of bourgeois morality is convincing. His further argument is also acceptable: that Nietzsche, Kierkegaard, Bergson and many other writers constitute 'a movement of intellectual revolt against the classical faith in reason of the eighteenth and the nineteenth centuries'. The movement, according to Mann, has done its work; what remains to be done is 'the reconstitution of human reason upon a new basis, the achievement of a concept of humanity of greater profundity than the complacently shallow view of the bourgeois age'.

Mann does not put any confidence in a new Aestheticism, if

only because 'aestheticism, under whose banner freethinkers turned against bourgeois morality, itself belonged to the bourgeois age'. To move beyond this age means 'to step out of an aesthetic era into a moral and social one'. An aesthetic ideology, he insists, is powerless to meet the problems we must solve, though he acknowledges that whatever we have learned of the daemonic elements of man's nature must be incorporated in any new sense of human life.[17]

X

With Mann's essay on Nietzsche we approach tendentious matters. We would approach them just as inescapably if, making a fresh start with Pater and Wilde, we thought of Hardy and then of Lawrence and of Lawrence's Hardy as a guide to *The Rainbow* and *Women in Love*. When Mann writes of incorporating the insights of Kierkegaard, Nietzsche and Bergson in a new Enlightenment or a new Humanism, he might just as powerfully say: 'Take Lawrence seriously in any new dispositions you think of making.'

In the present company of Ian Gregor's friends it is unlikely that Lawrence's extraordinary bearing upon art and morality will be misunderstood or slighted. So I may end with a few remarks consistent with my attention to Pater and Wilde. The question at issue, that of Aesthetic Ideology, is still in dispute. For a while, it looked as if we could simply agree with Walter Benjamin in denouncing the introduction of aesthetics into politics. Had we not the example of Pound, and indeed of Yeats, who judged societies by criteria mainly aesthetic, and ignored in their post-Nietzschean zeal the price exacted by heroes from their victims? 'The logical result of Fascism,' according to Benjamin, 'is the introduction of aesthetics into politics.' A few sentences later he said that 'all efforts to render politics aesthetic culminate in one thing: war.' But he also said, in the same famous essay, 'The Work of Art in the Age of Mechanical Reproduction':

'Fiat ars – pereat mundus,' says Fascism, and, as Marinetti admits, expects war to supply the artistic gratification of a sense perception that has been changed by technology. This is evidently the consummation of *'l'art pour l'art'*. Mankind, which in Homer's time was an object of contemplation for the Olympian gods, now is one for itself. Its self-alienation has reached such a degree that it can experience its own destruction as an

aesthetic pleasure of the first order. This is the situation of politics which Fascism is rendering aesthetic. Communism responds by politicizing art.[18]

Benjamin's essay was first published in 1936. The defeat of Mussolini's Fascism has not in any way reduced the force of Benjamin's argument, if only because the application of aesthetic criteria to politics is a perennial temptation. The fact that we are again in a 'Communist' phase of critical theory and *praxis* is as clear as it is dismal. One of the most insidious conditions under which we teach and write is the assumption, as widespread as it is virulent, that a work of literature is merely an illustration of a prior ideological formation. Largely as a consequence of this condition, our students are losing the ability to read, and we are losing confidence in our ability to teach them how to read. It is becoming more difficult to show that reading is not the simultaneous translation of a poem or a novel into a political lesson.

There may soon be a reaction against the blatant reductiveness which the politicization of the work of art entails. Apart from other considerations, there is the fact that the political lesson to be drawn from such a work is invariably banal. Of course we must denounce Aesthetic Ideology. But we have also to recover our sense of the work of art as irreducible. How to do that is the problem. My own prejudice, under some degree of provocation, is that the part of Aestheticism which we must save is its concern for the particularity of form, in every given instance. Pater implied this sense when he spoke, in *The Renaissance*, of one's search to find the *virtue* of each object of attention, the particular quality by which it is that thing and no other. Unfortunately, he thought of that virtue in psychological rather than in formal terms, and hoped to come upon it by describing the impressions a particular work, or a number of works attributed to the same painter, made upon him; upon Pater, immersing himself in their tones and atmospheres. It is not enough. James is a better guide in this search, because he does not dissolve the consideration of form in psychological description of the author. His debate with Wells and the Prefaces to the New York edition of his fiction make the best elucidation of a possible Formalism – because that is what it comes to – we have or are likely to get. It would be absurd to say that James's Formalism has gone unnoticed: there is a splendid range of considerations of it, from Blackmur's *The Lion and the Honeycomb* (1955) to Sharon Cameron's *Thinking in Henry James* (1989). But there is little evidence of a criticism or a pedagogy founded upon James in the sense that there is much evidence of a criticism founded upon Eliot and regnant in that character for many years.

XI

Pater, Wilde and James: but the differences between them must be acknowledged. It was Pater's prejudice to believe that thinking could be released from the drastic criteria of knowing. Even if you couldn't know anything for sure, you could still employ your mind in thinking. In particular, you could brood upon your own sensations in trying to know. That was Pater's prejudice, just as it was his embarrassment to discover that consciousness couldn't account for the whole of his experience. The next best consideration was that he could work his consciousness hard enough to produce the most intense moments of that experience, and settle for those exaltations in default of continuous splendour. Wilde worked on much the same assumption, but rather than internalize his thinking, as Pater did, he externalized it, performing acts of consciousness for all to see. In his plays, speaking dares to be as free as the thinking that precedes it: the shock of his paradoxes and conceits is that they are audible. What Pater merely thought, in private, and wrote down in a style for adepts and ephebes, Wilde turned into *coups de théâtre*: he displaced the conventional ethical concerns of the theatre by the production of appearances, sufficiently accredited by the free play of the mind that conjured them. In their otherwise different styles, both Pater and Wilde circumvented Arnold's morality, which was indeed founded primarily upon respect for objects and only secondarily upon respect for the mind that proposed to know them. To see the object as in itself it really is is Arnold's formula for that sequence.

When we think of James in this context, we continue to mark the supreme privilege of consciousness, but also the criterion according to which it is required to issue in an object, a composed form, a picture, a novel. Supreme value, according to

James's aesthetic, is that of an unusually capable imagination which keeps on going, through every instance of muddle, till it achieves a form distinct from itself; achieves such a form by imagining situations, characters, relations, disclosures and finalities. Sharon Cameron has argued that there is a discrepancy between James's aesthetic in the Prefaces – which mark a retrospect, a revision, a replacement of what is in the novels by what he wishes were there – and the novels. In the novels, especially in *The Portrait of a Lady*, *The Golden Bowl* and *The Wings of the Dove*, consciousness is often found defeated by crass circumstance or, nearly as bad, is found corruptly victorious, becoming not the highest form of spirituality but the mere power of manipulating other people. 'In *The Golden Bowl*,' Cameron argues, 'any transgression can be committed if it is kept out of speech.'[19] James's late style is among other things a device for creating other modes than speech for consciousness to inhabit, there to take action and exert power.

The argument is far more complex than I have suggested. It is bound to darken our sense of the character of thinking, so far as thinking is James's way of fending off the final darkness. It is likely, too, to complicate one's sense of form in James's novels. No form is innocent; no formalist emphasis in criticism is worth talking about if it doesn't take that darkness, and that way of fending it off, into account. Form, as Mark Schorer said, is 'achieved content'. We need each of the words to redeem the penury of the other. Or if we want another formula, we may think of Susanne Langer's *Feeling and Form*, and especially of the passage in which she says that a work of art is an object offered only or at least chiefly for perception: its mode is what she calls 'virtual'. It is the virtuality of a work of art that should keep us from translating the work into an ideology. Only a formalist criticism has any hope of remembering this, when the time of reading the work comes. The problem then becomes one of giving the notion of form every manner and degree of life, such that there can be no question of having our formalism intimidated, as Aestheticism has been intimidated, by a dismissive irony.

There is more than enough in Pater, Wilde and James to sustain an unapologetic Formalism, especially when we reflect upon their refusal to submit to the conditions at large, or to accept that reality was merely what it was commonly declared to be. In their different styles, their works are antithetical, as a matter of principle, to the conditions that supposedly constitute reality. Only a vulgar politics finds these writers compromised by the social conditions at large. But critics on the Left, with a few notable exceptions, persist in denouncing as inhuman and unreal the aesthetic impulse in Pater, Wilde and James. Or rather, the second and third generations of neo-Marxist critics have, with few exceptions, denounced this impulse. The first generation of Marxists or neo-Marxists have a far more honourable record in this matter than their successors. I am thinking of Herbert Marcuse, for instance, who argued that art is a force for liberation only so long as it holds out a vision of a better life than the one we live, and so long as it is indeed autonomous. Ernst Fischer is another exception, who recognized in the 'will to form', as Marcuse refers to it in *The Aesthetic Dimension*, the negation of that which is merely the prescribed case. Ernst Bloch, too, saw that the saving grace as well as the enabling force of art is always utopian. Art is always imagining a better life; it is not merely annotating this one. Form is that to which the utopian impulse aspires. Finally, I include T. W. Adorno's assertion, in *Aesthetic Theory*, that 'art is beautiful by virtue of its opposition to mere being'.[20]

XII

It would be pretentious to propose a new Formalism, except that some of the existing ones are open to objection. Formalism is unacceptable if it means the prejudice according to which man creates objects in his own image and holds that that image is eternal. Or if it demands that appearances represented in a work of art as external be answerable to concepts derived from subjectivity. Or, worst consideration, if it demands that works of art exhibit the closure which, as in a closed society, denotes that the meaning is accepted because it is the meaning given. All of these axioms are suspect. An aesthetics of form, as Adorno rightly says, is feasible only if it breaks with an older kind of tradition which was spellbound by form because it had totalized it. Adorno is especially useful in this context because he helps to hold the considerations of form and content in tension: 'All that appears in the work of art is potentially both content and form; but specifically form is that through which phenomenality is determined, whereas content is that which determines itself.'[21]

Adorno argues that form represents freedom, whereas empirical life represents repression. The manner in which this freedom is exercised bears upon the spirit in which the constituents of a work of art are organized. Form, according to Adorno, is 'the non-repressive synthesis of diffuse particulars'. Mozart is Adorno's exemplar of this freedom, as Dostoevsky is Bakhtin's. In *The Marriage of Figaro* the form is not such as to subsume particulars; rather, as in the finale of the second act of the opera, form is 'a configuration of interconnected segments that changes with the dramatic situation on the stage'. The organization of such a work is intimate with the disintegration it acknowledges as a truth in rivalry with its own.

NOTES

1 Walter Pater, *The Renaissance*, edited by Donald L. Hill (Berkeley, University of California Press, 1980), p. xix.
2 *Ibid.*, p. 42.
3 Oscar Wilde, *Complete Works* (London, Hamlyn, 1963), p. 873.
4 Harold Bloom (ed.), *Selected Writings of Walter Pater* (New York, New American Library, 1974), p. 264.
5 W. B. Yeats, *Autobiographies* (London, Macmillan, 1961), p. 313.
6 Henry James, *The Figure in the Carpet, and Other Stories* (Harmondsworth, Penguin Books, 1986), pp. 352–3.
7 James Joyce, *A Portrait of the Artist as a Young Man* (New York, Viking, 1947), p. 433.
8 Quoted in Eric Warner and Graham Hough (eds.), *Strangeness and Beauty* (Cambridge University Press, 1983), Vol. II, pp. 261–2.
9 Quoted in Linda Dowling, *Language and Decadence in the Victorian Fin de Siècle* (Princeton University Press, 1986), p. 133.
10 T. W. Adorno, *Kierkegaard: Construction of the Aesthetic*, translated by Robert Hullot-Kentor (Minneapolis, University of Minnesota Press, 1989), p. 10.
11 *Ibid.*, p. 15.
12 J. L. Borges, *Labyrinths*, translated by James E. Irby (Harmondsworth/Penguin Books, 1970), p. 223.
13 Yeats, *Autobiographies*, pp. 302–3.
14 T. S. Eliot, *Selected Essays* (London, Faber and Faber, 1932) 'Arnold and Pater' in p. 442.
15 Richard Ellmann, *Oscar Wilde* (London, Hamish Hamilton, 1987), p. 2.
16 Thomas Mann, *Last Essays*, translated by Richard and Clara Winston

(London, Secker and Warburg, 1959), p. 175.
17 *Ibid.*
18 Walter Benjamin, *Illuminations*, translated by Harry Zohn (New York, Schocken Books, 1969), p. 242.
19 Sharon Cameron, *Thinking in Henry James* (Chicago. University of Chicago Press, 1989), p. 110.
20 T. W. Adorno, *Aesthetic Theory*, translated by C. Lenhardt (London, Routledge & Kegan Paul, 1986), p. 76.
21 *Ibid.*, pp. 209–10.

3 Voices Across the Echoing Straits. Dialogue, Translation and Irony in Arnold and Clough

Miriam Allott

'The function of bridges may be described as the starting of a stream of human traffic hitherto impossible; the surmounting of a barrier, the linking up of two worlds divided by a gulf . . .'
   'Bridges', Encyclopaedia Britannica, 14th edn

*. . . surely once, they feel, we were
Parts of a single continent . . .*
   Matthew Arnold, 'To Marguerite – Continued'

All ages, we say, are ages of transition but in the midst some appear more transitional than others. A couple of decades ago, some twentieth-century feelings about this were sufficiently acute to produce talk about Apocalypse and Last Things, when presumably the process would stop for ever. The pair of nineteenth-century friends and fellow writers who figure in this essay did not permit themselves to contemplate anything so extreme. But they might have done had they not had instilled into them from youth the belief that adversity must be met with fortitude and that against all signs and portents moral stamina would see to it that good would be found on the other side of travail.

It was the stoical struggle to face up to 'these bad days' – 'Who prop, though ask'st, in these bad days my mind' is the earnest if inelegant opening of an early sonnet addressed by Arnold to Clough – and to master their own responses, complex and painful as they were, that shaped the life and work of these distinguished products of Dr Arnold's grand old fortifying educational system. That unforgettable Rugbeian discipline was itself an ingredient in the tribulations afflicting the more sensitive moral sensibilities which it had helped to forge. The lost generation of the 1840s, the thoughtful who with Arnold and Clough were at that time in their early twenties, had to accept the chilling fact that a vast and ever-widening gulf was opening up between the age that had produced the system, and was identified with their youth, and the forces making for the 'bad days' of their unsettled maturity.

The unique character of this sense of change lay partly in the difficulty of grasping the scale of what was happening, the rupture with the old simple certainties being, it seemed, irretrievable. But it lay still more in the impossibility of making even an informed guess about what might lie on the other side of the gulf. The 'bad times' were in fact rather good times for the sort of bridge-building which that brilliant engineering age could take in its stride. But no bridge – arched, suspension, cantilever or any other – could be built without knowledge of how the land lay on the two sides waiting to be linked. The knowledge could be won and the bridging possibilities assessed in a physical world, whatever the dangers and difficulties, but no amount of charting helped to bridge the gulf between the past and the present, the present and the future and, for some early wanderers in the contemporary 'No Man's Land', even between one individual and another. The best that could be done was to find some way of securing a purchase on the shifting sand. 'The doom of the Old has long been pronounced, and irrevocable,' Carlyle had said as early as 1831, 'but, alas, the New appears not in its stead.' By the 1840s, it has been pointed out, 'the idea of the age as a spiritual No Man's Land was a commonplace among Arnold's circle'.[1] Matthew's brother Tom, still believing in divine beneficence while wandering uneasily between the new and the old worlds and between new doubts and the old faith, told Clough in 1847:

> Our lot is cast in an evil time; we cannot accept the present, and we shall not live to see the future. It is an age of transition, in which the mass are carried hither and thither by chimeras of different kinds, while to the few, who know the worthlessness of the chimeras, and have caught a glimpse of the sublime but distant future, is left nothing but sadness and isolation.[2]

This was some seven years before Matthew published his 'Stanzas from the Grande Chartreuse' (1855), where the poet is seen alone on an alien strand, mourning lost faith,

> Wandering between two worlds, one dead
> The other powerless to be born...

and with little consoling sense that the 'other' represented a 'sublime future', however distant. The old world was the world of orthodox belief and the world not yet born was the secular world, and it was impossible to see how it would fare with those who were unable, as Arnold said later, to do without religion but were equally unable to do with it as it was.

It is hardly surprising in the circumstances that his poems should be full of images suggesting isolation, the difficulty of communication, regret for the lost past and the need somehow to get on without giving way to despair, all of these familiar to his readers as the informing features of his individual elegaic style. They appear early; for instance, in the themes and the title of 'Resignation. To Fausta' (1849), which records the difference in feeling experienced when a journey made in youth is made again in later years. The circumstances direct us to the poet's oblique dissenting dialogue with Wordsworth's 'Tintern Abbey', which also tells of revisiting in company with a favourite sister a place known and loved in youth. Wordsworth's poem invests Nature with eternal powers of wisdom, beauty and consolation, which afford for those who respond to her a constant stay against the chances and changes of life. Arnold's Nature, on the other hand, seems 'to bear, rather than rejoice' and is no more immune than human beings to 'the something that infects the world'. Again, for his lovers in the 'Switzerland' sequence the problems of passion are compounded by difficulty in communicating across unbridgeable spaces. 'Ah, what heart knows another?', sighs the poet, 'Ah! Who knows his own?'. Perhaps there was unity long ago – 'surely once ... we were / Parts of a single continent?' But human beings and physical nature now alike suffer the same arbitrary law ('A god, a god, their severance rules') which ordains that they remain isolated like islands in an open sea. The brief moments of respite come with spring-time in nature and the ephemeral experience of romantic love in human life. Then 'lovely notes' may be heard for a while across 'the sounds and channels'.

Pessimistic dissent from the idea of harmony between man and nature is revived by the reflections on Wordsworth's death in 'The Youth of Nature', a less circumspectly eulogistic tribute than Arnold's first elegy, 'Memorial Verses'. He now laments not only the loss of Wordsworth but also the loss of the age he grew up in, his failure to understand the age he survived into, and the nature of this new age in which millions 'darken in labour and pain' and the 'sacred poets' have no place because the times 'can rear them no more'. The poem, moreover, is cast in the form of a dialogue where Nature replies to questions about her independent existence as a source of beauty and truth, questions certainly set moving by the recent publication in 1850, the year of his death, of Wordsworth's *The Prelude*. Nature speaks up for herself in reply: through the vicissitudes of time and change 'I remain'. Yet the poet's question whether she and her attributes may exist only in a Berkeleyan manner through the poet's vision, aided perhaps by moments of insight into the 'gulph' of his hidden self, remains like an objection overruled in court but unexpunged from memory and ready to be taken up again, as indeed it is in the companion poem 'The Youth of Man'.

To extend this listing would be to do no more than rehearse the kind of themes which Arnold's poetry deals with. The manner in which the themes, the reader and the poet are engaged is the product of the special situation which brings the poems into being in the first place, and is thus essential to the various meanings they help to create. It is not merely the liking for a conventional rhetorical device that makes Arnold put the opening line of his sonnet to Clough, quoted above, in the form of a question. The line, further, is itself a reply to a previous question, one put by Clough about how to respond to the inescapable 'bad days' – *'diesen schlecten Tagen'*, as Goethe saw them in 1824, and, according to Carlyle in 1843, 'French Revolutions, Chartisms . . . That make the heart sick in these bad days'.[3] The only unquestioning statements possible in such days are statements that they are indeed 'bad'. Everything else is uncertain, including how one stands with oneself, with others and with the external world. The question is a logical form of expression for such 'days'. If it gets a reply, this itself may be another question or else a proposition which engages with other existing propositions to form part of a continuing debating dialogue. The dialogue may be internal – 'the dialogue of the mind with itself'

– or it may be conducted with others. If the former, it may involve setting forward and playing against each other conflicting views of the 'life liveable'; for instance, in Arnold's 'Resignation', 'Switzerland', 'The Forsaken Merman' or 'Empedocles on Etna', and in Clough's 'Easter Day', *The Bothie of Tober-na-Vuolich*, 'Amours de Voyage' or 'Dipsychus', each of these representing some variety of dramatic form. If conducted with others, the dialogue may be explicit, as in Arnold's use of his own and Obermann's 'voices' in his 'Obermann' poems, or it may be oblique, as in his dissent from Wordsworth in 'Resignation'. Or else again, in the struggle to bridge the cultural gap between the barren present and the rich past, between English parochialism and European intellectual enterprise, it may take the form of wrestling with the problems of translating a text and its meaning from one language to another. This process is in many respects potentially the most intimate dialogue possible between one mind and another; but, with the voices of other translators of the same text haunting the air, it can also present itself as a quintessential example of the intercourse identified with a particular kind of Bakhtinian dialogism. *On Translating Homer* is the most extensive but not the only instance of Arnold's profound concern with this process. Perhaps the most sophisticated, in some cases radically transforming, of these non-affirmative 'dialogic' forms of expression is the use of ironical wit, rare in Arnold's poetry but adopted as a prominent strategy in his prose and emerging supremely in Clough's brilliant and original 'Dipsychus'.

All these devices for securing a degree of purchase on shifting shores are found in some form in both Arnold and Clough. They constitute in many respects a continuation of the lifelong dialogue with each other which began with the establishment of their intimacy at Oxford. Some idea of its nature and the purposes it served for their individual needs is conveyed in the letters Arnold wrote to Clough from 1845 until shortly before Clough's death in 1861, and from the group of five poems, four of them sonnets, which Arnold addressed to him in 1848–9. This was the time of public upheaval, when Clough went over to France to catch a glimpse of 'these blessed revolutions' without which 'I should sink into hopeless lethargy', and of private dilemma, when Clough eventually took the decision to resign from Oriel because of scruples about religious subscription. His engagement in the dialogue is preserved in one letter to Arnold (his side of the correspondence has not otherwise survived), his letters to other members of their circle, his own poems and his prose, particularly his review of Arnold's 1852 volume, *Empedocles on Etna, and Other Poems,* the collection which was to make its dramatic reappearance in 1853 minus the leading poem and plus the notorious preface explaining why.

Clough, one must remember, was the elder of the two by some three years, a considerable gap in early youth. As Dr Arnold's prize pupil at Rugby and the homeless boy whose holidays were spent in the kindly protection of the Arnold household, he had been a daily presence in Matthew's life from the summer of 1829, when he came up to Rugby at the age of ten to join his brother Charles. (Charles was later removed to another school.) Matthew's position resembled that of a younger brother following behind a brilliant sibling in the same school. He saw Arthur shouldering with his habitual profound earnestness the huge responsibilities with which Dr Arnold burdened his praepositors – this being a key element in his disciplinary system – and regular features of his life included constant acclaim for Arthur's achievements at school and confident forecasts (which were not fulfilled) for a still more dazzling academic future. The culminating accolade came with the final prizegiving, when another boy had to help Arthur carry away all his prize books. By the time Matthew eventually caught up with him at Oxford in 1841, it was Arthur who was appointed to act as Matthew's tutor. The close bonds then formed were to be simultaneously deepened and rendered more testing by the independent movements of their developing creativity. Moreover, the search for an individual poetic voice was complicated by common uncertainty about the sort of voice a poet ought to adopt in the 'bad days'.

The anxieties explain the abrasiveness marking some of their public and private exchanges in the years following 1848, when Clough published his popular *The Bothie of Tober-na-Vuolich*, and 1849 when Arnold published his first collection, *The Strayed Reveller, and Other Poems.* By then Matthew had himself become a fellow of Oriel (1845) and then private secretary to the Whig elder statesman Lord Lansdowne (1847–51), but in earlier years it was probably the attraction and resistance in his attitude to an elder contemporary, who was now also his tutor, that shaped Matthew's version of undergraduate rebellion. His adoption of the insouciant dandyism which masked his subterranean *crises de conscience et d'âme* – the revelation of his hidden dialogue of the mind with itself in *The Strayed Reveller* more than surprised his friends – was not deterred by, and very likely had one eye on, the high seriousness of his universally respected ex-Rugbeian tutor. But the tutor engagingly recorded the tutee's carryings-on: 'Matt is full of Parisianism; theatres in general, and Rachel in special: he enters the room with a song of Beranger on his lips – for sake of French words almost conscious of tune.' Matt's degree of demoralization is indicated by his letting his hair grow in foreign style ('guiltless of English scissors'), having breakfast at noon and making a point of regularly cutting chapel, this youthful French phase clearly anticipating the cosmopolitanism with which he would later attempt to open up for his embattled countrymen a bridge across the philistine wastes.[4]

The manner of the letter, written to a mutual friend, is characteristically affectionate, like the tone of Matthew's letters to 'my dear Clough' which respond, often with open endearments and much gaiety, to the tone of those to which they reply, signing off with flourishes like 'Goodbye my love', or 'my own good man farewell', or 'your incorrigible and affectionate M.A.'. But the mutual attachment coexisted with – took much of its nourishment from – temperamental differences, mutual nagging and momentary upsets. In the running dialogue Matthew nagged Arthur for his 'irritating' attempt in his poems to try to *'solve* the universe', for his being a 'mere d—d depth hunter in poetry', for not settling to his *'assiette'*, for not discovering what he truly wanted to say, for the fact that he never could 'finally . . . "resolve to be thyself"'. The latter is taken from Arnold's self-admonishing poem 'Self-Dependence', which sets the voice of restless self-inquiry against that of calm self-knowledge, and it should call attention, if nothing else does, to the fact that these and other pronouncements, far from being dogmatic assertions, are parts of a continuing exploratory style of inquiry which moves to and fro between different environments, and involves other 'voices' as well.

Clough's cool review of Arnold's 1852 collection, as we shall see, widens the debate into the public sphere, but parts of it read like a continuation of the private in the public. The piece was designed to introduce some modern poets to readers of the *North American Review* and couples Arnold with the Spasmodic poet Alexander Smith, whose 'Life Drama', though 'imperfect' and not equal in poetic quality, had a modern subject and might be welcomed – the tone is characteristically tentative – as more in keeping than Arnold's 'literary' themes with the taste of the day in general and with the popularity of the modern novel in particular. The occasion allows Clough to nag Arnold in his turn for his overdelicate themes, for his introspection and melancholy, for the 'dismal cycle of his rehabilitated Hindoo-Greek theosophy', for, in other words, most of the qualities which Arnold had already touched on in their correspondence and which eventually made him send the introspective Empedocles into exile and replace him in 1853 with the 'animating' and 'ennobling' figures found in the ancient Persian legend of Sohrab and Rustum.

The reference to Arnold's allegedly glum 'Hindoo-Greek theosophy' resumes earlier stages of the debate reflected in the poems addressed to Clough in 1848–9. The title of the first, 'The World and the Quietist', announces the general theme, for Arnold had recently been captivated by the advocacy in the *Bhagavad-Gita* of mental detachment from worldly passions while engaging in action, and had married this with the Stoic thinking to which he was temperamentally strongly drawn. He tried out this new 'quietist' stance against Clough's new 'activism', putting up against the latter arguments for stoical patience and perspective as important 'props' for the 'bad days'. 'Religious Isolation. To the Same Friend' argues that one should not, as Clough was doing over the matter of his resignation, keep worrying away at whether or not the 'holy secret, which moulds thee' is also 'Nature's great law', for 'To its own impulse every creature stirs'. That this too is addressed as much to the writer himself as to his 'Friend' we know from his many times expressed need to discover the 'mystery of this heart that beats / So wild, so deep in us', his belief that calm comes only from finding one's 'own true impulse' in the depths of the 'buried self', and grief that the discovery is rare, given if at all in some brief 'lull in the hot race' for the 'flying and elusive shadow'.[5] The conversational sonnet 'To a Republican Friend, 1848' embraces Clough's political leanings – 'God knows it, I am with you' – if they mean concern for 'the armies of the homeless and unfed' and feeling for 'the long heart-wasting show', but the conditional mood and inquiring tone indicate that threads are being picked up from an informal debate which has been going on some time and is expected to continue. 'If these are what you are', he winds up, 'then I am yours, and what you feel I share', and the formulation suggests that whatever the forthcoming reply, it is unlikely to be a straight yes or no.

Clough's review takes up their dialogue from another position, one which had also engaged members of their circle at Oxford and by the early 1850s was beginning to surface in the periodical press as a new battle of the books. The review is really an attempt to add to discussions about the merits of modern over classical literature, a topic which a few years later Arnold would publicly extend to take in the need to know more about the literature of countries other than England and ancient Greece if the nation's cultural health was to survive its sojourn in the desert. Clough's lead-in to the subject of the modern novel turns on knowledge of, and characteristically questioning engagement with, the putting of such ideas into practice:

Studies of many a distant age or country; all the imitations and *quasi-*translations which help to bring together into a single focus the scattered rays of human intelligence; poems after classical models, poems from Oriental sources, and the like, have undoubtedly a great literary value. Yet there is no question, it is plain and patent enough, that people much prefer 'Vanity Fair' and 'Bleak House'. Why so?[6]

'Poems after classical models' and 'poems from Oriental sources' are aimed directly at Arnold, whose 'Sohrab and Rustum', which replaced 'Empedocles on Etna', nevertheless remained an example of both, and was in fact as firmly rooted in 'the folk' as some contemporary advocates of this kind of poetry for the people could have wished. (Arnold took his episode from the *Shah Nama*, the Book of Kings, which the Persian poet Firdousi had compiled from ancient oral heroic traditions, thus winning the title of the Persian Homer and encouraging Arnold to plunge his version deep into Homeric similes and narrative parallels with the *Iliad*.) His earlier verse narratives, moreover, had included 'Mycerinus' and 'The Sick King in Bokhara', both from traditional 'Oriental sources' and thus remote from Smith's 'Life Drama' or, say, Elizabeth Browning's modern theme in 'Aurora Leigh', published in 1857, the year of Arnold's inaugural lecture on 'The Modern Element in Literature', in which he put forward his own definition of 'the modern'. Not confined to any period, this 'modern' was above all an attitude of mind, an idea which immediately gave a new turn to the meaning of the word 'classic'.

From today's perspective, Clough's demurring reference to the introduction of various kinds of translation to help 'to bring together' from 'distant age or country . . . the scattered rays of human intelligence' looks like a flier for this and others of Arnold's first lectures at Oxford, while the lectures themselves could be taken as offering in reply a series of exemplars. Apart from dealing with the problems of translating Homer, which were in any case a matter of lively debate among classicists at the time and engaged Clough as well, Arnold saw to it that his lectures would deal exclusively with foreign writers, some famous, some not, but all of them owing the degree to which they were known at all in England to editors and translators, to whom he gave a good deal of attention on their own account. The current debate about the primacy of the modern novel has a strong bearing on Arnold's cosmopolitan reply about 'what to read'. Clough's handling of the matter, true to form, sets out its own series of questions, especially about the consoling possibililties of the new 'realism':

Is it simply that we have grown prudent and prosaic, and should not welcome, as our fathers did, the Marmions and the Rokebys, the Childe Harolds and the Corsairs? Or is it, that to be . . . popular, to . . . shake the heart of man, poetry should deal . . . with . . . ordinary feelings, the obvious rather than the rare facts of human nature? . . . Could it not . . . introduce into business and weary task-work a character and a soul of purpose and reality . . . Could it not console us with a sense of significance, if not of dignity, in that often dirty, or at least dingy, work which is the lot of so many of us to have to do, and which some one or other, after all, must do?[7]

If the modern novel could bring this order of consolation to inhabitants in the 'Waste Land' who 'darken in labour and pain', maybe it should be poetry's business to follow suit in providing an appropriately tailored literature for the people.

Among Oxford friends who joined in the inquiry – the closest included the future historian James Anthony Froude and the classical scholar William Young Sellar – there was John Campbell Shairp, temporary master at Rugby in 1846, Professor of Latin and Principal of United College at St Andrews in 1861 and 1867, and, with Arnold's support, in 1877 Professor of Poetry at Oxford (he was reappointed in 1882). His voice may be detected mingling with Clough's in this matter, since he was then beginning to shape his own views about a proper poetry for ordinary people in the changing times. He had reported to Clough in April 1853 (the review appeared in July), 'Mat, as I told him, disowns man's natural feelings, and they will disown his poetry.' Poetry for this new age, modern poetry, should in his view be drawn from the folk and firmly rooted in a native culture. The Greek tragic writers who were Arnold's great models could hold no interest for anyone in England or Europe today. But in fact the literary position separating Shairp from Clough was quite as unbridgeable as the attitude which separated him from Arnold. The essential feudalism of Shairp's ideas about 'the people', already latently discernible, became clear in his critical writings of the 1870s and 1880s, when he praised Scott for discovering 'the peasant' and his noble virtues, Wordsworth for creating a new 'aristocracy' of the simple, and made it plain that 'ordinary people' could not possibly appreciate anything more than 'rude but genuine poetry' like ballads. Arnold, in contrast, as a recent critic shrewdly puts it in her study of Arnold's idea of poetry in a democratic age, held throughout life to the belief that 'in a democratic poetry the best poetry was none too good for the people'.[8] The great Greek writers had flourished in such a soil, their audiences were sharers in their creative activity and poetry for the people from any age, holding out such appeal to the great abiding experiences of life, will always be classical because independent of time and place. That to produce the 'classic' was not merely the prerogative of the ancient Greeks was what his *Essays in Criticism* aimed to show.

Clough's feeling for 'the people' had manifestly more in common with these Arnoldian democratic ideas than with Shairp's, and indeed some of his major work takes him a good way outside the range of either, but his vivacious long vacation poem *The Bothie of Tober-na-Vuolich* was fastened upon for what seemed to Shairp and other friends its commitment to the modern subject and the needs of the modern reader. For some present-day modern readers, its working-class heroine, its description of Liverpool workmen cutting through the stone for Lime Street Station (Clough was born in Liverpool), and the departure of the well-born hero with his Scottish lass for a working life in Australia, render the work ideologically impeccable, a reading encouraging the idea of Arnold and Clough as a political Punch and Judy, with the populist Clough beating the élitist Arnold. In this critical arena, Arnold's irritated response to enthusiastic talk in Oxford circles about the newly published *Bothie* is evidence for the prosecution. But his outburst has less to do with the poem's quality – his admiration for Clough's poetry in general, and his feeling for the *Bothie* itself, are expressed elsewhere – than with its being singled out because it seemed to fit in with a not properly thought out and voguish view of what poetry should be in *'diesen schlecten Tagen'*. It probably didn't help that he was still struggling with his own less light-hearted poems, which would not make their appearance in print until the following year. 'I have been at Oxford the last two days,' he wrote to Clough from London in November 1848:

and hearing Sellar, and the rest of that clique who know neither life nor themselves rave about your poem gave me a strong almost bitter feeling with regard to them, the age, the poem, even you. Yes I said to myself something tells me I can, if need be, at last dispense with them all, even with him: better that than be sucked for an hour even into the Time Stream in which they and he plunge and bellow. I became calm in spirit, but uncompromising, almost stern. More English than European, I said finally, more American than English: and took up Obermann, and refuged myself with him in his forest against your Zeitgeist.[9]

The passage is native to the Clough–Arnold exchanges in its sharp debating tone and underlying humour, as also in its confident friendship. It continues, 'But in another way I am glad that Macpherson [the Oxford publisher] gave a very good account of the sale' and closes with the customary cheerful farewell ('When are you coming up hither love?' A letter sent a little earlier ends, 'Farewell my well known love').[10] But brief as it is, the passage affords a glimpse of the self-dialogue that accompanied all the other exchanges and the sensitivity about the 'Zeit-geist' which prompted some of the self-communing. Moreover, the juxtaposing of Senancour's Obermann and a 'stern' dismissal of what was more English – and, worse, more American – than European, keys us in, to use unArnoldian jargon, to ideas which would surface from the interior debate when he launched his polemical assault on 'the great British public' and, as a lecturer and then a writer for the periodical press, began his lifetime effort to wrest a few answering noises from 'that powerful but at present somewhat narrow-toned organ, the modern Englishman'.[11] Of the mixture of well-known and lesser-known writers figuring in the lectures collected in *Essays in Criticism. First Series* (1865), the book which is at once his sense of the past and his passage to Europe, the famous include Heine, Marcus Aurelius and Spinoza – in other words, a modern German, an ancient Roman of the early Christian era and a seventeenth-century Spanish Jew. The minor figures – Maurice and Eugénie Guérin, Joubert – are all French. The editors and translators who help to make their work known are essential agents in the taskforce helping to lead the potential 'children of light' out of the badlands ruled by their 'strong, dogged, unenlightened opponents', which was the original definition of the Philistines, a German term adapted from the Bible which Arnold now took over and used publicly for the first time in his Heine essay.

The 'children of light', for their part, could be found in any age or country, their modernity itself illuminated by those – translators in every sense – who were themselves sufficiently gifted to make them understood across the ages, across the seas and across the curious barriers set up between the famous and the unknown, between those whom custom had placed in the canon and those it had not. In a passage that should serve as an *aide-mémoire* for anyone selecting texts for the literature syllabus in academies,[12] he explains that his 'minor' figures – Joubert is one of them – are chosen because they have 'a genuine gift for what is true and excellent, and are therefore capable of emitting a life-giving stimulus'; because 'from what is new to us there is most to be learnt'; and because there is a better chance of engaging directly with such writers than may be the case with the familiar great. With these it is possible to be captivated less by their time-hallowed genius than by the 'turns, vivacity, and novelty' of our commentaries upon them, a remark which in view of some latterday literary habits, may get home where it hurts.

The best 'translators' for Arnold include those who distinguish what is truly 'modern' from what is not; those who fail in this have at least the distinction of helping to elicit from him for the first time publicly the play of his native ironic wit. Among his most cherished figures was Marcus Aurelius, 'perhaps one of the most beautiful figures in history', with 'a special interest "for us moderns"': 'he lived and acted in a state of society modern in its essential characteristics, in an epoch akin to our own ... Marcus Aurelius thus becomes for us a man like ourselves, a man in all things tempted as we are.'[13] Melancholy and troubled as he is, 'we see him wise, just, self-governed' and that we 'see him' so clearly in our day is owed to his recent translator, the distinguished classical scholar George Long (his translation of *The Thoughts of the Emperor Marcus Aurelius Antoninus* appeared in 1862). Long's great achievement is to treat the remains of Greek and Roman antiquity 'not as dead and dry matter of learning, but as documents with a side of modern applicability and living interest'. He deals with 'the modern epoch' of Caesar and Cicero,

> not as food for schoolboys but as food for men [who are] engaged in the current of contemporary life and action, so in his remarks and essays on Marcus Aurelius he treats this truly modern striver and thinker not as a Classical Dictionary hero, but as a present source from which to draw 'example of life, and instruction in manners'. Why may not a son of Dr. Arnold say, what might naturally here be said by any other critic, that this lively and fruitful way of considering the men and affairs of ancient Greece and Rome, Mr. Long resembles Dr. Arnold?[14]

Why not indeed? Especially since it is to our purpose to notice with respect that Thomas Arnold, besides striving to inculcate this sense of the past in his boys, did all he could to lay the foundations for some degree of cosmopolitan knowledge in the next generation by struggling to get modern languages efficiently taught at Rugby. He succeeded to the extent that French and German were established in the three higher forms, and French in the forms below, though by 1840 he was still wrestling with the practical problem of how '*all* the boys of a large public school can be taught modern languages'.[15]

It seems in keeping that his son's French was always good, his spoken and written German more halting (lamented by him the more because of his feeling for Goethe and for Heine). With Italian he had to start from scratch. He found a child of light in John Carlyle, whose 1849 prose translation of the *Inferno* gave him not only his first intimate knowledge of Dante but also a *point de repère* for his assault on the ineffable child of darkness, Theodore Martin, whose edition of Dante's *The Vita Nuova* was published with introduction and notes in 1862. For Martin, Dante's Beatrice is a replica of Wordsworth's 'Phantom of Delight':

> The perfect woman, nobly planned
> To warm, to comfort, and command,
> And yet a spirit still, and bright
> With something of an angel's light . . .

Martin 'is ever quoting these lines,' says Arnold, making the most of this fatuous comparison with 'the creature not too bright and good' of Wordsworth's domestic hearth. Dante here is a 'true-hearted gentleman', and the tradition that he lived unhappily with his wife is for Martin unacceptable because his feelings were 'noble' and 'manly'. She provided the 'support of a generous woman', which 'must have elicited from him a satisfactory response'; and so, 'without prejudice to the wife's claim on his regard', he could 'entertain his heavenward dream of the departed Beatrice . . .' Arnold's amused verdict – 'This Dante is transformed in Mr Martin's hands into the hero of a sentimental, but strictly virtuous novel!' – gestures towards the debate about the modern in general and modern fiction in particular. 'Modern readers' of the poem, he says, 'insist on seeing in the "worship of a woman" as they call it', something to do with 'modern relations in life between the two sexes . . . making out of Dante's adoration of Beatrice a substantial modern love story, and . . . arranging Dante's real life so as to turn it into the proper sort of real life for a "worshipper of a woman" to lead.'[16]

Martin's stuff is so crass that to quote it is mostly enough, but the gulf between the profound spirituality of the poem and this editor's crude antinomian actualizing of its subject matter is lit up by the ironical play that belonged with what Arnold called his 'vivacities'. 'I use irony so much,' he wrote in 1868, 'because the ordinary Englishman is so hard, strong and pugnacious, that he will contend with you, instead of weighing your words, if you appear to expostulate with him directly.'[17] He explained it defensively to the members of his family up at Fox How, whose 'vein of strictness' made them as he knew 'a little averse to that sort of style'. 'I see more and more,' he told his mother in 1867 when preparing her for *Friendship's Garland*, his most successful achievement in 'that sort of style',

> what an effective weapon in a confused, loud talking and clap-trappy country like this, where every writer and speaker to the public tends to say rather more than he means, is *irony*, or according to the strict meaning of the original Greek word, the saying rather less than one means. The main effect I have had on the mass of noisy claptrap and inert prejudice which chokes us has been, I can see, by the use of this weapon; and now when people's minds are getting widely disturbed and they are beginning to ask themselves whether they have not a great deal to learn that is new to them, to increase this feeling in them irony is more useful than ever.[18]

By 'now' the repercussions of the social and religious upheavals of the 1830s and 1840s had been added to by, among other things, *The Origin of Species*, *Essays and Reviews* and *Das Kapital*, from all of which there was indeed 'a great deal to learn' that was new and no less disturbing than before. In the context, the resort to irony, with its inherent problematics, underlines yet again that the sense of discrepancy and difference was itself still its own most powerful subject. The weapon in the hands of the self-styled 'Liberal of the Future' certainly needled people into response, but this could be as entrenchedly hostile as that of George Sala, the 'Young Lion' of the *Daily Telegraph*, who had prompted some of Arnold's most sardonic attacks on journalistic vulgarity. It was thus as often misunderstood then as now (Arnold is still widely regarded as one of the deeply unfunny Victorian heavies). More, it could only mask, never resolve, the unbridgeable division between the sanguine liberal idealist and the 'buried self' who sensed the demonic in life and, like Conrad after him, felt himself able to do little more than move gingerly in the dark, perhaps carrying a small light.

All the same, there are moments in both Arnold and Clough when irony brought them near to a synthesizing tension which normally lay well out of reach. In Arnold this happens only in *Friendship's Garland*. He never uses this kind of irony in his poetry, and his other prose is usually too discursive and strategically repetitive – he wants to get his points home – to achieve the interior tautness and witty use of inversion that distinguish his remarkable letters addressed to 'My Countrymen'. Clough's formal prose in reviews and lectures is disappointingly flat; his letters are certainly not so, but their humour is united with a fine journalistic flair (his eye-witness accounts of the undramatic feel of the great revolutionary moments in Paris and Rome have the authenticity of the battlefield experiences recorded by Tolstoy's Pierre and Stendhal's Fabrice). The story is different when it comes to his poetry. 'Dipsychus' is the single Victorian poem to treat with ironic wit the plight of the divided soul torn between belief and doubt, with the voices of the divided self, instead of echoing disparately across the boundless straits, now beginning to effect a 'modern' interplay between inner complexity and outer detachment.

In Arnold's equivalent major poem, although Callicles's closing lyric celebrates universal calm, the unbridgeable crater still lies between himself and the ravaged Empedocles (the eternal want of repose and resolution in Arnold's invocations of calm was always apparent to his shrewdest Victorian admirers). There is no such separation between the insouciant worldly pragmatism of the sardonic Spirit, the comic Mephisto who is Dipsychus's interlocutor, and the 'two-souled' Dipsychus himself. The dualities and contradictions in both figures provide the poem's continuous comic commentary on the human need to synthesize, a preoccupation which paradoxically brings to the balancing of contraries a sense that we may be hovering on the verge of an unprecedented resolution.

But in the true spirit of a modern fiction, the work remains open-ended. We are not finally to know whose advice is followed by whom or what moral or religious idea is the one on which to rest; the mystery remains and is interior to itself.[19] *That* voice, we may agree with mixed feelings, is one which still seems to be heard across echoing straits.

NOTES

1 Thomas Carlyle, 'Characteristics', 1831, in *Critical and Miscellaneous Essays*, Vol. 3, *Works*, edited by H. D. Traill (London: Centenary Edition, 1896–99), Vol. 28, pp. 29–30. The comment by Kenneth Allott is recorded in Kenneth Allott, *The Poems of Matthew Arnold* (London, Longman, 1965).
2 Letter to Clough, 16 April 1847, in F. L. Mulhauser (ed.), *The Correspondence of Arthur Hugh Clough* (Oxford University Press, 1957).
3 Goethe's *Conversations with Eckerman*, 2 July 1834; Carlyle's *Past and Present*, 1843, *Works*, edited by Traill, Vol. 10, p. 36.
4 See Clough's letter of J. C. Shairp, 22 February 1847, in Mulhauser (ed.), *The Correspondence of Arthur Hugh Clough*, Vol. 1, pp. 178–9; H. F. Lowry (ed.), *The Letters of Matthew Arnold to Arthur Hugh Clough* (London, 1932), pp. 24–5.
5 See 'The Buried Life', lines 52, 391, 393 (*Poems* 289, 291). For the 1848 poems to Clough, see *Poems* 106–112.
6 Blanche Clough (ed.), *The Poems and Prose Remains of Arthur Hugh Clough*, 2 vols. (1869), Vol. 1, p. 360.
7 Clough (ed.), *The Poems and Prose Remains of Arthur Hugh Clough*, pp. 360–61.
8 Mary W. Schneider, *Poetry in the Age of Democracy. The Literary Criticism of Matthew Arnold* (University Press of Kansas, 1989), p. 242.
9 Lowry (ed.), *The Letters of Matthew Arnold to Arthur Hugh Clough*, p. 95.
10 Ibid., pp. 93, 95.
11 Matthew Arnold, *Essays in Criticism. First Series* (1865).
12 Ibid., 'Joubert'.
13 Ibid., 'Marcus Aurelius'.
14 R. H. Super (ed.), *The Complete Prose Works of Matthew Arnold* (Ann Arbor, Michigan: University of Michigan Press, 1960–77), Vol. 3, p. 136.
15 A. P. Stanley *The Life and Correspondence of Thomas Arnold*, 2nd edn (1890), pp. 78–9.
16 Super (ed.), *The Complete Prose Works of Matthew Arnold*, Vol. 3, p. 6.
17 Letter to Thomas Spedding, 18 January 1868 (Wordsworth Trust Museum).
18 Letter to Mrs Mary Penrose Arnold, 5 December 1867 (Balliol College).
19 The fragmentary sequel, 'Dipsychus Continued', in which the action takes place after 'an interval of thirty years', is closer in moral style to the later, more conventional *Mari Magno*, the series of tales written in 1861 during Clough's last travels abroad.

4 Seriousness and Triviality: Towards The Importance of Being Earnest

Brian Nicholas

The ambiguities of Wilde's subtitle, 'A Trivial Comedy for Serious People', offer us a playful challenge to define his own seriousness in a way he would have found acceptable, or to convict him of triviality on grounds which he had not already anticipated. And the 'lord of language' invites further literary scrutiny, especially after an excess of attention to his personality and biography.[1] But we have to admit from the start the limitations of a purely literary–critical approach. As we read, the obtrusive personality reminds us constantly that Wilde must in some measure remain an historical figure, a figure in opposition, whose stature may finally depend on our estimate of what he opposed.

Certainly any worthwhile consideration of Wilde must be through the forms in which he expressed himself. But the more dazzling the forms – particularly those of paradox and epigram – the more sharply we are directed back to 'content'. 'Work is the curse of the drinking classes' may seem, according to our own stance, a liberating and humane reversal of the Protestant ethic or a cheap comment on a complex historical issue. A favourable response to Wilde may ultimately depend on our sharing his belief in the concrete existence, and objectionableness, of that shadowy monster, Victorianism; on agreeing that sententiousness is synonymous with hypocrisy, and that overactivity of the moral sense is the English disease. As to the aesthetic alternative proposed, there may be elements of pose and exaggeration in Wilde's amoralism ('there are only two sorts of people, the tedious and the charming', 'any preoccupation with what is right or wrong in conduct is a sign of arrested intellectual development', and so on); on the other hand, his call for a revision of values and his rejection of the primacy of the ethical cannot, any more than Nietzsche's, properly be watered down into a tame and easily acceptable reformism.

So much for the irreducibly ideological and controversial element in Wilde; but there is still plenty of room for a more specifically literary examination. Wilde's output does not, in fact, consist just of contentious opinions 'illustrated' by witty formulas. The essays, in which he was most at home, show a far closer and more suggestive unity of form and content than the detached epigrams might have led us to expect. And we may want to do our critical best for Wilde for another reason: in art, as in life, he was often his own worst enemy. The comedies on which his reputation rests in some ways do him a disservice, and prove ambiguous documents for his 'seriousness'. The subject matter conspires against him. If the mixture of problem play and sentimental melodrama in the first three leads to their being judged 'dated', *The Importance of Being Earnest* by its very perfection qualifies all too readily for the unhelpful epithet 'timeless'. In both cases grounds are to hand for isolating the cleverness and establishing a category of 'pure' wit, into which the reader can channel his admiration (or distaste) for the verbal technique. This, of course, is to reduce or to reject the plays' significance.

Yet such is the moral confusion of the problem plays that appreciation of their wit can seem a generous response to the undertaking. It was natural, in the literary climate of the times, that Wilde should be drawn towards this form in order to express his hatred of the man-made law which, in the words of the *Ballad of Reading Gaol*, 'But straws the wheat and saves the chaff / With a most evil fan'. But dramatizing the Wildean point of view, so convincing and stimulating in the essays, presented unexpected hazards – and for a fundamental reason. The mode of dramatic conflict is in direct opposition, to a much greater degree than Wilde realized, with what is most essential in his amoralism: the distaste for envisaging and adjudicating particular moral issues. The enemy of earnestness has to get involved in what – in the words of Lord Illingworth in *A Woman of No Importance* – is the normal concomitant of earnestness: 'taking sides'. And, inexperienced and ultimately not very interested as he is in this very Victorian skill, Wilde manipulates his characters and situations with a nonchalance which is bound to lead him into trouble. Yet what we have in this and his other 'problem' plays is not necessarily a final proof of Wilde's moral hollowness; perhaps more an endearingly naïve playing into the hands of the enemy. None of them forms a coherent whole, but they are successive attempts to solve an artistic problem in a borrowed form. To show the continuity of these preoccupations will be to claim for Wilde at least one sort of artistic seriousness; and *The Importance* will gain in stature by being seen not as an isolated triumph but as the culmination of the whole effort, the more remarkable since the Wildean point of view looked like proving incommunicable in dramatic form.

What the Wildean viewpoint *is* can be got at only through illustration, perhaps most relevantly from *The Soul of Man under Socialism* (1890), the fine essay which immediately precedes the plays. Here Wilde maintains the necessity of Socialism for the development of the individual, at present impeded by the competitive spirit which the unequal distribution of wealth provokes. There is a radical attack on the whole basis of society; a rejection of palliatives like philanthropy; contempt for rationalizations in favour of the *status quo*, such as the notion of the 'good poor' or of pain as a 'mode of perfection'. A sociological view is taken of crime – 'starvation, not sin, is the parent of modern crime'. With the removal of poverty crime will disappear and the way will be clear for a new valuation of the individual, in which the charitable and the ethical – 'sympathy' and moral judgement – will give way to more flexible and liberating criteria. We must learn a task harder and more rewarding than sympathizing with suffering – that of sympathy with a man's success and with the 'joy and beauty of life'.

Such ideas recur in the utopian and progressive thought of the century, but they are renewed and personalized by the Wildean manner. The cumulative effect of this is difficult to communicate, but the opening sentence already sets the style: 'The chief advantage that would result from the establishment of Socialism is, undoubtedly, the fact that Socialism would relieve us from the sordid necessity of living for others which, in the present condition of things, presses so hardly upon almost everybody.'

The obviously relished paradox – Socialism as a means to individualism – distinguishes Wilde's approach from the start. The casual use of 'sordid' assumes the reader's complicity in a scale of values very different from those of socialist brotherhood. And dissent from the idea of moral retribution as a valid motive in social reform is emphasized in the assertion that the problem weighs on everybody. Capitalism must be got rid of on grounds not only of injustice but of sterility. The point is expanded a little later:

Some years ago people went about saying that property has duties. They said it so often and so tediously that at last the Church has begun to say it. It is perfectly true. It involves endless claims on one ... If property simply had pleasures we could stand it; but its duties make it unbearable. In the interest of the rich we must abolish it.

Here a well-worn cliché is taken up and we are prepared for its demolition. A passing jest on the way in which 'earnest' opinion is formed – and the cliché is proclaimed to be true; but only in a way which prevents another sort of reader settling into an equally self-righteous posture. The point is reinforced by a reminder of the criterion of pleasure; and the rich, who are always asking for sympathy, are playfully accorded it. The 'thought' is never less than serious – an aesthete's variant, as it were, on the difficulty of the rich man's entering the kingdom of heaven. But Wilde manages through stylistic means actually to embody in his discourse the intellectual and moral virtues he is preaching, rather than merely to substitute one sort of pretentiousness for another. To start with the rich man's plight is itself a blow at cant, and the whole nimbleness of approach, never hardening into an attitude of indignation or moral superiority, declares Wilde's concern with the positive and creative, rather than the ethical and retributive aspects of the problem he is considering. At the same time the interrelationship between Aestheticism and humaneness is convincingly established, and paradox acts with ease in the service of both: in the passages on social agitation ('Disobedience is man's original virtue') we feel it performing its most legitimate function of cutting through a whole system of reactionary rationalization and merging with complete naturalness into less epigrammatic argument.

The Soul of Man seems to me the best vindication of Wilde's thought and manner, and it is unlikely that anyone who finds its tone completely uncongenial will want to go further with him.

What emerges for the sympathetic reader is not a set of values but an attitude of mind in which we can distinguish positives of genuine humanity, unpretentiousness and unvindictiveness; and these Wilde manages with conscious ingenuity to make consistent with the doctrine of total hedonism which his horror of cant makes the only acceptable premise for reform. But total hedonism is a dangerous commodity and, if the liberating purpose of *The Soul of Man* is achieved, it is because Wilde remains completely unpractical and does not lead us to envisage any concrete moral or political situation. The difficulties start when he tries to embody the Wildean point of view in a Wildean character, involved in a personal situation.

A common theme of the three plays preceding *The Importance* is the humanizing of a puritan. Lady Windermere and Hester both revoke the rigorous standards by which they would have condemned Mrs Erlynne and Mrs Arbuthnot, and Lady Chiltern comes to accept the real instead of the 'ideal' husband that she had always assumed Sir Robert to be. In general *Lady Windermere's Fan* (1892) is a success in that it avoids any open conflict of values. Wilde injects into the easily sentimental theme of the salvation of a marriage some of his own more ironical and astringent attitudes. Lady Windermere owes her initiation into a more flexible moral outlook to the Wildean Lord Darlington – but his impulse to enlighten her is bound up with the possibility of seducing her; she ends by characterizing Mrs Erlynne as 'a very good woman' – but it has been made clear that Mrs Erlynne's gesture belongs to the field of style rather than of sincerity. However, the reality of Lady Windermere's goodness and the worthwhileness of her marriage are not seriously at odds with her being not so much a convert to, as a dupe of, Wildean style and philosophy.

But in *A Woman of No Importance* (1893), though it is a more interesting play, Wilde gets into deeper water. Here we are introduced to a fatuous country-house society in which Lord Illingworth is the reigning dandy-philosopher. He has just offered the post of secretary to the son of a pious widow, Mrs Arbuthnot. Watching these developments is Hester, a visiting American puritan who detests Illingworth and finds in Mrs Arbuthnot a lone example of simplicity and virtue. After she has expressed her views strongly and publicly, Gerald turns out to be Illingworth's illegitimate son. The play ends with her becoming engaged to Gerald and recognizing that Mrs Arbuthnot's virtue is not discredited by a single distant fault.

Here we have the authentically Wildean undertaking of confuting puritanism and moral absolutism. But Wilde takes a more decisive step than with the ultimately non-active Darlington and makes the spokesman of the anti-puritan cause into the villain of the piece. Now, Illingworth is the mouthpiece for a large number of the 'views' which Wilde expressed in his discursive works. Thus the question of philanthropy and the notion of the sterility of 'sympathy' come up in this skirmish with the caricaturally 'earnest' politician Kelvil:

KELVIL: You cannot deny that the House of Commons has shown great sympathy with the sufferings of the poor.
ILLINGWORTH: That is its special vice. That is the special vice of the age. One should sympathise with the joy, the beauty, the colour of life. The less said about life's sores the better.
KELVIL: Still, our East End is a very important problem.
ILLINGWORTH: Quite so. It is the problem of slavery. And we are trying to solve it by amusing the slaves.

Considered on their own Illingworth's views would seem qualified to dominate the action of the play. For not only his aphorisms but his arguments in dramatic contexts express the Wildean viewpoint. In the recognition scene Mrs Arbuthnot's objections to the career proposed for Gerald are answered with the charge that sentiment is being used to conceal selfishness; and Gerald's present discontent is proclaimed good in the way that political subversion is defended in *The Soul of Man*:

MRS ARBUTHNOT: He was not discontented till he met you. You made him discontented.
ILLINGWORTH: Of course I made him so. Discontent is the first step in the progress of a man or a nation.

Now, whatever 'seriousness' we may allow these views, the context can only make them look cynical, flippant, callous. In the first example because Illingworth is not sufficiently dissociated from the purely fatuous world around him, which regards the politician's work with snobbish incomprehension; in the second because our involvement with Mrs Arbuthnot's plight prevents us from giving the father's views the weight they might deserve in a discursive context. His dicta, therefore, since they never become fully integrated in a supporting action, acquire the character of isolated witticisms.

Yet Wilde's irony supports to the end not only Illingworth's views but to a large extent his analysis of the situation. He tells Mrs Arbuthnot that Gerald's upbringing will make him judge her if he ever finds her out; and it is in fact Gerald's cool comment on her third-person account of her past that makes her resign herself to letting him go. Similarly, it is the exaggerated reactions of Gerald and Hester to Illingworth's realization of his ambition to 'kiss the puritan' that provoke the revelation of his identity. 'Style', we are led to feel, might have ordered things better. And Illingworth's discomfiture is left so late that Wilde has rather hastily to make him act in a brutal and uncharacteristic way in order to secure the final sentimental resolution. But what works against Illingworth throughout, despite the vigour of his ideas, is the fact that, though Mrs Arbuthnot's 'goodness' has little real substance for Wilde, is hardly more than a convenience for initially recommending her to Hester, she engages his sympathy from another point of view. With his deep (and prophetic) horror of social ostracism he has a ready, if stagy, sympathy for any sort of pariah, and gives Mrs Arbuthnot some of his lushest prose with which to describe her sufferings. The effect, of course, is to make Illingworth's style seem still more brittle and inhuman.

With his basic indifference to problems of moral adjudication Wilde fails to see that they will raise themselves in the most damaging way if he tries to present ideas (and too many at once) through the medium of personal conflict. While the action is proving to Hester that a formally bad woman may be essentially good, Illingworth is suggesting to the audience that a formally good woman may be essentially selfish. Both are impeccably 'serious' Wildean notions, but there is something perversely cavalier about trying to illustrate them both with the same set of characters. By moving from the world of attitude to that of action, Wilde almost wilfully draws attention to the practical shortcomings of his philosophy; and to many readers the demonstration will be conclusive. The misfortune is not that the philosophy is not vindicated but that it does not even get a chance, that the play invites us from the start to consider the crudest of moral questions – is it better to be clever or good? The enemy of moral adjudication has invited us to exercise – and then confusedly – the very indignation that it was his avowed aim to diminish.

An Ideal Husband (1895) throws further light on Wilde's problem, but from a different angle. Here the Wildean figure, Lord Goring, is also the hero, successful both in saving Chiltern from disgrace and in converting his wife to a more charitable view of human weakness. The discrepancy here is between Goring's spontaneous impulse to help Chiltern and his implicit indifference to, even distaste for, all that Chiltern's life represents. So insistent is this that, in the discussion of Chiltern's past, Goring, by an ironic reversal, takes on an almost moralizing attitude to the falseness of its assumptions ('a thoroughly shallow creed'), while Chiltern uses the Machiavellian and hedonistic arguments about power that we might rather have expected to hear from the Wildean character. When it comes to action, however, Goring's approach to 'this dreadful business' is strictly practical:

The money, if you will allow me to say so, is . . . awkward. Besides, if you did make a clean breast of the whole affair you would never be able to talk morality again. And in England a man who can't talk morality twice a week to a large, popular, immoral audience is quite over as a serious politician.

The criticism of philanthropy recurs:

CHILTERN: I have paid conscience money many times . . . The sum Baron Arnheim gave me I have distributed more than twice over in public charities.
GORING: In public charities? Dear me! What a lot of harm you must have done, Robert!

Chiltern complains of his flippancy, but Goring airily sticks to his point. And at the very end his response to Lord Caversham's comment on the (again caricaturally earnest) *Times* leader on Chiltern, 'They will never say that about you, sir', is a heartfelt, 'I sincerely hope not, father'.

It is at such points that the underlying problems of the plays come to the surface. Clearly, when Goring talks to Chiltern of charity, or Illingworth to Mrs Arbuthnot of selfishness, there is a whole Wildean dialogue ready to burst out of the dramatic framework; but all we can be allowed to hear of it are a few fragments suspect of triviality or insensitivity.

Wilde is in fact severely paid off for the very concessions he has made to his public. Without subscribing to a fairly conventional notion of the 'good' woman and the 'serious' politician, he probably felt that he could not get a hearing at all. The concessions once made, Goring is available to be judged by conventional standards – as at best a generous but dilettante-ish moral freelance, whose verbal lapses in critical situations show a fundamental lack of taste. (And it is typical again of Wilde's naïveté or perversity that he not only puts Goring on the easiest terms with the villainous Mrs Cheveley but gives him a former engagement to her, 'for three days . . . nearly'.) Yet judged by Wilde's and Goring's own values, Goring's conduct must look even more arbitrary – indeed it strongly resembles one of those *ad hoc* acts of charity which are condemned in *The Soul of Man* as helping to perpetuate a corrupt and philistine system.

If these objections do not obtrude during our reading of the play it is because – as in the case of Mrs Arbuthnot – there is an authentic Wildean motive at work: to save Chiltern from the gloating hypocrisy of public opinion is a good in itself, irrespective of the ultimate value of his political life. It is easy to hear Wilde's (again prophetic) voice through Mrs Cheveley's gleeful evocation of 'the hypocrite with his greasy smile penning his leading article, and arranging the foulness of the public placard'; and in Goring's rejection of the moralist's claim that the scandal will expose the 'real' Chiltern. Here, in apposite dramatic context, are echoes of the reviling in *The Soul of Man* of the press's 'dragging before the eyes of the public some incident in the life of a great statesman' and inviting them 'to discuss the incident, to exercise authority in the matter . . . in fact to make themselves ridiculous, offensive and harmful'. But what, there, is a supporting argument for the privacy of the artist is hardly enough to sustain the coherence of a play in which the coexisting alliance and unlikeness of the main characters are already causing problems. It is precisely some evaluation of the 'real' Chiltern, some content for the notion of the 'great statesman', that the situation leads us to demand – but that it would be impossible to supply without gravely compromising Goring's position. Once again the reader's mind, instead of being able to absorb an unsystematic mood, strays dangerously on to questions too specific for Wilde to be able or to be expected to answer.

In short the Wildean viewpoint, whatever its value, inevitably suffers by the attempt to communicate it through action and conflict. The dandy as villain is an obvious naïveté. The dandy as hero is more subtly damaging. Goring's action may suggest to some a tribute more or less consciously paid by vice to virtue. At best he exposes the unsystematic nature of Wilde's philosophy, the unlikeliness of its application without inconsistency in a specific ethical context. Wilde's ideal, as he says, is of being rather than doing: his central aim the communication of a liberating and positive mood rather than the redirection of an existing morality. And it is this aim which he achieves, with hardly a single provocative discord, in *The Importance of Being Earnest* (1895).

Wilde's greatest success is not just a flight into fancy or a retreat into mere words – the alleged 'pure' wit of the earlier plays transferred to a context where we are not moved to accuse it of triviality or inadequacy. It is the logical solution of the artistic problems raised by them. In this last play we move from specific moral issues to the single, general issue of earnestness itself. And the theme is treated not by way of personal conflict, with its attendant dangers of witty blackmailers and boring saints, but by a tone which permeates the whole texture of the play. This very homogeneity, however, has led to a spectrum of interpretations: at one extreme the dominantly satirical reading, at the other the escapist and idyllic. If neither is complete, the implicit disagreement as to whether we laugh 'at' or 'with' points to a capital quality of the play: the critical and the positive are woven inextricably together; it is both an attack on earnestness and a concrete embodiment of its opposite.

A framework of farce, with an inevitably happy ending, makes it possible for Wilde to tilt at overactivity of the moral sense without involving us in a drama where we risk generating any indignation ourselves. Secure from the threat of real conflict, from the temptation to make ourselves 'ridiculous, offensive and harmful' by harbouring dissentient moral judgements, we are free to listen to a parody version of that compassed, self-righteous touchiness which is the characteristic manner of the morally indignant or complacent. The stage directions 'stiffly', 'sententiously' give the key to the first conversation between Algy and Jack. Thus the resort to convention and precedent as an explanation for conduct, coupled with the oblique accusation of social ignorance, is echoed in Algy's reply to Jack's 'Eating again?': 'I believe it is customary to take some slight refreshment at five o'clock.' Jack's 'It's a very ungentlemanly thing to read another man's cigarette-case' merits the foreseeable Wildean reply that it's absurd to have hard and fast rules about what one should and should not read. Jack makes a claim to superior moral sensibility in remarking that Cecily calls him uncle 'for reasons which it would be impossible for you to appreciate'. The first encounter between the two girls provides a similar mock-heroic edition of moral indignation. The systematic echoing of the clichés of normal, complacent speech removes the play from the world of fancy to something much more contemporary. But – questions of tone and intention apart – to call this *social* satire is already to tie it down too exclusively to a single social class. If two at least of the characters are critically observed social types, they are still presented, primarily, as variants of the earnest posture. More than anything it is the echo of sententiousness that Wilde is concerned to catch. Thus the very punctuation of Lady Bracknell's sentences reveals at once the rigidity and the hollowness of the formal pose. She speaks a sort of aristocratic officialese. We have, with the same superb confidence, cattiness masked as superior discretion – 'It [Lady Harbury's hair] certainly has changed colour. From what cause, I, of course, cannot say'; emotions treated as business – 'When you do become engaged to someone I, or your father, should his health permit him, will inform you of the fact'; and history reduced to the status of an inconvenience to the titled classes – 'And I presume you know what that unfortunate movement [the French Revolution] led to'. Chasuble embodies up to a point a specific satire of that England where the Church could be called the Tory party at prayer. But, while the domestication of religion receives a comic thrust ('Sprinkling is all that is necessary, or indeed I think desirable. Our weather is so changeable'), it is the meticulously punctuated manner, divorced from any response to event, which is most pointedly reproduced; while the exclamation about Ernest's desired burial place – 'In Paris! I fear that hardly points to any very serious state of mind at the last' – echoes an inveterate bit of English folklore. What we are listening to is not a particular class but earnest humanity at large, a superbly imaginative extension (for nobody ever talked quite like Lady Bracknell and Chasuble) of Flaubert's recording of *idées reçues*.

Yet we must already feel the incompleteness of the notion that the play is purely critical. The opening scene, for instance, is seen by Eric Bentley as 'a prelude to the jokes against class society which run through the play'. But surely it is much more than this:

ALGERNON: Did you hear what I was playing, Lane?
LANE: I didn't think it polite to listen, sir.
...
ALGERNON: Oh! ... by the way, Lane, I see from your book that on Thursday night ... eight bottles of champagne are entered as having been consumed.
LANE: Yes, sir; eight bottles and a pint.
ALGERNON: Why is it that at a bachelor's establishment the servants invariably drink the wine? I ask only for information.
LANE: I attribute it to the superior quality of the wine, sir. I have often observed that in married households the champagne is rarely of a first-rate brand.

The opening exchange works in two ways. The notion that to listen to piano-playing could be rude may suggest a satirical purpose, or at least a reminder of the extent and arbitrariness of the restrictions placed on servants. But at the same time a more positive point is being made: Lane is seen to be the Wildean ideal butler in that he appreciates that a man's playing may be as intimate an expression of his personality as his speech or his letters. In this bizarre example of apparent subservience Wilde both echoes critically the lifeless, automatic quality of the normal master–servant relationship and embodies a more positive, liberating ideal. The ensuing exchanges develop this ideal. They are the living antithesis of the 'serious' world of moral rights and duties, with their concomitants of cunning, dissimulation and suspicion. Algy's disinterested inquiry ('only for information'), Lane's precise correction, the notion of servants as connoisseurs, these take us into a world at once of frankness and formality, beside which we may sympathize with Lane's very Wildean formulation – that the 'real' world of his personal relations is 'not a very interesting subject'.

Wilde obviously has a double view of the social world he is portraying. Far from dismissing it, he is fascinated by it (note his fussy, sometimes snobbish stage directions). And while he has no illusions about the social forms as they at present exist, he sees them as a starting-point for the embodiment of his own ideas. It is this which provides a realistic social basis for that fusion of the critical and the positive which is the play's particular triumph. For though the parody of indignation is an important element, the concrete expression of the unearnest virtues also sets a dominant tone. A common movement in the dialogue is from indignation or pretension to a frank avowal of hedonism or egocentricity which delights us by its reversal of the normal moral façade. Thus Gwendolen, explaining her fears of Jack's infidelity, declares that 'Modern, no less than Ancient History, supplies us with many most painful examples of what I refer to.' But pomposity gives way to the ingenuousness of the young girl who has found her lessons hard going: 'If it were not so, indeed, History would be quite unreadable.' Jack, listing Algy's misdemeanours, complains that 'under an assumed name he drank an entire pint bottle of my Perrier-Jouet, Brut, '89; wine I was specially reserving for myself'. And Lady Bracknell triumphantly proclaims her own unreasonableness when she silences discussion on the grounds that arguments are 'always vulgar and often convincing'.

Up to a point these transitions strike us as deliberate manipulation, exploiting to the full the licence afforded by the conventions of farce. And the complete unity of tone of the opening scene is not achieved or even attempted at every point in the play. But in general what distinguishes *The Importance* is the skill with which Wilde combines established formulas such as self-revelation (as in high comedy) and self-deflation (as in farce) for his own purpose. Far from finding the transitions from critical to positive too abrupt or artificial, many readers, while aware of the presence of the two elements, may well find it difficult to decide on the category to which a particular remark belongs. Consider, for instance, Chasuble's offer to christen Jack:

In fact I have two similar ceremonies to perform at the same time. A case of twins that occurred in one of the outlying cottages on your own estate. Poor Jenkins the carter, a most hard-working man.

The final remark strikes us as endearingly unearnest, a humane alternative to pulpit cant about the blessings of fecundity. But it also springs (as does the use of the word 'occurred') quite naturally from the character of the life-fearing, hypochondriac celibate who recommended sprinkling rather than immersion. The speech could almost form part of a consistent classical comedy of self-revelation. But the effect is more complex: if it is lack of self-awareness which leads to complacency – and the comic defect of rigidity and automatism – it is lack of self-consciousness which leads to frankness – and the Wildean virtue of freedom from cant. And every character benefits from the blurred line of demarcation between the two. Even Miss Prism, in some ways that most traditional of comic butts, the embittered spinster: her heedless defiance of the normal convention *de mortuis* – 'this [Ernest's death] seems to me a blessing of an extremely obvious kind' – makes its impact in the context as a blow against hypocrisy rather than as a piece of self-revelation. If the formal device of exposure is used, the chief thing exposed is the reassuring fact that all the characters partake of something of Wilde himself.

In high comedy we only rarely get examples of egoism and its by-products used to such exhilarating effect. When, in *Le Bourgeois Gentilhomme*, M. Jourdain's philosophy master suggests that they study '*la Morale*', which teaches man to moderate his passions, his pupil rejects it out of hand: '*Non, laissons cela. Je suis bilieux comme tous les diables, et il n'y a morale qui tienne.*' We feel the same warming to the character as with Chasuble and Miss Prism. But Jourdain shines only by the introduction of another term of comparison: a fool and a snob beside the *honnête homme*, he has a realism amounting almost to true philosophy when placed next to the pedant. The peculiar ambivalence of self-centredness in Wilde's code makes his personages more constantly available to embody his values, while at the same time he can use them allusively as a means for attacking the earnest world. Wilde may not be concerned with the traditional dramatist's business of 'creating character', but he certainly succeeds in saying all he wants to say without making us feel that the notion of character is being grossly violated, that we are just listening to a collection of detached witticisms, brought together by mechanical manipulation of their spokesmen. Even 'indignation', which looks as if it is being set up merely to be wittily knocked down, proves to have a legitimate life of its own. Consider Jack's explanation of his double identity:

> My dear Algy, I don't know whether you will be able to understand my real motives. You are hardly serious enough. When one is placed in the position of a guardian one has to adopt a high moral tone in all matters. It is one's duty to do so. And as a high moral tone can hardly be said to conduce very much either to one's health or one's happiness . . . I have always pretended to have a younger brother . . .

While this is formally an example of the manipulated move from pretension to self-deflation, it also has a coherence of tone (whether we like the tone or not) which comes from the play on the word 'serious'. 'You are hardly serious enough' seems at first to belong to the parody of indignation, but taken in conjunction with what follows it becomes part of a Wildean charge that Algy is neglectful of the refinements of hedonism. If indignation has any place in Wilde's world it is as a reaction to a lack of his own sort of 'seriousness'; and its partial legitimation furthers that merging of the critical and the positive, the formation of that continuous, elusive tone in which both elements make themselves unambiguously felt without our needing or being able to separate them analytically.

In such a climate paradox and epigram can be perfectly absorbed into the texture of the dialogue. Paradox becomes the token of honesty, not the signpost of frivolity. The girls court their dandies with a frankness and purposefulness which provoke in each case the stage direction 'looks at her in amazement'; and the technique in each case is the reversal of conventional sentimental assumptions ('I wish that, in public at any rate, you had been more demonstrative', 'a very young girl's record of her own thoughts and impressions, and consequently meant for publication'). Such robustness has nothing to fear from, and would no doubt endorse, Algy's 'cynical' critique of cosy conjugal life ('in married life three is company and two is none') and displays of conjugal affection ('simply washing one's clean linen in public'). Wilde has found a context for the wilfully brittle dicta of the *Phrases and Philosophies for the Use of the Young*, and it is a measure of his success in creating a mood that Gwendolen, consistently with her emancipation from conventional romanticism, can pronounce one of them verbatim at a dramatic juncture: 'In matters of grave importance style, not sincerity, is the vital thing.' She has 'grave doubts' about Jack's account of the deception practised on her, but 'I certainly intend to suppress them. This is not the moment for German scepticism'. Epigram and paradox are assimilated and vindicated in the play, rather than thrown into discordant relief as they had been earlier. In fact the epigram, the detached moral or amoral formula, turns out to occupy a smaller place in the play than one's memory would suggest. Paradox may be ubiquitous to the point of irritation. But even so it often gains its point by being pushed a term further than we expect, so that we have an impression of an unresting yet effortless campaign not to be caught out in the earnest posture ('What shall we do?' / 'Nothing.' / 'It's awfully hard work doing nothing. However, I don't mind hard work where there's no definite object of any kind.') Paradox is only one of a multiplicity of verbal techniques (including the 'absurd' non sequitur which still echoes the rule of thumb oppressiveness of the moral world: 'We have already missed five, if not six trains. To miss more might expose us to comment on the platform'); all of which, from different angles, illumines the general theme of earnestness.

In *The Importance* Wilde has come completely to terms with his talent and has found the perfect dramatic form for projecting many of his 'views'. We are not presented with a situation of conflict in which we are invited to envisage a particular moral issue or to take sides. We listen to a tone. But, if the tone is one from which the development of ideas has been banished, those informing ideas are sensed at every turn. *The Soul of Man* has a vehement attack on paternalistic notions of the 'good poor' ('to recommend thrift to the poor is both grotesque and insulting... Man should not be ready to show that he can live like a badly fed animal'). When Jack asks Chasuble whether 'you know how to christen', Miss Prism intervenes with: 'It is, I regret to say, one of the Rector's most constant duties. I have often spoken to the poorer classes on the subject. But they don't seem to know what thrift is.' Wilde's rejection remains unambiguous, and the association of the idea with a particular psychological type is the opposite of trivializing. At the same time the mood remains legitimately genial. Life has nothing to fear from Miss Prism.

SERIOUSNESS AND TRIVIALITY

Wilde includes her in his happy ending – the forthrightness and unselfconsciousness which accompany her earnestness win her a place there. As we saw earlier, most of the characters are accorded enough Wildean virtues to be accommodated in the idyllic frame. And this idyllic aspect is itself vindicated. The world of the play – in which there are no worse vices than addiction to muffins – combines sophistication and innocence in an extraordinary but credible way. Evil is not denied but plausibly kept at bay. Having given his characters the capacity to represent both what is to be criticized and what is positive, Wilde's use of them can be in harmony with Lord Illingworth's dictum (which echoes *The Soul of Man*) that we should sympathize with 'the joy, the beauty, the colour of life', and that 'the less said about life's sores the better'. The idyllic complements the satirical as the vision of the ideal complements the critical analysis in *The Soul of Man*. But that broad vision could not be dramatized. Wilde's seriousness as an artist consists in the discovery that a large part of his purpose could best – could only – be served by a 'trivial comedy'.

NOTE

1 This imbalance has in fact been substantially redressed in recent years. Ian Gregor's own article, 'Comedy and Oscar Wilde', *Sewanee Review*, July 1966, was reprinted in the useful *Oscar Wilde's Comedies: A Casebook*, edited by William Tydeman (London, Macmillan, 1982). There have been several critical studies, the latest of which, Peter Raby, *Oscar Wilde* (Cambridge University Press, 1988), contains an up-to-date bibliography. Scholarly editions of all four comedies by Russell Jackson and Ian Small (London, 1980–83) have provided, through the evidence of variants and reworkings, another kind of testimony to Wilde's 'seriousness' as an artist. Richard Ellman's monumental *Oscar Wilde* (London, Hamish Hamilton, 1987), though generous and perceptive about the works, is essentially a biography and an evaluation of the man – and the best sort of reminder that the pendulum might swing too far in the direction of pure criticism.

5   Thresholds and Verges: Hardy Imagines Imagination

Barbara Hardy

I
Introduction

Liminal metaphors are active in Hardy's poetics of creativity. Not surprisingly they often take an architectural form, but we should not lay too much biographical stress on that. Donne, Herbert, George Eliot, Henry James and D. H. Lawrence also allude to doors, arches, windows, gateways, interiors and exteriors in their imagining of creativity. Entrance and exit, passages, walls, barriers and windows are common conveniences of vision as artists imagine and re-imagine the efforts, successes and failures of imagination.

II
Inner and Outer Self

Even in an early poem, Hardy can portray the gradual contamination of the inner life, which he imagines as the self at its least public, least conditioned by social experience. His superficially naïve love poem 'At A Seaside Town In 1869', subtitled 'A Lover's Reverie', is concerned with the traffic between the private and the public worlds in which what we call the self forms, changes and dies. He presents the effects of a to-and-fro crossing as a gradual process of undesirable socializing, a form of psychic and social osmosis in which the flow of fluid through tissue is a two-way action and consequence. The poem images the self as interior and society as composed of public relationships and pastimes in an exterior environment both social and natural. The narrative is dependent on images of barrier, threshold, crossing and divided space. The love story is a simple narrative, but a not so simple way of imaging image-making and its vulnerability. The poem tells its story in an incremental structure which gives more and more space to the public action, less and less to privacy. At first this privacy is an honoured space; at the end it is regretted as a vacated sanctuary. The first four stanzas set up an equal division and oscillation between inner and outer life.

> I went and stood outside myself
>   Spelled the dark sky
>   And ship-lights nigh,
> And grumbling winds that passed thereby.
>
> Then next inside myself I looked,
>   And there, above
>   All, shone my Love,
> That nothing matched the image of.
>
> Beyond myself again I ranged;
>   And saw the free
>   Life by the sea,
> And folk indifferent to me.
>
> O 'twas a charm to draw within
>   Thereafter, where
>   But she was; care
> For one thing only, her hid there.[1]

In the first paired stanzas preference is clear, in 'shone' as against 'dark', and the 'grumbling winds', though there is a slight tip of the balance with the epithet 'free' in the next pair. All the explicit judgement is on the side of the inner life, which is matchless, lit, exercising charm, soliciting care and opposed to the 'folk indifferent to me' in the external world. There is a sense of active but free and easy traffic: 'I went and stood', 'Beyond myself again I ranged', 'O 'twas a charm to draw within'.

The fifth stanza suggests a more passive and involuntary movement from inner to outer life: 'But so it chanced, without myself / I had to look'. And with compulsion comes a longer span of extroversion: 'And then I took / More heed of what I had long forsook'. 'Forsook' introduces the first sign of divided loyalty and attachment to the public region. Formal proportions endorse and demonstrate this shift: three stanzas are now devoted to the outer world, whose desirability increases, though the growth is slow, even reluctant. Neutral images of 'boats, the sands, the esplanade' are followed by 'the laughing crowd', and then 'Light-hearted, loud / Greetings from some not ill-endowed', in which understatement conveniently marks a transition to genial social life while quietly reserving value. Communication, allure and art are now present in the social world; charm is no longer the preserve of privacy, as 'talk', 'Hailings', music, dance, the 'sunlit cliffs' and 'keen sea-salts' join in appeal.

> The evening sunlit cliffs, the talk
>   Hailings and halts,
>   The keen sea-salts,
> The band, the Morgenblatter Waltz.

Then the ration of private contemplation is reduced and the ambiguous implications of that first 'hid' reinforced: 'Still . . . / Forward she came, / Sad, but the same . . .' This is an unlit image, timed 'at night', a night neutrally presented so that any amorous implications are balanced by suggestions of sleep and diminished energy. The next return shows the actor more passive, and now the external force is clearly and competitively amorous – 'as by force, / Outwardly wooed / By contacts crude' – though exteriority is denigrated as it is empowered. There is a return to the even division of the beginning, with the next stanza showing a decision to move back from 'This outside life' to 'the pure / Thought-world'. The allegory declares itself here, but creativity appears both abstract and sensual: the pure thought world is imagined, in a fine oxymoron, as a basking in 'her allure'. The end of the poem devotes three stanzas, including the one just quoted, to preferred innerness, and so balances the earlier three registering the takeover by exteriority. But the conclusion is one of absence and loss. The return to self is enfeebled – 'Myself again I crept within' – the verb marking a change from that early smooth passage and access. The images of privacy, seclusion and light return to be negated, as the seeker scans 'The temple where / She'd shone', but can 'not find her there'. The last stanza inexorably doubles repetitions of effort and failure: 'sought and sought' and 'is gone, is gone'.

The poem can be read as a story about the loss of love, but the imagery of passage and interaction carries larger implications. The poem is a reverie, but also about reverie, contemplating the strength and enfeeblement of image-making, seen by Hardy (as it was more analytically by Yeats) in love and art. It is also a grim psychological study of the dangers and impossibilities of the divided self, like Stevenson's *The Strange Case of Dr Jekyll and Mr Hyde* or Wilde's *The Picture of Dorian Gray*, which also use liminal imagery but have a stronger and more specific ethical emphasis. This short poem, however, is capable of articulating ideas about imagination, privacy and the social interference with creativity. It is a model for Hardy's varied but sustained meditation on imaginative effort.

A similarly constructed poem, where naïveté is a deceptive cover for subtle suggestiveness, is 'Self-Unconscious'. Its title offers a coinage to stand beside the now indispensable but then less well-worn 'self-conscious'. Self-unconsciousness may be thought of as a creative advantage, but not in this poem. Once more Hardy creates a divided action, though the threshold between vision and the expense of mind in a waste of fantasy is never crossed. It is presented as a barrier and a limit, retrospectively recognized as passable. The outer world is imaged in sparkling naturalistic detail of colour, motion and energy, as Hardy imagines an imperative which is perilously ignored, the solicitation of an outer world of natural dynamism:

> Bright yellowhammers
> Made mirthful clamours,
> And billed long straws with a bustling air,
> And bearing their load
> Flew up the road
> That he followed, alone, without interest there.
>
> From bank to ground
> And over and round
> They sidled along the adjoining hedge;
> Sometimes to the gutter
> Their yellow flutter
> Would dip from the nearest slatestone ledge.
>
> The smooth sea-line,
> With a metal shine,
> And flashes of white, and a sail thereon,
> He would also descry
> With a half-wrapt eye
> Between the projects he mused upon.

Thresholds are compounded. In this story the mind is cut off from both the phenomenal world of Nature and from an apprehension of self, by a detached and distracted attentiveness to plans, projects and fantasies. The threshold uncrossed is also that which separates real time, in the present, from abstract time, in the future, both remembered as time past. Creativity is active, indeed 'limns' reverie, but ignores the live moment, the elusive present tense, which offers a vision of wholeness and significance. The creative mind is dramatized as dangerously rootless, suspended between inner recognition and attention to the outside world. The brilliance of the natural world condemns that suspension. It would be a pity, I think, to be too interested in the fact of origin (the poem's location is subtitled as 'Near Bossiney') since the particular might blind us – like the character in the poem – to a larger meaning. What the poem suggests is the powerful transient passage of that present moment, so honoured by Hardy's admirer D. H. Lawrence, who constantly said, and used poetry to show, that we should trust the glimpse and the momentary manifestation, true to affect, spontaneous, unselfconscious and sensuously alert. Perhaps the title suggests that to be self-conscious is sometimes to lose true consciousness of self. Once more, Hardy uses a short lyrical narrative to analyse, as well as to utter, psychic experiences. In this instance fantasy, which might be considered imagination's proper work, is less creative than wise passiveness, which responds to nature's springlike creativity – 'Earth's artistries' – and in a moment, catches wholeness. If there is autobiography behind the poem's narrative reserve, that reserve allows an emphasis on 'clear-eyed distance' and a 'conning' of the whole that would have seen 'A thing . . . / That loomed with an immortal mien'. Like many of Hardy's poems, it gives incisive visualization, reminding us of Coleridge's strongly visual landscape in 'Dejection: An Ode' and that disturbance of imagination which brings 'the whole soul of man into activity', in unbalanced insistence on heartless seeing: 'I see, not feel, how beautiful they are'. Though Hardy sometimes presses with Coleridgean (and Wordsworthian) power and sense on visual excess (in 'Overlooking the River Stour', for instance), here the visualization acts differently, to suggest, from the point of view not available in the past, a negative capability responsive to the world outside self and to the self lost in reverie. The missed moment is defined through exteriority, with the elated building of yellowhammers and luminous sea and sail, but its interiority is characteristically left undefined: 'that self / As he was, and should have been shown that day'. The imagery of perspective – seeing at a distance, and seeing whole – involves a space between the seer and the thing seen. There is also an image of seeing 'into', 'To see therein'. The poem suggests a barrier between whole vision at a particular time, in a particular space, and a future-orientated creativity, which saw nothing. No simple opposition here between inside and outside, as in 'At A Seaside Town', but this too is a poem using inside-outside imagery to discover imaginative lapse, and imply imaginative power.

The poem's action offers holistic knowledge to the reader, who is forced into extreme attentiveness to the bird and sea images. But the reader is also faced with the generalized vagueness of the language of wasted and wasting creativity, the dulled abstract words: 'shapes that reveries limn', 'projects that he mused upon' and 'specious plans that came to his call'. The poem turns out to be a teasing structure. What is told to the reader is less than what is not told. The vision which might have been, and was not, seen is not specified. The reader is left on the ignorant side of a narrative threshold, denied access to wholeness, fed with specificities of the non-human phenomenal world, but offered nothing else. Like the 'I' in the poem, the reader also misses revelation, and like the mind in the poem looking back with hindsight, ultimately shown 'that self / As he was, and should have been shown, that day', we know that something big was missed, but not what it was. A poem about limits of vision for the reader. In 'At A Seaside Town' we are also given overspecific images of the exteriority which destroyed interiority, but given only image, not character and history, not interpretation.

Hardy's poetry about threshold and limits is truly about itself. It creates an active and thwarted response for its reader. There is variety of invitation: to press questioning against the barrier set up by the poem, to transgress in crossing (as biographical critics may do, treating the poem that does not tell all exactly like the poem that does tell all), to refuse to question, or to imagine a tentative step across the barrier but decide that the territory beyond is alien, no sooner sensed than inhibited. The last response seems the most likely for the biographically informed, (but not for the biographically fanatical), who can recognize that reticence, if respected, has rewarding resonances. The poem creates a category of trespass, fencing off forbidden territory. Limits may mimic thresholds.

Poetry which imagines loss or lapse neighbours that which imagines success. The well-known poem 'The Self-Unseeing' suggests loss, but sees it as an impulse to new retrieval.

> Here is the ancient floor,
> Footworn and hollowed and thin,
> Here was the former door
> Where the dead feet walked in.
>
> She sat here in her chair,
> Smiling into the fire;
> He who played stood there,
> Bowing it higher and higher.
>
> Childlike, I danced in a dream;
> Blessings emblazoned that day;
> Everything glowed with a gleam;
> Yet we were looking away!

The image of the child dancing 'in a dream' is the recognition of hindsight; the image of the 'Blessings' that 'emblazoned that day' is the judgement of nostalgia; the gleam with which 'Everything glowed' was not part of the pleasure in smiling, dancing and bowing, but memory's creative vision of what could not have been sensed in the present that is past. The poem turns on a form of *occupatio*, occupying an absence with a passionate presence. The vision grasps significance incompatible with the self-engrossed creative joy, in a newly accrued creative impulse, a gain of distances. Like many of Hardy's poems, this one contains an extra image of threshold and limit, a signature of theme within the poem. It begins with a reminder of a past beyond the past re-enacted here, in the image of a 'former' door, closed in the past he remembers, representing anterior pastness.

The third and fourth lines of the first stanza form a miniaturization of the poem's action, in which dead limbs are revived by creative memory. The part stands for the whole, in the images of the door and of dead feet walking. The threshold between looking and looking away is a creative facility: some joys are not compatible with whole seeing, some visions must be retrospective. The articulation of this threshold between experience and reading is made by the attentive reader, given two points of view and impelled to move between them and make the connection which the poem does not utter and even seems to deny, in 'Yet we were looking away'. Crossing this threshold, we temporarily convey the 'Yet' into a 'Because', but understand why 'Because' could not be in the poem. It is written within nostalgia's limits, but in a way which recognizes them. There is no Proustian sense of loss but a strong Proustian sense of creative recovery, marked in the boundary between characters (including narrator) in the poem and the poem. There is a difference between the gains in memory in Hardy and Proust: Hardy knows that the past experience cannot be exactly or wholly retrieved, but can be made different, new or enlarged. He is with Proust in revealing how the creations of memory are acts of imagination.

III
Human and Non-human Nature

In 'Self-Unconscious' the sustained and particularized imaging of nature represents the animal, vegetable and mineral individualities as they can be perceived by the attentive human senses, not anthropomorphically but in creaturely companionship. Perhaps companionship is not a safe word: Hardy sees the nest-building birds, the sunny sea and the journeying sail as exhilarated, probably springlike, but separate. There is a sense that the missed moment, long ago, was an experience of youth. He writes many poems which mark, define and respect the boundary between human and non-human nature, focusing comprehensively on the natural world. His site for imagination, as he imagines its work, is often located on the verge of the inhuman phenomenal world. Despite his compassion for this other world, he does not usually imagine on behalf of flora and fauna. When he does, as in 'Ah, Are You Digging On My Grave?', he uses speech to present a cool animal neutrality and put down the sentimental hope of fidelity from pets. Hardy does not impute human passion and mind to other species. 'An August Midnight' is one of many poems in which he is warm towards animal characters, but he respects their vitality and refuses to cross the barrier between human and non-human experience. This poem creates a theatre: 'On this scene enter' apparently humble *dramatis personae*. The stage is a page on which almost half-way through the poem a fly is discovered rubbing its hands ('mid my page') and is then joined by the rest of the cast. The human presence is confirmed as that of a writer, in 'new-penned line' and asserts a sense of mixed company.

> Thus meet we five, in this still place,
> At this point of time, at this point in space.
> – My guests besmear my new-penned line,
> Or bang at the lamp and fall supine.
> 'God's humblest, they!' I muse. Yet why?
> They know Earth-secrets that know not I.

It is a poem which creates a full apprehension of the moment. The 'beat of a clock', the theatrical images and the repetition – 'in this still place / At this point of time, at this point in space' – insistently concentrate the attention of the speaker in the poem and the reader of the poem. The three 'thises' suggest that the page is the page of this text, more obliquely and ambiguously than Ted Hughes in 'The Thought Fox'. On this occasion the poet has his reverie but is allowed to revise it: the sense of quaint companionship sees the creatures as humble and sets them on a scale of being, compassionately but hierarchically. Immediately, with the word 'muse', which implies inspiration and thought but also openness, the thinker retracts his categories and admits the limits of his knowledge. On one side of a natural division lie his acts of mind, on the other is the animals' mystery. He acknowledges an equality and otherness of being, in an utterly unpatronizing way. Someone was shocked because Hardy didn't know the names of flowers (though he knew a few), but he knew something more important – how to look at the non-human world with intentness and respect. He honours the space between the self and its creature-visitors, celebrating the limits of imagination, hospitably allowing the insects to come uninvited into the poem as they come on to the page in the story within the poem. They collaborate randomly, smearing his ink, dying matter of factly as they bang into the lamp that lights his page, to make the poem write itself. It marks the separateness of the human and non-human worlds in a heartfelt joke against romanticism.

Another poem which respects the limits of the non-human animal is the wondering 'Shelley's Skylark'. Shelley's lark enters in two forms: as a surviving morsel of matter and as an image in Shelley's poem. We cannot read the poem without reading Shelley too: it truly enters into a dialogue with another text, meditating on Shelley's famous apostrophe, 'Bird thou never wert'. Hardy disagrees, insisting that Shelley's skylark must indeed have been a physical individual. Hardy imagines the bird precisely as Shelley did not, as a real bird that died, whose body became materially recycled.

> Somewhere afield here something lies
> In Earth's oblivious eyeless trust
> That moved a poet to prophecies –
> A pinch of unseen unguarded dust:
>
> The dust of the lark that Shelley heard,
> And made immortal through times to be; –
> Though it only lived like another bird,
> And knew not its immortality.
>
> Lived its meek life; then, one day, fell –
> A little ball of feather and bone;
> And how it perished, when piped farewell,
> And where it wastes, are alike unknown.

Shelley's skylark, in Hardy's poem, is like those insects landing on the page who couldn't know they were getting into a poem, and whose individuation was too alien and inhuman for them to get in as symbols or metaphors. Hardy rewrites Shelley in order to insist on the uncrossable threshold between the human and the animal creature, the more powerfully because Shelley so exuberantly denied limits to make the bird into spirit and symbol. The mystification provokes the unromantic poet's matter-of-fact and demystifying imagination, but Hardy asserts limits with such subtle restraint that readers don't always understand the sheer revisionary cheek and humour of the poem. He doesn't criticize, but counters the original and originating poem with his commentary and his praise of bird and poet. It is a backhanded compliment, but still a compliment. Shelley magnificently makes Hardy make us imagine that his lark had once – one way or another – been a real bird, and Hardy makes us reread Shelley.

The triolet 'Birds At Winter Nightfall' teems with tender humours.

> Around the house the flakes fly faster,
> And all the berries now are gone
> From holly and cotoneaster
> Around the house. The flakes fly! – faster
> Shutting indoors that crumb-outcaster
> We used to see upon the lawn
> Around the house. The flakes fly faster,
> And all the berries now are gone!

It is witty, fanciful, affectionate; an imagined act of naming done from the bird's-eye view, yet not attempting to cross the threshold. From the animals' viewpoint the human being is reduced to the instrumental 'crumb-outcaster', not a bad providence, less dignified and more reliable than most, and marvellously re-created in the birds' nonce act of naming, which is amusingly rhymed with a horticultural mouthful. There is something delicately odd yet apt in converting birdsong to a small, repetitive but intricate metrical form. Such a firm line drawn between human and other animals plays a more ambitious part in 'The Darkling Thrush', Hardy's most famous bird poem, a poem of sympathetic nature, almost but not quite imaginatively overcoming natural limits. The aged gauntness of the thrush and his brave unseasonal song are used expressively to convey sterile wintriness and energy, elderly gloom and a kind of hope. Hardy makes as if to move across the threshold dividing human nature from other nature, but it is only a gesture of crossing. The thrush's symbolic scrawniness is thoroughly particularized, asserting a physical presence which gives good cover for symbolism, but appearances are preserved. The threshold is not crossed, nor is animal privacy penetrated. We feel the human imagination trying its best – if best's the word – to press against limits of perception and invoke sympathetic nature, but in the end Hardy's appreciative and scrupulous recognition of the animal's separateness, vividly articulating physical vividness, stays on the agnostic side of Nature's division. The poet keeps the categories intact and presents only the possibility of taking the thrush as a symbol. 'Some blessed hope' is imagined lovingly: it is longing, but candidly vague and tentative. Hope's blessed presence is permitted by the reservation, by the assertion of that knowledge that the inner and affective life – Earth's secrets – of the bird must remain a mystery. So too must the future and metaphysical meanings. The speculative tremor of anthropomorphism reinforces the tremulous cosmic hope. The poem imagines a pressure against bounds out of a desire to break them. It ends with a refusal to be too humanly imaginative about birdsong – traditionally so tempting to poets' identification. It also refuses to be either pessimistic or optimistic about futurity. The poem is a firm demonstration of the meliorism which, like George Eliot, Hardy insisted was his stance, and which itself constitutes a recognition of speculative limits.

IV
Phenomenon and Noumenon

An agnostic poet, Hardy constantly images the spiritual world.[2] His passionate inclination is fired by unbelief. As he asserts in that bitterly brilliant parody of hymn 'The Impercipient', unbelief is not caused by blindness to belief's advantage. This unbelieving poet writes out of a longing for the impossible supernatural object of desire. Hardy records the phenomenology of disbelief, explicating various experiences of unfaith, almost as flexibly as George Herbert re-imagining faith. Hardy did not always write at the imaginative pitch of 'The Impercipient' and 'A Sign-Seeker', and some of the dialogues with God or imagined monologues of God are crudely, if touchingly, propagandist. But his best poetry of noumenal desire is not only imaginative in richly emotional and argumentative ways but contemplates imaginative effort. 'A Sign-Seeker' beautifully articulates the scientific piercing of veils and the thwarted energy of spiritual or spiritualist vision. (His drawing in *Wessex Poems* emblematizes the doubled seeking in stars and a huge comet in the dark sky.) The speaker spends nearly half the poem on completed apprehensions of the phenomenal world, in all tones, slightly more than half imaging the unimaginable survivals. These are personal, 'heart to heart returning after dust to dust', but politically and ethically significant: 'when Earth's Frail lie bleeding of her Strong' he longs for 'one plume as pledge that Heaven inscrolls the Wrong'. The story teems with images and incidents of imaginative scope in order to mark its limits.

> Such scope is granted not to lives like mine . . .
> I have lain in dead men's beds . . .

The domestic and physical directness and simplicity of statement are poignant, the occupation of dead men's beds a common occurrence and a desperate investigation. The sad near-rhyme of 'dead' with 'beds' has its part to play in the conclusion. The final line is characteristically both generalized and dramatic, conceptual and physical; abstraction's speech is dead simple as it instances and affirms mortality: 'And Nescience mutely muses: When a man falls he lies'. The poem presses hard, but not tirelessly, against limits.

In 'The House of Silence' Hardy uses the image of piercing the material screen, as a metaphor and a metonymy for penetrating to the noumenal world. Child and adult stand outside the house, in an immediate rendering of limit and pressure. The child is unWordsworthianly unimaginative, stubbornly stopping at appearances and needing to be informed that the silent house is teeming with imaginative business. The walls through which nobody is visible are transformed into a screen of matter, pierced only by those who 'bear / The visioning powers of soul' and 'who dare / To pierce the material screen'. The appearance of the house is one of funeral enclosure, but as the instructive dialogue proceeds we move within, only to discover a further threshold and limit. Inside are figures not visible to the child: 'funereal shades that seem / The uncanny scenery of a dream,' but perform a festival of music and laughter and light for the spinning brain. The poet's vision, implied at the start in the spinning brain, is formally identified at the end. It is not indeed explicitly said to be supernaturally visionary, but passes the limits of death and time, comprehends visions of past and present, Earth and Heaven, compressing 'an aeon in an hour'. The thresholds of outside view are set up to praise creative scope, and the poet's, not the philosopher's, imagination is allowed passage between the material and the immaterial. Hardy imagines his necessary angel as a poet's compensation for agnosticism.

Such thresholds are crossed in Hardy's many ghost poems, though most of his ghosts, however personal their returns and hauntings, achieve only a biological continuity. In 'Transformations' the dead are imagined 'not underground, / But as nerves and veins . . . / In the growths of upper air,' and in 'Proud Songsters' Hardy contemplates not postmortal but premortal life: 'a year ago, or less than twain', when the finches and nightingales and thrushes were 'particles of grain, / And earth, and air, and rain'. As James Richardson observes in *Thomas Hardy. The Poetry of Necessity*,[3] Hardy created a 'magnificent spiritualism', showing that 'The past fights its way to its own energy, struggles back into human awareness, back into its immortality.' It is a spiritualism which wryly and powerfully asserts a lack of scope and an inexorable limit.

The elegiac imagination has seldom been imaged with more tact and reserve, on behalf of self, than in 'Afterwards'.

> When the Present has latched its postern behind my tremulous stay,
>   And the May month flaps its glad green leaves like wings,
> Delicate-filmed as new-spun silk, will the neighbours say,
>   'He was a man who used to notice such things'?

The image of the door is, like everything in the poem, gentle and soft, the postern latched as if going were as tremulous as staying. The controlled sibilants and the metaphor of latching create an unobtrusive and modest exit, leaving the scene without disturbance, welcoming the hubbub of spring and May, though May's leaves insist on delicacy and fragility. Hardy writes about life and leaving life, bestowing the utmost tenderness on the objects of the natural world but also spreading solicitude for his own modest request for memorial. He can be pathetically immodest too, as in 'A Poet', which speaks of a poet but asks that he should be remembered as beloved by 'two bright-souled women'. 'Afterwards' is the obverse of such honest sultanlike wishes for memorial. Its speaker is treading difficult ground, speculating on the touchy subject of our own posthumous memorial. Prominent in this anticipation of becoming a memory is the absence of any mention of what Thomas Hardy is remembered for. The poet leaves out his writings. He creates an absence which truly draws attention to itself and we read the poem, observe what he does not wish us to remember him for (the 'us' subsuming those who knew him and those who did not) and then look for traces of the expected desire. As we contemplate the images afresh, absence becomes presence in a delicate transformation.

If it be in the dusk when, like an eyelid's soundless blink,
    The dewfall-hawk comes crossing the shades to alight
Upon the wind-warped upland thorn, a gazer may think,
    'To him this must have been a familiar sight'.

If I pass during some nocturnal blackness, mothy and warm,
    When the hedgehog travels furtively over the lawn,
One may say, 'He strove that such innocent creatures should come to
    no harm,
    But he could do little for them; and now he is gone'.

If, when hearing that I have been stilled at last, they stand at the door,
    Watching the full-starred heavens that winter sees,
Will this thought rise on those who will meet my face no more,
    'He was one who had an eye for such mysteries'?

And will any say when my bell of quittance is heard in the gloom,
    And a crossing breeze cuts a pause in its outrollings,
Till they swell again, as they were a new bell's boom,
    'He hears it not now, but used to notice such things'?

The new leaves, the flying hawk, the furtive small creature, the winter stars and the bell tolling are images belonging in his novels and poems, though also to common experience. The imagined moderate praise is sufficiently detached to come from acquaintances, or strangers and readers: 'He was a man who used to notice such things', 'To him this must have been . . .', 'He strove . . . could do little'. The 'eye for such mysteries' is a testimony to his yearnings and his recognition of limits. It is not necessary to see the images as recapitulations, but they are, recalling such episodes as the wonderful Mayday at the end of *The Return of the Native*, the starry night when Gabriel Oak watched his flock, Marty's, Jude's and Tess's fellow-feelings for the vegetable and animal world, and many passing bells. The images also assert typicality, reminding us of particulars but also of general tendency – 'such things'. The old familiar Hardy images are being made new, in the poem. Phenomena are imagined by soft-fingered perception, 'delicate-filmed', 'like an eyelid's soundless blink', 'mothy', by seasoned observation and routines, 'the dewfall-hawk . . . The wind-warped upland thorn', and loving apprehensive sympathy, for the hedgehog travelling 'furtively'. Like the mysteries, each detail is appropriate, and the projected memorial compounds the good traditional habits of obituary enumeration. The ego's elegy is made psychologically exact and alert by its wondering and self-cheering tone: 'What will they say?' it implies, and 'perhaps it won't be too bad, at least they could say this'.

Hardy's attempt at the complex emotional projection from living to dying, self to other and human to non-human nature is brilliantly compounded. To meditate an elegy for his own passing summoned up the desires and wrung recognitions of a lifetime. His attempts to imagine the dead, or to imagine the dead seeing the living, were at their most specifically dramatized and experientially varied in the poems written about his first wife's death. For Hardy, bereavement involved a sense of many barriers, and many kinds of desire to break them down. The elegies are poems of limit in which limit becomes unbearable. Just as Hardy's poetry of unbelief is never static but reflects and renews longings, thwartings, indignations and ironies in a continuum, so the poetry of bereavement continues the experience and re-experience of loss, remorse, restorations and desires.

In 'The Haunter' – to take one of many examples – he imagines death from the ghost's viewpoint, to invoke an intolerably tantalizing sense of barrier, in images of proximity.

> He does not think that I haunt here nightly:
>   How shall I let him know
> That whither his fancy sets him wandering
>   I, too, alertly go? –
> Hover and hover a few feet from him
>   Just as I used to do,
> But cannot answer the words he lifts me –
>   Only listen thereto!
>
> When I could answer he did not say them:
>   When I could let him know
> How I would like to join in his journeys
>   Seldom he wished to go.

> Now that he goes and wants me with him
>   More than he used to do,
> Never he sees my faithful phantom
>   Though he speaks thereto.
>
> Yes, I companion him to places
>   Only dreamers know,
> Where the shy hares print long paces,
>   Where the night rooks go;
> Into old aisles where the past is all to him,
>   Close as his shade can do,
> Always lacking the power to call to him,
>   Near as I reach thereto!
>
> What a good haunter I am, O tell him!
>   Quickly make him know
> If he but sigh since my loss befell him
>   Straight to his side I go.
> Tell him a faithful one is doing
>   All that love can do
> Still that his path may be worth pursuing,
>   And to bring peace thereto.

The ghost claims to 'Hover and hover a few feet from him', and read in isolation the repeated verb sounds ghostlike in position and motion. But it is weirdly transformed to a memory of earthly habit – 'Just as I used to do' – presenting the hover as a shocking metaphor for a distance and hesitancy in daily life. Though the poem ends with consolation, the ghost beneficently assuring him of fidelity, wishing him well and bringing him peace, the shifting image of limits sets up a strong undertow. The ghost's benison (needed by the poet-widower as posthumous forgiveness) is a frailer presence in the poem than the recollection of the rift between the living pair. Perhaps the poem tells a truth in spite of willed reticence and desired sweetening: once that hovering has been translated into remembered daily separateness all the repeated words of closeness – 'Close as his shade' and 'Near as I reach' – resound with deepened irony. The sense of threshold and limit is compounded and converted, to make the poem no generous haunting but a ghost's reproach, aptly muted but clearly audible. The tug away from reproach only makes clear the hearer's unwillingness to hear all the ghost would say, as if Emma Hardy had influenced the pen in a real haunting. It was as dangerous for Hardy to invoke ghosts as for Lady Macbeth to invoke unsexing spirits.

V
Telling and Not Telling

In 'The Haunter', and others, the reader is offered a subtext. The combination of reserve and suggestiveness stamps Hardy's lyrical poems of spareness and understatement. Some of the other elegies depend on narrative gaps, preserving but threatening the threshold between lyric and narrative. A story is told, up to a certain point. Reserve may be the result of an unconscious tug against willed conclusion, as in 'The Haunter', but it is more often an effect of control and restraint, a grim or melancholy teasing that fits a mourning mood and the poet's moody inclinations. In 'Castle Boterel', for instance, the implied but untold story resembles that in 'Self-Unconscious', though with an unmistakable note of praise: what they did and said as they climbed, 'Matters not much, nor to what it led' (which draws attention to the absorption in a moment), 'But was there ever / A time of such quality, since or before, / In that hill's story?' Despite the wary admission of subjectivity – 'To one mind never' – the declaration is probably the most powerful utterance of love in these love poems. The poem offers a simple model of suggestiveness, a pregnant lyrical moment aptly forming words for a pregnant moment in life – 'It filled but a minute' – to give that sense of teeming overflow with which this poet can astonish us, like his wintry thrush. Another instance of expressive understatement is 'After A Romantic Day', where the lack of romantic landscape, beyond a minimal moonlight, is welcomed by the mind and heart brooding on day's overflowing experiences. And there is the magical 'Lyonesse', which asserts a sense of future – 'No prophet durst declare' – and of past 'When I came back . . . / All marked with mute surmise / My radiance rare and fathomless'. The subjects of romance and secrecy, like the refreshed metaphors of enchantment, draw richly on the legends of the Arthurian drowned city. The barrier is set up between the onlooker's 'mute surmise' and the speaker's radiance, 'fathomless'. This is an early love poem, and what vibrates across the threshold between wondering spectator and secret lover is unequivocal. It reminds us that the habit of not telling appears early and adapts itself to later passions and purposes, rather than originating in experiences and emotions better kept secret, or in habits of domestic silence. Such silence is the subject of many poems of barrier, in which a couple do not communicate, do not share or do not comprehend the meanings of the moment, as in 'The Division' or 'Overlooking the River Stour'.

Hardy does not just write about experiences of crossing or failing to cross the threshold in ways that challenge and limit our passages. He constructs thresholds which the reader too may cross or fail to cross. 'In Her Precincts' uses one of Hardy's favourite threshold and limit images: the window. A shut-out lover first interprets the darkness of the windows as reciprocal gloom, then sees it change to light, to become an image of 'severance'. Threshold becomes limit as the poem moves into its second part, the space between the two stanzas becoming a threshold which gives access to meanings and to a final fixing of limit. This creation of structural threshold is more complex in 'Before And After Summer'.

I

Looking forward to the spring
One puts up with anything.
On this February day
Though the winds leap down the street,
Wintry scourgings seem but play,
And these later shafts of sleet
– Sharper pointed than the first –
And these later snows – the worst –
Are as a half-transparent blind
Riddled by rays from sun behind.

II

Shadows of the October pine
Reach into this room of mine:
On the pine there swings a bird;
He is shadowed with the tree.
Mutely perched he bills no word;
Blank as I am even is he.
For those happy suns are past,
Fore-discerned in winter last.
When went by their pleasure, then?
I, alas, perceived not when.

The gap between the stanzas is large and eloquent. It contains the spring and summer, and their passage, the months between sharp February and shadowed October. The heart of the poem lies in that absence. The thresholds of time are cruelly marked, as the speaker ignores the present in his February anticipation of spring and 'sun behind', and looks back from autumn to the past 'happy suns', whose passing he did not perceive. It is a moving failure to catch and keep the present moment, the momentary happiness. It is also a complex memory of anticipation, an enactment of time limits for the poet and narrative limits for the reader.

These are only a few of many poems in which the reader is denied access to the full story, and in some, like 'Before And After Summer', there is no story told. Hardy, a great storyteller, often creates a negation of specific narrative, an absence of persons and actions. The reader is like Hardy looking at the five insects or listening to the darkling thrush. True, we understand the poet's language, but it is used to preserve its heart secrets and mysteries. We are confronted with a feeling utterance but denied the causes or the objective correlatives. Like Hardy feeling for the insects, from this side of the boundary between self and other's inner vitality, we release an outgoing sympathy but recognize limits of knowledge. Hardy makes importantly reduced claims for the imagination's grasp of truths and unities. Such reduction is congenial to modern readers practised in the appreciation of openness, fracture and displacement, and wary of wholeness, harmony and closure. Hardy should also remind us that Victorian writers,[4] despite current fictions about their enclosed idealism, have a capacity for tentativeness and provisionality, may hesitate before the noumenal and the visionary, can admit imagination's temptation to idealize, civilize, blend and make whole. Thomas Hardy uses his poetry to embody the difficult, frustrated and fatigued efforts of imagination, in ways that require the reader to experience checks and halts, limited access and impassable boundaries.

NOTES

1. This and all quotations from Hardy are from *The Complete Works of Thomas Hardy*, edited by Samuel Hynes (Oxford University Press 1982–5).
2. For the best discussion of this subject see Samuel Hynes, *The Pattern of Hardy's Poetry* (Chapel Hill, NC, 1961).
3. James Richardson, *Thomas Hardy. The Poetry of Necessity* (University of Chicago Press, Chicago and London, 1975, 1977).
4. I have discussed this subject in 'George Eliot on Imagination', *Particularities: Readings in George Eliot* (London, P. Owen, 1982, 1985).

6 Odd Man Out? Henry James, *The Canon* and *The Princess Casamassima*

A. Robert Lee

This, please, for the delightful young man from Texas, who shews such excellent dispositions . . . I suggest to give him as alternatives these two slightly different lists:
1. *Roderick Hudson.*
2. *The Portrait of a Lady.*
3. *The Princess Casamassima.*
4. *The Wings of the Dove.*
5. *The Golden Bowl.*

1. *The American.*
2. *The Tragic Muse.*
3. *The Wings of the Dove.*
4. *The Ambassadors.*
5. *The Golden Bowl.*

The second list is, as it were, the more 'advanced' . . .
        Henry James to Mrs G. W. Prothero, 14 September 1913

I

On more than just one occasion James spoke with considerable appreciation, if not envy, of the use in France of *'Maître'* as a term of honour for its men of letters.[1] It was anything but mere vainglory on his part. For a writer whose circle of literary friends had once included Flaubert, Maupassant and Zola, and whose own mastery of the language might as readily have led him to Paris as to London, it could hardly have been thought inappropriate. Casting back, too, over a lifetime's creative effort, not least as he saw it being embodied in the twenty-four volumes of the Scribner/New York Edition (1907–17), he had even more substantial grounds to think himself worthy of the French honorific.

But would he have reacted with pleasure or suspicion to the idiom of a later age, which almost by reflex has taken to pronouncing him 'canonical'? He may not literally have used the term himself, but on the evidence of his letter to Mrs Prothero few would accuse him of not having run well ahead of the game. There, in plainest fashion, he offered his own appointed canon – indeed, not one but two – his own willingness to create representative and even alternative hierarchies for his fiction. One can, further, readily enough imagine him savouring the scriptural resonance of the term, his place at the head of a broad (or perhaps more to the point in his case) a high church of literature. Given, too, how dismayingly unread he knew himself to be at his death in 1916, it would also represent a certain amends, a yet further, if posthumous, recognition of the unflagging expenditure of energy he had given to his chosen vocation. He might, in addition, have relished stepping free from any mere coterie following of *The Yellow Book* variety, a writer at last to be savoured by an overdue more general readership.

At the same time, who doubts that the critical intelligence capable of producing the Prefaces or essays like 'The Art of Fiction' or 'The Future of the Novel' would not immediately have detected the less favouring implications of 'canonical', its imputation of a top place in the hierarchy simply by privilege of caste or gender? Would he not also have found the term too chill or distant, the product of a time when the asseverations of academic theory threaten to inhibit any unmediated contact with the work at hand? But whatever his, or anyone else's, caveats, 'canonical' has become virtually required usage, attributed, furthermore, with barely a hint of reservation to the whole body of his fiction, be it early, middle or late.

What, then, happens when an agreed canonical writer like James produces a novel which, though occasionally it arouses even passionate shows of interest, none the less seems to go absent or missing? That is, a novel precisely like *The Princess Casamassima* (1886), the one novel in either list which has had to exist in a kind of suspended animation, there but somehow not there. For however often James's story of London anarchism, with its cast of Hyacinth Robinson, the Princess, Millie Henning and the Muniments and their circle, has been given dutiful mention, acknowledged as an also-ran, far more often has it been discreetly stepped round or, as it were, left to its own devices. In other words, should 'canonical' apply simply across the board, even to novels like *Casamassima*, which whatever James's overall ranking, tend to remain unread and to feature only infrequently in school or college syllabuses?

Nor can it be said to be a question simply of early or apprentice work. A thoroughly full-length effort, *Casamassima* after all appears well after James hit his stride, no less than five years on from *The Portrait of A Lady* (1881) and within little more than a decade and a half of 'the major phase' of *The Wings of the Dove* (1902), *The Ambassadors* (1903) and *The Golden Bowl* (1904). Rather it might be said to share a fate with those novels which for one reason or another get stranded, or remain uninvited into the limelight, because they look on initial acquaintance to be out of kilter with the rest of the output, a kind of undeniable but wayward progeny.

One thinks, in this connection, of, say, Fielding's *Amelia*, which abandons the expected 'comic-epic' mould, or Charlotte Brontë's *The Professor*, which nicely inverts the Brussels love plot of the better-known *Villette*, or George Eliot's *Romola*, which breaks ranks and attempts historical romance, or Melville's *The Confidence-Man*, which opts not for sea adventure but for a forbidding and satiric Pilgrim's Progress through the New World, or Hardy's *A Pair of Blue Eyes*, which replaces Wessex with Cornwall, or Edith Wharton's *Ethan Frome*, a novel by James's great friend and countrywoman which moves out of her accustomed New York 'society' and into a puritan and provincialized New England. Taken along the canonical sightline, all these have been thought oddities, diversions from the main track. They all, too, have had to be refound, given new certificates of acceptability. More oddly still, in this light, almost every one of these texts represents a favourite offspring, a novel held in the most special affection by its author.

As to *Casamassima* in its own right, how to account for its relative neglect given its inherent drama as a story of would-be political insurrection; or its portrait of Hyacinth first as child and then artist *manqué* and sacrificial assassin; or its memorable portrait gallery of types and characters, not least of which besides Hyacinth is the title figure of the Princess; or the peculiar weight and density of its evocation of London as 'this huge, luxurious, wanton, wasteful city'?[2] Given, too, the routine charge that James sidestepped both politics and the sexual life, does it not, at however much a tangent, offer nothing if not 'political' and 'sexual' James? Why, in a further twist, does *The Bostonians*, which he also published in 1886 and which he thought a companion piece in terms of theme, tend to get invoked as being unarguably more alert to issues of social power struggle, or class, or gender, or even the relationship of art to politics?

Why, too, and again oddly given its interest in London as 'underground' and as a site for conspiracy and protest, has *Casamassima* none too often been nominated for the great line of Condition of England novels with which it shows an obvious affinity and which typically includes the likes of Dickens's *Bleak House*, Disraeli's *Coningsby*, Elizabeth Gaskell's *North and South*, Gissing's *Demos* and *The Nether World* and H. G. Wells's *Tongo-Bungay*? If not absolutely and unreservedly a 'missing' James novel, *Casamassima* cannot be said to have had anything like the best or most assiduous of attention, and assuredly not so when put alongside the other novels from the same list chosen by his own hand to be representative of his different principal 'phases' such as *Roderick Hudson*, *The Portrait of a Lady*, *The Wings of The Dove* and *The Golden Bowl*.

In sum, what is it about *Casamassima*, whether as a specimen text or in and for itself, which goes on making it the uninvited member at the feast, the cuckoo in the nest? The author himself would have felt no small consternation at the question. For why include it in either list had he not held it in the most considerable personal esteem? We do not know how Stark Young, 'the delightful young man' on whose behalf Mrs Prothero had written and who would go on to become the distinguished drama critic of the *New Republic* (he came, incidentally, from Mississippi not Texas), reacted to James's letter of reply. But his inquiry was not only timely in itself, it can be seen with perspective to have been made on far more than his own behalf alone. It also has the added bonus, be it in hindsight or not, of showing how uncannily James anticipated our latterday contemporary interest in canonicity and, implicitly or otherwise, in the fate of novels which indeed become odd men out in the manner of *The Princess Casamassima*.

II

Nor do matters get any less odd when a round of still closer coordinates is brought to bear. First, we have James's own Notebook entry for 10 August 1885, with its hint that there might in truth be something vexatious about the novel:

> It is absolutely necessary at this point I should make the future evolution of the *Princess Casamassima* more clear to myself. I have never yet become engaged in a novel in which, after I had begun to write and send off my MS., the details had remained so vague. This is partly – or indeed wholly – owing to the fact that I have been so terribly preoccupied – up to so lately – with the unhappy *Bostonians*, born under an evil star. The subject of the *Princess* is magnificent, and if I can only give up my mind to it properly – generously and trustfully – the form will shape itself as successfully as the idea deserves. I have plunged in rather blindly, and got a good many characters on my hands; but these will fall into their places if I kept cool and think it out. Oh art, art, what difficulties are thine? Without thee, for me, the world would be, indeed a howling desert. The *Princess* will give me hard, continuous work for many months to come; but she will give me joys too sacred to prate about . . .[3]

Whatever forward light these notes afford, it needs remembering that they emanate from an author still in the throes of composition. 'Vague', for instance, holds no necessary sway as a judgement on the eventual result, any more than James's having 'plunged in rather blindly'. His rhapsodic 'Oh art, art, art . . .', too, can be matched up with any other number of self-encouraging memos and asides in the Notebooks. The key observation, however, for present purposes, has to be 'The subject of the *Princess* is magnificent', his conviction that he was about major fare and a novel to elicit nothing less for him than 'joys too sacred to prate about'.

But on both sides of the Atlantic, *The Princess Casamassima* was to enjoy no better a fate than *The Bostonians*, much as the latter had gone on to win belated acclaim. In 1888 a mournful James would write of both to W. D. Howells: 'I have entered upon evil days . . . I am still staggering a good deal under the mysterious and (to me) inexplicable injury, wrought – apparently – upon my situation by my last two novels.'

Not only did this unflattering reception of novels matchingly given over to portraits of Boston and London – Tales of Two

Cities, so to speak – have much to do with his ill-fated venture into the theatre from 1890 onwards (he had adapted 'Daisy Miller' for the stage in 1882); his misgivings in the case of *Casamassima* would prove especially well taken. Truly a veil of silence, inattention at least, would descend, to persist with only the most occasional demur for well over half a century.

It took an Introduction written as late as 1948 by Lionel Trilling (and republished in 1951 in *The Liberal Imagination*) to get matters moving again.[4] Trilling spoke up uncompromisingly for the novel as 'an incomparable representation of the spiritual circumstances of our civilization', by which he had in mind James's observation to A. C. Benson in 1896: 'But I have the imagination of disaster – and see life as ferocious and sinister.' He also argued James to have been 'beautifully in control of his novel', 'warm' and 'fluent', and to have created a 'social texture' at once 'grainy' and 'knotted with practicality and detail'. Even so, and however timely or invigorating the intervention, it created anything but a consensus. On the contrary: in what debate there was to follow, the variance, indeed the outright disagreement, could not have been more marked.

Only a part of Trilling's admiration, symptomatically, would do for Irving Howe in his *Politics and the Novel* (1957).[5] James's 'flight – or descent – to the world of anarchist London in the 1880's' amounted to 'a bewildering mixture of excellence and badness'. Unlike Trilling, Howe could detect no 'commanding vision of the political life'. James, too, for all the virtuosity of individual portraits like Miss Pynsent or Millie or Paul Muniment or the Poupins, had written too much from the outside. His anarchist scenes were too unelaborated (and even unfactual, a Bloomsbury gathering-place and pub like the 'Sun and Moon' notwithstanding). The leader, Hoffendahl, came over as too shadowy, too much the silhouette and figure of mystery. As to the London poor and dispossessed, however keenly engaged his personal sympathies may have been, James had drawn them too much by implication, too abstractly.

But Howe was the very spirit of restraint when put alongside Maxwell Geismar, whose *Henry James and the Jacobites* (1963) saw in *Casamassima* 'James's own most abiding prejudices, social ignorance and infantine obsessions'.[6] The story, for Geismar, reveals James's 'baroque social conservativism', a 'dreamlike

ODD MAN OUT?

fantasy' which avoids all 'the true conditions of British social misery' in favour of portraying a foundling prince, a moneyed and implausible Fairy Queen (reincarnated out of the former Christina Light of *Roderick Hudson*) and an aesthete's retreat back to the life of art over political action. No half-measures, clearly, by this account, only Jacobite conspiracy.

Between views of *Casamassima* as on the one hand worthy of 'high estimation' (Gorley Putt) and unreservedly 'a great novel' (Walter Allen) and on the other a novel whose plot verges on 'the inane' (Yvor Winters), it has also been notable for its absence in a number of the standard accounts.[7] Neither F. R. Leavis's *The Great Tradition* (1948) nor Richard Chase's *The American Novel and Its Tradition* (1957), for instance, gives it space. Leavis, it is true, spoke passingly of it elsewhere, in an early comment praising its 'sappy vitality' but later condemning it as 'one of James's most embarrassing failures' – two responses from a single source which point up the novel's power to create contradiction.[8] More lately still it has been made subject to 'gender' and 'new historicist' dispensations, interpretations which see James as respectively 'patriarchal' (especially in the treatment of the Princess, Lady Aurora Langrish, and even Millie) and led by the inlaid biases of his class to his supposed horror at any upturn of the established political order.[9]

To these dissonant responses should be added a solid round of influence hunting – which more than anywhere has pointed to Dickens (above all in the portrait of Mrs Bowerbank and Hyacinth's childhood visit to his mother in the prison) and to the Turgeniev of *Virgin Soil* (1876), to whose plot line *Casamassima* demonstrably bears a resemblance and whose French version James had once reviewed.[10] Who, too, could resist the comparison of James's novel with Conrad's *The Secret Agent* (1907), two visions by fellow author-exiles of London as a City of Dreadful Night, a fallen and conspiracy-ridden modern metropolis? Little wonder, given such gyrations, that *The Princess Casamassima* goes on being called 'a kind of freak among James's other novels',[11] 'the least representative' of his works.[12] But has it, in truth, deserved to be James's conspicuously uncanonical text, his odd man out? Without wishing to turn things utterly on their head and to claim *Casamassima* as some unqualified masterpiece, I want to suggest three kinds of reason why this assessment does James's novel a genuine disservice and why in fact, for all its ostensible difference, it is utterly in line with the other landmarks of his oeuvre.

III

First, what at heart is *The Princess Casamassima* about? Debate has gone back and forth about whether James wanted simply to tell a Life (Hyacinth's), or a Fate (the taking of the anarchist vow – with the Princess and Paul Muniment there to aid and abet), or even a would-be political thriller (irradiating out from Hoffendahl through Muniment, Poupin, Schinkel and the rest). None of these is out of place or unreasonable. But my own inclination would be far more to discern in *Casamassima* nothing less than James's own version of *Culture and Anarchy*, his own deliberately pitched 'outsider' contribution to the great State of the Nation issue. Here, after all, was his adopted and admired England, whose dense, stubborn particularity had drawn him from the start. But it was also an England, a civilization, in danger from within, threatened by decadence, its own inertia and contradiction. A hub of Empire it may have been, a repository of history and culture, a political order evolved out of pragmatics rather than any Grand Scheme – but it was also at risk of turning predator against itself, its own victim of perpetuated antagonisms of class, of wealth, of unyielding and entrenched power.

'Beneath the vast smug surface', to cite James's description in his New York Preface, its focal point, London, as a result has become a hive, a sinister, conspiratorial underworld likely by design or blunder to erupt at any time. Much as James has been attacked for not knowing enough about anarchist politics, about Kropotkin, Bakunin, Blanqui, Nechaev, Tkachev and the rest, does not his 'little bookbinder', Hyacinth Robinson, addled as he may be about his mix of 'noble' blood and his reduced conditions, speak directly to the issue in an outburst like the following: 'It's beyond anything I can say ... there's an immense underworld peopled with a thousand forms of revolutionary passion and devotion. The manner in which it is organized is what astonished me ... And on top of it all society lives!'?

To this we might want to add James's sharp political awareness of English political and cultural decline, as expressed in his letter to Grace Norton in January 1885:

> ... the country is gloomy, anxious, and London reflects its gloom. Westminster Hall and the Tower were half blown up two days ago by Irish Dynamiters ... I find such a situation as this extremely interesting, and it makes me feel how much I am attached to this country and, on the whole, to its sometimes exasperating people. The possible malheurs – reverses, dangers, embarrassments, the 'decline', in a word, of old England, go to my heart ...

Having, to his own satisfaction at least, taken the measure in *The Bostonians* of what had become of America's founding New Englandism ('I wished,' he writes in his Notebooks, 'to write a very American tale, a tale very characteristic of our social conditions'), so he undertakes a similar task for 'Our Old Home', as Hawthorne called it. It was, too, in James's *Hawthorne* (1879) that he so lovingly enumerated the consoling 'textures' of English as against American life, the 'accumulation of history and custom', 'the complexity of manners and types', in all, to his novelist's eye, a necessary 'fund of suggestion'. *Casamassima*, thereby, represents both an act of homage and a cautionary tale, James's tribute yet also his critique and warning.

The novel's terms, however, have not been of a kind to satisfy those who look to James to have written the definitive 'English' political or revolutionary novel. His, rather, were the deeply Arnoldian concerns of culture, high culture as may be, of that 'sweetness and light' whereby society, and specifically English society, might avoid implosion and disaster. Not, then, for James, any more than for Arnold, any one or another political programme or formal ideology, but rather to offer in all the paradox of Hyacinth Robinson's life and death another kind of way forward. Deny imagination, the human will to self-expression, and you produce quite inevitably the 'ignorant armies' of opposition, be it a meretricious aristocracy, a philistine middle class, a desperate anarchist underclass, or victims (and even the well intended, like Lady Langrish) caught – indeed stranded – in the ensuing clash and confusion.

James's vision throughout the novel assumes with Arnold that 'culture' truly 'enlarges our whole view', thereby liberating us from all forms of the provincial – but the politics of the provincial especially, as exhibited by either a mandarin ruling-class, or a one-man sectarian leadership (Hoffendahl, pointedly, has a 'mutilated hand'), or 'hard' apparatchik-commissars like Paul Muniment, or sacrificial martyrs like Hyacinth (the resemblance with Conrad's Stevie in *The Secret Agent* is striking), or the expatriate 'republican' nostalgia of M. Poupin, or a moneyed Princess Casamassima in search of 'the real' and acting ultimately in anything but authentic good faith, or the confused and jargon-laden band of would-be terrorist plotters who gather at the 'Sun and Moon' (itself the perfect deflationary name). He writes, ironically, affectionately and with all his resources of pace and interplay of viewpoint, to decry an England turning too narrow – and in favour, implicitly, of the liberal order whose touchstones are those bound up in art. This, one emphasizes, favours no one or another 'politics', but rather a view of 'culture' as a process which offers awareness, self-individuation, in the first instance, and implicitly a way forward from there to political and economic justice. Nor does James exclude 'popular' culture – how else to explain the vital presence of Millie and her world? James, in all these respects, will always fall short for those who want from him a manifesto, a programme, a call to arms even. But he saw himself, as ever, about a drama, a novel, which tells its story implicitly, tacitly, from its own unswervingly Jamesian angle. Culture and Anarchy as a phrase from his own time, Culture and Society as a phrase from a time closer to now: James's *The Princess Casamassima* has fair claim to belong in that frame of reference – but nothing if not to its own kind of measure.

IV

Second, *The Princess Casamassima* offers itself as supremely a novel of place, but of a kind far different from that to be found in Zola or even James's admired George Eliot. As he recalls it in his Preface, the novel took form out of 'the assault directly made by the great city upon an imagination quick to react', a London at odds against itself and driven to insurrection 'from below'. The city, whose streets and byways he had subjected to the inspection of his never-ending walks, loomed for him as 'the great grey Babylon', 'a garden bristling with immense illustrative flora'. Hyacinth Robinson, in turn, and no doubt Millie, Miss Pynsent, Mr Vetch and the rest, 'sprang up for me out of the London pavement'. James, further, speaks of seeking to re-create 'London mysteries', of pursuing not only Hyacinth's own ordeal of consciousness but that of the world in which it has arisen, a consciousness, a politics, at work 'irreconcilably, subversively', beneath the city's 'vast smug surface'.

If it gestures towards a London of the Thames, Millbank, Belgravia, Oxford Street, Camden Town, and pubs and meeting-places like the 'Sun and Moon', not to mention mood-setting weather from sunshine to damp and fog, *Casamassima* even more depicts a London refracted through the senses and impressions. These include, typically, Hyacinth's own sense of crampedness, Miss Pynsent's shabby gentility and compensating worship of the gentry, the vernacular exuberance and sexuality of Millie Henning ('to her blunt, expanded fingertips, a daughter of London', 'the muse of cockneyism'), Captain Sholto's man-about-town knowingness, the Poupins's 'exile' republicanism, Lady Aurora's aristocratic well meaning, and the avidity of the Muniment and Schinkel anarchist circle. For all this plenty, however, James quite self-acknowledgingly aspires to no more than a selective picture, a limited if vividly particularized cast, a city seen through a single lens and only in part. Better than anybody, he indeed knew himself to be writing as an outsider and actually seeks to turn it to his own advantage (which may be why, easy as it is to overlook, *Casamassima* uses a first-person narrator). Despite its length and meticulous unfolding, this by design would not be a novel of London set forth in all its Dickensian zest, nor a London open to the test of a historical or literal map. Rather, it would be a city imagined through feelings of individual engagement and response.

Is there not, accordingly, a nice self-irony in the note he sent to his friend Thomas Perry in December 1884 as the novel was taking shape in his mind: 'I have been all the morning at Millbank prison (horrible place) collecting notes for a fiction scene. You see I am quite the Naturalist. Look out for the same – a year hence –'? One has only to dwell for a moment upon how James conjures into being the novel's different locales to discern not the city of the naturalist or historic realist but that of the literary impressionist. A Turner or Monet canvas, all controlled shade and indistinction, comes most to mind as a likely analogue.

Lomax Place, where Hyacinth is raised by Pinnie, sets the note. It typifies hole-in-the-corner London, a step up from tenement poverty but disabling, limiting. More still to the novel's deeper purposes, it serves as a place of Hyacinth's first and shaping impressions. He recalls it on Pinnie's death as a 'cold, stale parlour', for all her and Mr Vetch's kindliness, a place of 'impure air', 'mean window-panes' and a *chiaroscuro* he thinks of as having been 'dismal'. This is where he has been subjected to Pinnie's 'limited, stinted' outlook and to her unintendedly mocking glorification of his half-aristocratic parentage; where Mrs Bowerbank ('a towering woman') has made her entry as the emissary of Millbank Prison, within whose 'dusky mass' and 'brown, bare windowless walls' Hyacinth half-catatonically encounters his French mother, the murderess Florentine Vivier; where Hyacinth has come to know in the seamstress and the fiddler two surrogate parents and in Milly a warring but fond sister-companion; and where, amid the domestic round and eventual bookbinding at Crookenden's, he has done his early reading and shown himself the artist in waiting. Lomax Place, thereby, becomes a place of the most intimate past as well as present, the London of his beginning self.

Each subsequent staging-place works to like effect. Audley Court, where Paul and the crippled Rosa Muniment live, serves as a kind of testing-ground for Hyacinth's anarchist credentials. Here he must negotiate Paul's give-nothing-away 'hardness' and Rosa's tyrannical good cheer in the face of her physical disablement (she acts like a malign Jenny Wren), a rite of passage into adult companionship – even though, like the Princess, Muniment will eventually show bad faith towards Hyacinth. At Lisson Grove, the Poupin residence, he encounters a second home, a France abroad but also the place where Hoffendahl will send Schinkel to deliver his call to action. A once-safe haven has turned deadly, Hyacinth's own last courtroom. The 'Sun and Moon', with its 'hideously papered walls', its 'meeting club' where raillery and bluster substitute for serious politics, conjures up 'the shabby sinuous ways' of 'Soho, Islington, and Pentonville'. We see the Langrish home in Belgravia through Pinnie's astonished, admiring eyes as 'grand', 'noble', a 'higher' and 'other' London. It belongs with the *salon* the Princess

Casamassima establishes in South Street and with Medley Hall, the country estate where Hyacinth, reeling in its sumptuousness, sees a palace of art – books, heraldry, gardens, architecture and a deeply European Mme Grandoni to explain and guide. James, too, includes a lower-middle-class London, that of Madeira Crescent, the 'quiet little cockneyfied retreat' rented by the Princess as part of her resolve to plunge into the arena of revolution.

James's 'London' in the novel declares itself, thus, in terms of feeling, association, the shaping interaction of self and place. Its climate and streets become a part of Hyacinth, Millie, Muniment, Sholto and the others. In winter it issues dampness and fog, in summer 'the thick, warm air of a London July'. Much as Hyacinth at one point can be dazzled by London's Belgravia and West End, by the world of the galleries and museums and opera beyond his bookbinding at Crookenden's, so, too, even though he 'sees' euphorically and amid 'the loud, contradictory, vain, unpractical babble' of the politicos at the 'Sun and Moon', he can also conjure up a counter-London – one of 'the monstrosity of the great ulcers and sores' and 'sick, eternal misery'. This London he imagines mocked by 'granaries and treasure-houses and places of delight where shameless satiety kept guard'. 'Real' London, as sought by the Princess, will thus for ever be denied her. It lies within, on the pulse and in the senses and beyond any mere willed acquisition.

James, time and again (and it has brought him rebuke), adds to this 'felt' London. As the novel pursues its plot line at an unhurried rhythm towards the fulfilment of Hyacinth's vow, London exerts its presence in the scenes of a misted-over Thames, long, crepuscular streets (Hyacinth is said to engage in 'interminable, restless, melancholy, moody, yet all-observant strolls through London'), in obscure meetings (as when Muniment and Schinkel take Hyacinth to meet Hoffendahl) and in the haze of its West End lights and opera-house gaudiness (as on his visit with Millie) – in all, a city of half-lights and shifting colours. James also invokes Paris and then Venice ('an enchanted city', as he describes it in a letter to the Princess) in a matching impressionistic idiom as he has Hyacinth spend his Pynsent inheritance in order to break free of his past. The French capital becomes for the bookbinder one great 'boulevard', 'brilliant with illuminations', 'tremendously artistic and decorative', a place where Hyacinth, as James tells us,' felt his pulse and took stock of his impressions'. The latter phrase could not be more to the point. James's Paris, like his London, is a city transposed into feeling, sensation, into nothing other than a sustained and painterly 'impression'.

V

Third, and inextricable from the rest, *The Princess Casamassima* offers a Portrait of the Artist, or at least a portrait of the artist as would-be, the artist denied or in waiting. Hyacinth Robinson serves both as an instance in general of a Jamesian 'consciousness' and as a consciousness which reacts with a special creativity, an intense openness to (though not command of) all sides of experience. This causes 'his mixed, divided nature', his 'conflicting sympathies', 'his eternal swinging from one view to another'. The Princess herself calls Hyacinth 'a strange mixture of contradictory impulses'. In childhood he thinks of Mr Vetch as 'a privileged, magical mortal' because he plays in the theatre orchestra. He is said to be a child given to long silences, a reader, a storer-up of experience, as we learn from his startling prison encounter with his blood mother. This childhood, this childishness, carries over, James makes clear, into Hyacinth's ostensible adulthood, the suggestible and uncertain boy in the man. Millie, on her dramatic first visit as a grown woman to Miss Pynsent, nevertheless instinctively recognizes the unrealized artist in him – his ability to have learned French so quickly, his stylish 'blouse', his 'imaginative, ingenious' mind, and even his reticence or fright (and, let it be said, his very Jamesian reticence or fright) in the face of her willingness to make herself sexually available to him, not that either prevents his profound disappointment and shock at perceiving the signs of her liaison with Godfrey Sholto. Millie, importantly, observes from a selfhood which has found it own centre, a 'free temperament' in which 'many disparities were reconciled'.

Despite, too, his modest circumstances, he becomes on his walks a kind of *flâneur*, the observer-artist. At Crookenden's a Ruskinesque fervour overtakes him as, under M. Poupin's guidance, he acquires in his bookbinding 'the perception of beauty and the hatred of ugliness'. Accompanying Millie one time, he offers as assured opinion the view that Buckingham Palace yields nothing 'that a real artist would look at'. He also, frequently, 'authors' other identities for himself, as an artist *révolté* born through his mother's French nationality of the Revolution itself (a revolution he imagines as 'magnificent energy'), or, in English terms, as an enlisted artist-combatant against Victorian Gothic ugliness and slummage. In all, if he has any real politics, they lie in this will to make an artist of himself. The politics he finds himself obliged to take his part in, however, are those of infantilism, the deadly but story-book bravura of having to discharge his 'vow' by the assassination of a nominated aristocrat, a duke (a plot line, it should be added, perfectly in keeping with his sensibility and anything but 'inane').

There can, as a consequence, be little surprise in Hyacinth's eager capitulation to the Princess, his dazzling but ultimately spurious Europeanized muse and icon. James underlines the Princess's spuriousness in her whimsies, in the embittered witness of her banal Italian princeling-husband, in Muniment's brute admission that his group all along wanted not her but her money, and in her vaunted quest for 'the real'. Hyacinth, in his rapture, not inappropriately invents her as 'in a statue, in a picture, in a museum'. Likewise, he speaks true to form in pouring out to her his desperate resort to the pictures and exhibits at the British Museum and National Gallery. In like vein he reads Tennyson to her and confides his wonder at 'the glorious Louvre'. The narrator, with no small irony, designates him a 'genuine artist' not only in his bookbinding but in his professed desire to write – the very index of Hyacinth's need to inscribe his own creative signature on history but which cannot be other than denied by his life's circumstance. James shows a near perfect touch in so rendering the shortfall between Hyacinth's aspiration to become an artist and its actual enactment.

Politics as Hyacinth knows them – even Muniment, whom he thinks the exemplary man of action – also grow in proportion increasingly impossible and remote. Anarchism, with its onenote singleness of purpose, is transformed for him into 'the beastly cause'. Vetch's talk of 'a general rectification' and Muniment's of 'the great restitution' become parodic, as otherworldly as the Princess's 'foreign socialism'. But Hyacinth is left with his vow, the utter, reductive opposite of all he has it in him to become. His last act, suicide by the gun (and not, as some critics have thought it, murder), is a would-be artist's revenge, a final reclamation of his life by self-imposed extinction. It is literal death as the metaphor of the art, the creative existence, which has not taken form – be it Hyacinth as painter, writer, composer or representative 'author' of his own terms of being. The writer especially, he thinks, has access to 'wider fields of knowledge, still higher sensations'. He stands in this as the figure of life denied, James's own oblique but utterly striking way of expressing the consequence of a larger politics of division and repression.

VI

'Magnificent' as James himself may have thought his 'subject' overall, his novel goes on being charged with a lack of true cultural or political vision, a lack of achieved place, a weakly turned artist-hero. By these criteria, *The Princess Casamassima* represents a falling-away, an error. To anti-Jamesians, it proves what they had maintained all along: that James had neither the taste nor the stomach for anything but the delineation of the more rarified strata of society. To resolute Jamesians, it proves that he had moved too far outside his accustomed realms of 'psychology' or manners and not done himself justice. Differing perspectives they may appear, but each contributes to the same result. Only a few hardy souls like Lionel Trilling have put up a case for admiring the novel. The rest, for the most part, have looked on in silence or with the wish to advance as quickly as possible to the safer shores of the agreed 'canonical' fiction.

All these factors have helped make *The Princess Casamassima* an odd man out, uncanonical – or perhaps more accurately, a-canonical – James. Yet if my argument holds, the novel, whatever its reception, could not have been more Jamesian. In this one does not for a moment have to regard *Casamassima* as an unalloyed success. It can still be thought to have its longueurs, to come at its materials too much from an angle, to depict anarchism as too much a world afar, and to lay itself open to the charge of a certain contrivance and overdelay in delivering Hyacinth into his fatal cul-de-sac. Nor does it mean failing to recognize why the Princess and Paul Muniment, as the two

ODD MAN OUT?

principal figures alongside Hyacinth, have not always satisfied, the former too operatic and the latter too undisclosed. One can, too, like or dislike the values, cultural, political or otherwise, which may be assumed to lie behind the critique of British society (Irving Howe, no doubt rightly, speaks of James's 'comely conservativism').

But it serves nothing if we fail to see clearly the kind of novel James actually wrote or to attend scrupulously to the imaginative terms of reference in which it is cast. To do less is to assume a novel other than the one to hand, the one James set about to compose with all the resolve and exhilaration he registers in his Notebooks. That indeed means acknowledging his particular mode of portraying politics (with its emphasis more on feeling and personality), his impressionist's sense of place and his notion of art as a radical and highest form of self-expression, with all that such implies for the life of Hyacinth Robinson. It also means acknowledging the reasons for James's deliberateness of pace in the novel, its sometimes undramatic rhythm of observation. Taking these considerations together, the odd thing, then, about *The Princess Casamassima* becomes the fact that it ever became the odd man out in the first place.

NOTES

1. The one figure who did regularly address him as '*Maître*' was the French-speaking Joseph Conrad. See Frederick R. Karl, *Joseph Conrad: The Three Lives* (New York, Farrar, Strauss and Giroux, 1979), p. 407. Nor does translation into 'Master' or 'The Master' entirely fit the bill, notwithstanding its use as a title for the fifth volume of the standard biography. It fails to convey the Gallic sense of intimacy and cultural pride of possession so subtly woven into the wish to pay respect. See Leon Edel, *Henry James, The Master: 1901–1916* (Philadelphia and New York, J. B. Lippincott Company, 1972).
2. This and all subsequent quotations are from the 1886 text. See Henry James, *The Princess Casamassima* (Harmondsworth, Penguin Books, 1977).
3. Leon Edel and Lyall H. Powers (eds.), *The Complete Notebooks of Henry James* (New York and Oxford, Oxford University Press, 1987), p. 31.
4. Lionel Trilling, *The Liberal Imagination: Essays on Literature and Society* (New York, Viking, 1951).
5. Irving Howe, *Politics and the Novel* (Cleveland, Ohio, Meridian Books, 1957). Howe's reading of the novel might be compared with John Lucas, *Literature and Politics in the Nineteenth Century* (London, Methuen, 1971), pp. 173–221.

A. ROBERT LEE

6 Maxwell Geismar, *Henry James and the Jacobites* (Boston, Houghton Mifflin, 1963).
7 These judgements are taken from, respectively, Gorley Putt, *Henry James: A Reader's Guide* (Ithica, New York, Cornell University Press, 1966), p. 163; Walter Allen, *The English Novel* (Harmondsworth, Penguin Books, 1958), p. 273; and Yvor Winters, *In Defense of Reason* (Denver, Colorado, Alan Swallow, 1947), p. 333. I would add the following to the account: John Goode, 'The Art of Fiction: Walter Besant and Henry James', in David Howard, John Lucas and John Goode (eds.), *Tradition and Tolerance in Nineteenth Century Fiction: Critical Essays on Some English and American Novels* (London, Routledge, 1966); John L. Kimney: 'The Princess Casamassima and the Quality of Bewilderment', *Nineteenth Century Fiction*, 22, 1967–8, pp. 47–62; Sister Jane Marie Luecke, *The Princess Casamassima*: Hyacinth's Fallible Consciousness', (1963), reprinted in Tony Tanner (ed.), *Henry James: Modern Judgements* (London, Macmillan, 1969); Taylor Stoehr, 'Words and Deeds in *The Princess Casamassima*', *English Literary History*, 37, 1970, pp. 95–135; and Alwyn Berland, *Culture and Conduct in the Novels of Henry James* Cambridge University Press, 1981).
8 Cited by Putt, *Henry James: A Reader's Guide*, p. 164
9 Both points are nicely joined in Marta Banta, 'Beyond Post-Modernism: The Sense of History in *The Princess Casamassima*', *Henry James Review*, 3, 2, 1982, pp. 96–107.
10 This resemblance has been helpfully explored in Oscar Cargill, *The Novels of Henry James* (New York, The Macmillan Company, 1961), pp. 146–52.
11 Walter Dubler, '*The Princess Casamassima*: Its Place in the James Canon', *Modern Fiction Studies*, XII, 1, Spring 1966, p. 44.
12 Bruce R. McElderry Jr, *Henry James* (New Haven, Connecticut, Twayne Publishers, 1965), p. 68.

7 To the Sulaco Lighthouse

M. M. Mahood

One of the claims I was going out to settle was called the Aves Island claim. The Americans had gone to a rock of that name . . . to collect guano, and had been stopped by the Venezuelans, who maintain that the Aves Islands belong to them. For the loss caused by this demurrer, the Americans now claim one hundred and fifty-five thousand dollars of the Venezuelan government: a sum sufficient to have plated the whole island with silver instead of guano.

Venezuela (1868)

So observed Edward B. Eastwick as the *Isabel* bore him, in 1864, towards the coast of Latin America. Conrad possessed his book; it was one of several that he turned to for information after he had agreed, in February 1903, to make the tale he was currently writing into a novel of some 80,000 words. 'The story is very thin for such a large scale,' he told Galsworthy, adding, 'Still! I would be able to let myself go . . .' It appears that he had originally intended *Nostromo* to be a 'silly and saleable' novella of the *Karain* type. Although the synopsis Conrad sent to his literary agent has not survived, his allusions to it elsewhere suggest that it was to concentrate on a small group of Italian emigrants into a South American republic. Its focus was perhaps to be a contrast between the integrity that Giorgio Viola, the old Garibaldino, derives from the fact that he has been one of the *Mille* devoted to the ideal of Italian unity and the corruptibility of the man who breaks ranks. Nostromo is called 'one in a thousand', but as Dr Monygham in the finished novel perceives, he is nothing of the kind, but 'absolutely the only one', a solitary adventurer owing allegiance to nothing but his self-image.

From these limited beginnings, and seized by the desire to 'faire grand', Conrad indeed let himself go in creating the history and geography of an entire country, bringing to life a throng of its inhabitants, and engaging them, as he himself says, in more action than is to be found in any of his previous tales. The natural point from which the story could be made to grow was the revolution that occasioned the central character putting to sea with a lighter full of silver. Conrad, however, knew little about South American revolutions; his own experience of the continent was allegedly limited to a few days ashore on the Venezuelan coast in the 1870s. Books helped, often through the indirect suggestiveness represented by the extract quoted at the start of this chapter. But the greatest help came from his closest friend, the socialist journalist and politician R. B. Cunninghame Graham, who had a uniquely intimate knowledge of two of the more southerly South American republics. When appealed to in May 1903, 'Don Roberto' not only furnished Conrad with a rich, even overrich, mass of detail about South American life – though Conrad's controlling imagination prevented his laying on this local colour impasto, in the manner of Cunninghame Graham's own stories – but also imparted to him his own fierce bias against the United States's frequent interventions at the time in South American affairs. Graham's indignation over what he saw as the covert imperialism of America's 1898 war against Spain smouldered on for years in the correspondence columns of the *Saturday Review*, and was rekindled by the Venezuelan blockade of 1902–3 which ended with Britain's acquiescence to the United States's hegemony, as proclaimed in Theodore Roosevelt's renewal of the Monroe doctrine. Another event of early 1903 then fuelled it afresh. This was the treaty whereby Colombia undertook to cede to the United States the zone of the proposed Panama Canal. In Part One of the novel, written during the spring and early summer, the gigantic narrational arabesque which culminates in the involvement in the San Tomé undertaking of the San Franciscan financier Holroyd, with his belief that 'Europe must be kept out of this continent, and for proper interference on our part the time is not yet ripe', reflects, in this as in many other passages, the reaction of Englishmen of Cunninghame Graham's way of thinking to recent events in Latin America's northern republics.

But the Colombian senate was not willing to ratify the canal zone treaty. As a result, in early November, when Conrad had begun work on *Nostromo*'s second part, in course of which the secession of the Occidental Province from Costaguana is conceived by Decoud as a way of maintaining the economic stability of which American capital is the source, a 'real' revolution – if the term can be used of events that appear to have been stage-managed in Washington – broke out in Colombia's own most westerly province, Panama, to which the canal project had brought high hopes. The lives of American residents were held to be at risk, as was the American-built railway – or such was the pretext for dispatching a naval force to the area. The appearance outside Colon of the US cruiser *Nashville* effectively put an end to Colombian resistance to the secession of Panama. In this intervention the European powers, according to *The Times*, acquiesced 'cheerfully'. No less cheerfully, in the novel, Captain Mitchell recalls 'an international naval demonstration, which put an end to the Costaguana–Sulaco war'. As a neat underlining of the point that the advantage of those who have the guns remains the same through changing historical circumstances, the US cruiser, which in the novel is the first to salute the Occidental flag, is called the *Powhattan*.

Three weeks after these events Conrad, who was unwell and depressed, wrote disparagingly of *Nostromo* to J. M. Barrie. There is an element of pose in his self-deprecation, but what does sound genuine in the letter is the statement 'I've never felt that I had my subject in the palm of my hand. I've been always catching at it all along: and I shall be just catching at it to the end.' Was it that Conrad felt the *Ur-Nostromo* to be slipping from his grasp? If so, the reappearance of another figure in Conrad's life at this point still further distanced him from his initial psychological concerns with Nostromo as a man of the people. At the end of November Roger Casement, who had helped to open Conrad's eyes to the exploitation rife in the Congo at the time of his employment there, in his turn sought Conrad's help with publicizing the findings of his report on Belgian atrocities. The renewed contact excited Conrad: strong feelings about the exploitation of Africa returned to colour those already present, in the thinking behind *Nostromo*, about commercial imperialism in South America. On Boxing Day he commended Casement's cause to Cunninghame Graham as an active political journalist, strengthening his commendation by an allusion to the Dominican protector of the Indians, who was one of Graham's heroes: 'I have always thought that some particle of Las Casas' soul had found refuge in his indefatigable body.' The same letter reveals that Conrad was corresponding with the Colombian diplomat S. Perez Triana, his model for Don José Avellanos, who was even then himself denouncing, in letters to Cunninghame Graham, the United States government as 'highway robbers and land thieves'. And a highly rhetorical question concludes the body of Conrad's letter: 'what do you think of the Yankee Conquistadores in Panama'?

Conrad's method of working makes it difficult to pin down the writing of any part of a novel to a particular date. But just after his renewed contact with Casement, he mentioned to a correspondent that he had reached page 567 of his manuscript. Reckoning about three and a half pages of manuscript to one printed page of the Collected Edition this brings him to about a fifth of the way through Part Two. It is tempting to attribute to the reawakening of the passion that had inspired *Heart of Darkness* the amazing fourth chapter of this part of *Nostromo*. What Conrad would call his 'intentions' are here at their most sustained and concentrated. The narrative moves from Barrios's exhortation to the Europeans gathered to watch the embarkation of troops to 'Work, work': 'There's enough wealth in Costaguana to pay for everything – or else you would not be here'. (p. 164),* to the ambiguous glimpse into that work afforded by the telegraph poles. They are described as 'bearing a single, almost invisible wire far into the great campo – like a slender, vibrating feeler of that progress waiting outside for a moment of peace to enter and twine itself about the weary heart of the land' (p. 166), and 'twine' disturbs by its hint of strangulation. Then come the two encounters of the returning carriageful of patriotic champions of a regime financed by the mining concession – first with Viola, for whom the conscripts dispatched to the defence of material interests are savagely defined as 'esclavos', and later with the young English engineer whose zest for the undertaking recalls the dangerous innocence of the Russian in *Heart of Darkness*. So finally to the vignette that closes the chapter: as the

---

* This and all subsequent page references refer to Joseph Conrad, *Nostromo*, Collected Edition (Dent, London, 1947).

carriage enters the city, Decoud, the character who is most aware of exploitation, looks back to see 'the shrieking ghost of a railway engine fleeing across the frame of the archway, behind the startled movement of the people streaming back from a military spectacle with silent footsteps on the dust of the road', and to hear how 'when the ear-splitting screech of the steam-whistle for the brakes had stopped, a series of hard, battering shocks, mingled with the clanking of chain-couplings' make 'a tumult of blows and shaken fetters under the vault of the gate'. There could be no clearer foreboding of enslavement of some kind as the consequence of even the most seemingly beneficial intrusions of material interests.

To stay with the railway image, the parallel indignation of Cunninghame Graham and Casement at the mask of progress assumed by commercial interests fulfilled much the same purpose as the rails that gave Nostromo the necessary start for his situation-saving ride to Cayta. Added to Conrad's own first-hand experience of European enterprise in Africa and Asia, they afforded him the impetus into what he was to write of fifteen years later as 'the ever-enlarging vistas opening before me as I progressed deeper in my knowledge of the country'. Current happenings and contacts, then, changed the focus of Conrad's novel during its composition. It follows that our valuation of the enlarged undertaking rests on the issue of how successful Conrad has been in shifting our interest from the nature of a man to the nature of a society; how far he goes beyond the opening of picturesque vistas towards making us feel in our pulses the vulnerability of Costaguana; and how well this graft has taken upon the original stock of the 'Italian' story.

One difficulty impeding Conrad's determination to create a society in whose fortunes the reader could feel implicated lay in the composite nature of his fictional country. The Right-versus-Left pattern of Costaguanan politics, with its liberals and conservatives divided upon such issues as federalism and the disposal of Church property, belongs to late nineteenth-century Colombia. Its topography, however, derives in large part from Conrad's past glimpses of the Venezuelan seaboard and from his subsequent reading about that even more strife-torn country. We may perhaps take a hint from Don Pépé, being an old officer of Páez, to conceive of Costaguana as the fictional continuation of Bolívar's short-lived Gran Colombia. But of the fact that the northern republics are in tropical America, whose seaboard was encumbered with all the dangers and difficulties of a fever coast, there is virtually no hint, unless it be the recognition that not all the young English engineers will live to see the railway completed. The Sulaco mosquitoes give rise to nothing worse than a proprietorial pride on the part of Captain Mitchell. Sulaco's climate has been imported into the novel from more temperate regions known to Don Roberto and other travellers to Paraguay and the Argentine. At times the reader is bound to feel fussed by this eclecticism: we long to know where we are as precisely as we do in, say, *The Honorary Consul*. But Greene's precision belongs to an age of fast travel. Unable to respond to Triana's invitation to visit Colombia, Conrad had no way of adding to his fading memories of what he described as the dreary Venezuelan coast. Instead, he turns the very imprecision of his setting to good account by making sure of its wider applicability. The way of life in haciendas of the Costaguana campo has a strong affinity with that the Afrikaners felt was threatened by British mining interests in the Transvaal, as well as with that of Polish estates in an area made precious to Russia by its mineral wealth.

A more serious hindrance to our apprehending Costaguanan society is that it is at first presented to us as totally without cohesion. To begin with, in our search for the people of Costaguana we have to discount the title of 'man of the people' afforded to Nostromo in the story as it was first projected. Conrad seems to have intended it merely to mean 'without formal education'. He wanted to show the late and painful acquisition of self-awareness in a man – and his sea career furnished many models – who had not been trained to introspection. But Nostromo, though he basks in the admiration of the Sulacans, is no more a man of the Costaguanan people than are the Italian railwaymen who gather in a tight expatriate group in Giorgio Viola's bar. Viola himself has fought in Montevideo, under Garibaldi, for an abstract idea of freedom rather than for the common people, whom he treats with reserve and even scorn. When trouble breaks out, the Italian artisans fight for the lives of their English employers. It was a lucky circumstance for Sulaco, we are gravely informed, that 'the relations of those imported workmen with the people of the country had been uniformly bad'. The lightermen, or Cargadores, who under Nostromo also throw themselves into the fray in defence of the Europeans, though technically natives of the Republic, are described as 'an outcast lot of very mixed blood, mainly negroes'. Many of them are from the offshore islands and treat the riots of 3 May as the opportunity to pay off old scores. Nor are the townspeople themselves any more homogeneous as a group. 'Sullen, thievish, vindictive and bloodthirsty', their strength has been augmented by 'thieves and murderers from the whole province'.

Every so often, however, this effect of a social jungle is shot through with a suggestion, not usually intended by the speaker, of more human and humane feelings. In defining the Cargadores as 'an unruly brotherhood of all sorts of scum, with a patron saint of their own', the mysterious 'I' of Part One's final chapter at least attributes two kinds of devotion to the scum. The same narrator's approving account of Nostromo's strong-arm methods against absenteeism also affords us in passing a brief but appalling glimpse of the shanties the lightermen inhabit. Decoud is for the most part arrogantly dismissive of the people and their spokesmen; but he notices that the face of the corpse sprawled on the cathedral steps has been covered 'by the attention of some friend perhaps', and he relates the help given both by a negro Cargador and by the Italian Nostromo to the old lacemaker in her search for the body of her crossing-sweeper son – the exact occupations here contrasting with the contempt of *'leperos'*, which is the term in general use for such people when we see them through the eyes of those who look at Costaguanans from the seaboard. It is from hints such as this that we are brought to enter into the distress of the unnamed Cargador's wife, mumbling prayers and trying to force a piece of orange between his stiffening lips, as he dies in the Casa Gould, inner sanctuary of the material interests he has been coerced into defending.

But the Casa Gould is also another kind of sanctuary, from where Costaguanan society does not appear fragmented and cannibalized. In fact it is in the Casa Gould that readers of the novel are made Costaguaneros, and for this reason our first visit merits a leisurely recall. We find Don José taking tea with Mrs Gould:

Then giving up the empty cup into his young friend's hand, extended with a smile, he continued to expatiate upon the patriotic nature of the San Tomé mine for the simple pleasure of talking fluently, it seemed, while his reclining body jerked backwards and forwards in a rocking-chair of the sort exported from the United States. The ceiling of the largest drawing-room of the Casa Gould extended its white level far above his head. The loftiness dwarfed the mixture of heavy, straight-backed Spanish chairs of brown wood with leathern seats, and European furniture, low and cushioned all over, like squat little monsters gorged to bursting with steel springs and horsehair.

Albert Guerard regrets that *Nostromo* contains more descriptions of furniture than are usual in Conrad's work. But Don José's rocking-chair is an inspired touch. What supports him in his role of silver-tongued elder statesman is American money emanating from Holroyd. And just as this American rocking-chair is out of keeping with its surroundings, Don José is himself not quite at his ease with the comfort it affords him, any more than he is with Mrs Gould's English tea. Of the San Tomé concession, operated by an Englishman and financed by an American, he is wont to murmur *imperium in imperio* 'with an air of profound self-satisfaction which somehow, in a curious way, seemed to contain a queer admixture of *bodily discomfort*'. The steel-sprung little monsters are also good: the disturbance they cause in the harmony of this traditional setting – we never catch Antonia sitting on one of them – echoes that created in the country at large by bulkier products of the developed world's mastery of metals, the imported railway tracks and mining machinery.

As the description continues, however, Guerard's impatience may begin to appear justified:

There were knick-knacks on little tables, mirrors let into the wall above marble consoles, square spaces of carpet under the two groups of armchairs, each presided over by a deep sofa; smaller rugs scattered all over the floor of red tiles; three windows from ceiling down to the ground, opening on a balcony, and flanked by the perpendicular folds of the dark hangings. The stateliness of ancient days lingered between the four high, smooth walls, tinted a delicate primrose-colour; and Mrs Gould, with her little head and shining coils of hair, sitting in a cloud of muslin and lace before a slender mahogany table, resembled a fairy posed lightly before dainty philtres dispensed out of vessels of silver and porcelain.

Impossible not to wince here. The profusion is perhaps necessary to make the point that the Goulds are now affluent – amid all this clutter, we recall the one broken gilt chair furnishing the room in which we first saw them together – but after that, 'primrose', though it may be intended to hint at the woodland atmosphere Conrad tries to create around Emilia Gould, only adds an appalling *Homes and Gardens* flavour of gracious living to the paragraph, which appears to end on a painfully arch note of Edwardian whimsy. But though Conrad may here give the impression of being perilously close to losing control, he knows what he wants to achieve with this picture of rarified domesticity: its purpose is to render the opening of the next paragraph the more shocking:

Mrs Gould knew the history of the San Tomé mine. Worked in the early days mostly by means of lashes on the backs of slaves, its yield had been paid for in its own weight of human bones. Whole tribes of Indians had perished in the exploitation; and then the mine was abandoned, since with this primitive method it had ceased to make a profitable return, no matter how many corpses were thrown into its maw.

Mrs Gould *knew*. Wielding her antique silver teapot, she is well aware what has been the past cost of tearing treasures out of the earth. If Conrad seems here to have pulled himself out of a skid, it is because he always has difficulty in standing outside of Emilia Gould and looking at her; partly, no doubt, because of the uneasiness he shows in the presence of so many of his women characters, but also for the much more valid reason that her vision is in a large part his vision. When she first appears in the book, she is called patriotic by the visiting railway magnate, and this patriotism for her adopted country springs from an idea of society that contrasts sharply with the concepts underlying the vision set before us elsewhere in the book, of a society split laterally in a way that, on the principle of divide and rule, can freely be exploited.

The nature of Mrs Gould's vision is made clear to herself only very late in the book, in the thought that Eloise Knapp Hay has rightly described as being fraught with high political significance: 'for life to be large and full, it must contain the care of the past and of the future in every passing moment of the present'.

It has, however, been clear to the reader ever since the novel's seventh chapter, which describes her travels through the interior of the country, where Gould is recruiting labour for the mine. Here are to be found two unchanged, traditional ways of life, in the great haciendas 'where masters and dependants sat in a simple and patriarchal state' and in the pueblos of peasants whose 'great worth' is their tenacity in sustaining and handing on life in defiance of the 'absurd devils let loose upon the land with sabres and uniforms and grandiloquent phrases', for whose armies they can be lassoed like cattle. If the thought crosses our minds that even if this society were undisturbed it would still be a 'colonial' society of rich Spaniards and poor Indians, we find that Conrad has taken care of that too. Just as Mrs Gould knows of the Conquistadores' enslavement of labour for the mine, she is aware in even the most idyllic landscape of the oppressions of the imperial past: 'The heavy stonework of bridges and churches left by the conquerors proclaimed the disregard of human labour, the tribute-labour of vanished nations'. 'How one is faithful to the past without confirming its errors never becomes quite clear,' Hay comments on Mrs Gould's reflections. But in *Nostromo* (and perhaps there is relevance here in Dr Monygham's 'idealization' of what he sees as his past failure as the basis for heroic action in the present) fidelity to the past consists of the redemption of its failures as much as the sustentation of its achievements.

So Mrs Gould throws herself into the reopening of the mine, itself a way of redeeming the unhappy recent past of Gould's father. The mine is to be for men, not men for the mine. And the mining community as we first see it in the novel, viewed through the eyes of Mrs Gould's devotees, Don Pépé and Father Romàn, who share her basic vision, is organic, self-renewing. The 'small, staid urchin', cigar in mouth and mother's rosary looped over his stomach, lingers long in the reader's memory, not as a picturesque detail but as the child of parents from whom he has purloined both objects, parents whose identity the priest and the Gubernator gravely dispute. Like all the other children of the community's 'innumerable Marias and Brigidas', he is part of a lineage and so the symbol of that stability which, in the early days of the concession, appears to Mrs Gould, and to Charles Gould, who is still in love and sees everything through her eyes, as the whole purpose of their undertaking. And again, it is through her sensibility that we experience the emergence of the first ingot, 'still warm' from the mould as a new birth, arising from a 'justificative conception' of peace and justice for a society that has known little of either.

From this point in the story, the centre of Mrs Gould's life shifts to the city. Here the Casa Gould has already been presented to us through her eyes as representative of life sustained and handed on. On the patio, equivalent to the hearth in other cultures, is the cistern, watering man and beast and the living greenery of the corridor that surrounds it; among all the domestic comings and goings, trays of fresh bread emerge from the bakehouse. The same patio becomes a place of healing for those injured in the riots. But the strongest impression of social cohesion comes at the moment the church bells crash out their greeting to the Monterists and the whole household, believing this a signal for massacre, takes instinctive refuge in the room where the Goulds are at breakfast. For the first time Charles Gould realizes the extent of his household, ranging from the 'big patriarchal head' of the porter who witnessed his uncle's execution to 'old hags' of whom he had been unaware, and children too – 'he had never before noticed any sign of a child in his patio'.

This is not surprising. Charles Gould's life has grown apart from that of the Casa, much as his objectives have changed from sustaining a community to sustaining a contract with a San Francisco financier. The river of life issuing from the paradisiacal gorge has been diverted into the ore-shifting flumes of the mine, and he seeks no renewal at the cistern. For the most part, the reader is made aware of his presence in the house only by the fetter-like sound of his silver spurs as he comes and goes between the mine and the hard-lit room which is no more than an extension of the mine. It is a sign of his isolation from the society he once thought to stabilize that, at the height of the crisis, he is prepared to blow up the mine, like a buccaneer throwing a match into his magazine, rather than 'let it be wrenched from his grasp'. To Holroyd's response that he must put his trust in God, Gould's reaction can be summed up, he tells the chief engineer, in a local proverb: 'God is very high above.' But this desperation is countered by the brief paragraph which follows and which closes the chapter: 'The engineer's appreciative laugh died away down the stairs, where the Madonna with a Child in her arm seemed to look after his shaking broad back from her shallow niche.'

Here is one child Gould has never noticed on his patio. Despite the opposition of 'shallow' to 'broad', the statue – so idolatrous to Holroyd's way of thinking – represents a determination (in every sense) for the future more effective than the silver which has become Gould's fetish. To protect their future, the miners with their wives and families sweep down from the mountain to join in the final defeat of the Monterists.

That society coheres vertically, through a natural piety towards the past by which it conserves its values for the future, rather than horizontally, through the bond of brotherhood between its different elements, was at the root of Conrad's Burkean form of conservative thinking. Fraternity, he told Cunninghame Graham in a letter of February 1899, 'means nothing unless the Cain–Abel business'; it serves only to 'weaken the national sentiment, the preservation of which is my concern'. And for a direct expression of his own preservation of a sentiment which appears to have no possible outcome in action, he turns to the second language of his childhood: *'Moi je regarde l'avenir du fond d'un passé très noir et je trouve que rien ne m'est permis hormis la fidélité à une cause absoluement perdue, à une idée sans avenir'*. So, too, Mrs Gould's reflection that 'our daily work must be done for the glory of the dead and for the good of those who come after' exposes her to a great wave of sadness which is more than regret for her childlessness. Her ideas also have no progeny: the good fairy, 'weary with a long career of well-doing', is aware that her philtres have not wrought the transformation she strove for in her involvement with the San Tomé mine, and this for the reason that Dr Monygham has left with her: 'There is no peace and no rest in the development of material interests.' Caught between the devil and the deep blue sea, the internal and the foreign exploiters, Costaguana is no place for the patriotism that puts first continuity and tradition, the rootedness of a stable order.

Among those who throng into the Goulds' dining-room when the bells clash out are two other children, Linda and Giselle Viola. They have been brought to the house from their dying mother's bedside by Mrs Gould. Hardly yet realized as characters, they are to be given a symbolic role in the story by virtue of Teresa Viola's last cry, 'Save the children.' The words, we are given to understand, move Nostromo, more than does Monygham's appeal to his vanity (an appeal of the kind he has heard once too often), into undertaking the ride to Cayta, which leads to the relief of Sulaco and the founding of the new republic. In heeding the appeal, he is fulfilling the wishes of the woman who has been a mother to him and the man who has made him a substitute for his lost son. Loyalty to a past generation is here again a setting right of the past, in that Nostromo is guilt-ridden at having refused, through his eagerness to prove his daring to the Blancos in taking away the silver, to bring a priest to Teresa. Now, in undertaking a new exploit, he is instinctively putting the principle of natural piety, even though it is not natural in the full genetic sense, before the instinct of comradeship, before his obligation to the stranded Decoud. When he sights the empty boat and swims out to this patent sign that Decoud has perished, he sees in the distance the ships he has set in motion steaming on to save those he now despises as his taskmasters; but also, clinchingly, 'to save the children'.

I offer this both as an example of one of many motifs in which Conrad attempts to link the Italian story to the political part of the novel, and as an example of the way such couplings repeatedly sound forced and contrived. Most contrived of all are the disastrous two final chapters, in which Conrad returns to the story in which, as he said early in 1903, Viola's two daughters were 'to take a great space'. The events on Great Isabel – where Nostromo's enslavement to the silver hidden on the island causes him to become betrothed to the sister who acts as lighthouse keeper while secretly pursuing the other, and finally to his being shot as an intruder by old Giorgio – jar less by their inherent improbabilities (one can imagine Hardy making something of those) than by the desperately strained artifice of the prose in which they are narrated. Yet there are ample signs throughout the novel that the scenes at the lighthouse were the planned climax to a tale in which there are a number of light and dark houses.

Behind all such images lies the phrase most often used at the turn of the century to justify commercial enterprise in what we now call the Third World: it was to bring light into dark places. The bright lights of industrial workings, which lend a sense of awe at human mastery to any empty landscape, and never more powerfully so than when the landscape is part of a 'backward' country, appear to the Goulds as the ray of hope through 'a rift in the appalling darkness of intrigue, bloodshed, and crime' which Gould's father despaired of ever seeing. The altarpiece Mrs Gould gives to the miners' chapel, 'a figure soaring upwards, long limbed and livid, in an oval of pallid light, and a helmeted brown legionary smitten down', has for her more to do with Charles Gould's mission of enlightenment than with the Resurrection. And at the end of a crucial day, when the political tide has ebbed out of the Casa Gould, the master of the house is left 'standing motionless, like a tall beacon amongst the deserted shoals of furniture'. Twice in the course of the same evening we have been made to feel that power emanates from the Casa Gould, as its windows cast their light 'defiantly' on the street and fling 'their shining parallelograms upon the house of the Avellanos' – henceforth to remain dark, as Don José's concern for national unity is eclipsed by the drive to secession as a way of safeguarding the mine's resources. Antithetical to this beacon effect of the Casa Gould is the darkness of the Violas' house of exile, the fortress of old Giorgo's lost hopes. Only lights from without throw up the sad irrelevance of Albergo d'Italia Una. No light comes from it the night of Giorgio's vigil with his wife's body, and instead of making straight for home, Nostromo, stripped of his hitherto refulgent sense of identity by the failure of the silver exploit, is lured by the glimmering candles in the windows of the Custom House.

All this interplay of strong and feeble lights and total darkness should converge on the setting of the last two chapters: on the lighthouse which throws no light to Sulaco but faces the ocean for the guidance of fresh Conquistadores; on Linda, steadily guarding the light, which is magnified by many reflectors such as have in the past fed the vanity of the 'magnificent' Capataz de Cargadores; and on the light that draws him in his present darkness, the candle at Giselle's window. The potential here is surely great, and the question has to be asked why the final effect is so disastrous. There are hints of two possibly valid answers in two details of the third and final part of the book.

When Sotillo withdraws his troops from the Custom House, he leaves lights in the room where Hirsch has been interrogated: 'The light of the two candles burning before the perpendicular and breathless immobility of the late Señor Hirsch threw a gleam afar over land and water, like a signal in the night.' Here is at first sight another ironic ikon, the body of the tortured Jew flanked by votive candles, to set beside the Madonna and Child and the altarpiece. But in neither expression nor applicability does it have the vigour of those earlier images, and we sense the repetition of effect which characterizes tired or hurried writing. Conrad in fact wrote almost all of Part Three, half the novel, in five months and under the double pressure of the need to keep up with the book's serialization and the need to earn enough to repay an overdraft on his bank, which had failed. The effort was heroic; the writing suffered. But more destructive than anxiety was the shift of focus which has been my concern here.

As the work, nourished by events contemporaneous with its writing, grew into a political novel, Conrad lost interest in his eponymous hero: 'But truly N is nothing at all – ' he wrote to Cunninghame Graham after the book had been published: 'a fiction – embodied vanity of the sailor kind – a romantic mouthpiece of "the people" . . . I do not defend him as a creation.' And transformed by Conrad into Costaguanan patriots, we too cannot regain our interest in the group of Italian characters when Conrad returns to them in the last two chapters of the book. This is made plain when, just before, they are reintroduced to us in the course of conversation between Dr Monygham and Mrs Gould: the doctor has witnessed an impassioned exchange on the wharf between Linda and Giselle's suitor, Ramirez. But his description evokes only gesticulating figures that seem to belong to a toy theatre; what really catches our attention is Monygham's reason for being on the wharf at the time. He had been 'called to an urgent consultation by the doctor of the German gun-boat in the harbour'. The chapter has been full of foreboding of further unrest, of the kind of instability which was the pretext for the Anglo-German blockade of Venezuela. Have sharks at last got inside the Gulfo Placido? As Costaguanans, we care – as we cannot bring ourselves to care about the involved relationships of the four people isolated on the Great Isabel.

Moreover, we go on caring. The novel retains its hold upon us decade after decade, because, whatever his exhaustion, Conrad's political insight enabled him to write as a prophet new inspired in all his hints of events to come in Costaguana. There the next upheaval, we gather from Antonia, will be from an alliance of intellectuals and priests with the workers, and we know as well as Dr Monygham what reaction that will evoke from the House of Holroyd – and indeed from the White House. The lasting social relevance of *Nostromo* can be traced into all the ramifications of Costaguanan affairs, even into one detail that Conrad appears to have forgotten. Charles Gould's father bequeathed him something else beside the San Tomé mine: 'a vague right of forest exploitation in a remote and savage district'. There too we assume there is no rest and no peace.

NOTES

I am very grateful to Hans van Marle and Cedric Watts for casting a critical eye over this essay, which is also indebted throughout to Cedric Watts's edition of *Joseph Conrad's Letters to Cunninghame Graham* (Cambridge University Press, 1969), and to Norman Sherry's *Conrad's Western World* (Cambridge University Press, 1971). I have also made much use of *The Collected Letters of Joseph Conrad*, Vols 2 and 3 (Cambridge University Press, 1986, 1988), edited by Frederick R. Karl and Laurence Davies. Among critics, I am grateful to Eloise Knapp Hay for *The Political Novels of Joseph Conrad* (Chicago University Press, 1963), Avrom Fleishman for *Conrad's Politics: Community and Anarchy in the Fiction of Joseph Conrad* (Baltimore, Johns Hopkins Press, 1967), and Benita Parry for *Conrad and Imperialism* (London, Macmillan, 1984). Quotations from *Nostromo* are from the 1947 Collected Edition (Dent, London).

8 Late Turner, Hardy's Tess and Lawrence's Knees

Howard Mills

I

'Eh, Jack! Come an' look at this girl standin' wi' no clothes on, an' two blokes spittin' at 'er.' That, says Lawrence, is how 'the English Tommy' sees Botticelli's Venus; whereas the highbrows 'get a correct mental thrill' while their bodies 'stand there as dead as dustbins'.[1] This dim view of English responses to art reminds us of George Eliot's description in *Middlemarch* of a Puritan bride bewildered by the orgy of art run riot in St Peter's which is to haunt her like 'a disease of the retina' – while her pedant of a husband can only advise her that Raphael's paintings 'are, I believe, highly esteemed ... He is a painter who has been held to combine the most complete grace of form with sublimity of expression. Such at least I have gathered to be the opinion of cognoscenti.'

Two years after that was written, Rome was visited by another honeymoon couple, Thomas and Emma Hardy. One picks up by way of echo the first cracks in conjugal bliss, but also the provincial girl's distress at Michelangelo's David wi' no clothes on. And one might be tempted to push the parallel further by recalling that the bridegroom – admittedly eleven years earlier – betrayed a Casaubon-like turn of mind by copying into his notebook a series of reach-me-down, out-of-date definitions of the 'Schools of Painting'.[2] But recalling this would be unfair because around that time Hardy had also begun reading Ruskin's *Modern Painters*, and before his marriage had developed a first-hand, extremely varied and idiosyncratic taste in art. After his marriage emerged a liking, which he was conscious went against the current of cognoscenti, for 'the much-decried, mad, late-Turner rendering'.[3]

Hardy went to many of the exhibitions that Henry James

reviewed. James's response to Turner was usually enthusiastic, but in 1873 he felt able to refer casually to 'Turner's later eccentricities'.[4] And although James elsewhere maintained that Ruskin's championing of the artist was too extreme and too violent,[5] Ruskin largely agreed with James. For it was Ruskin who, in the mammoth sort-out after Turner's death in 1851, topped and tailed him – supervised the burning of erotica *and* put away many ultra-etherial late works as eccentricities or uncompleted colour-beginnings. So that although Hardy in 1889 could mention seeing several specific late works, 'Norham Castle, Sunrise' was, like many others, gathering grime in the National Gallery cellars until displayed at the Tate in 1906. (More were exhumed for a further Tate extension in 1910.)

In 1911, D. H. Lawrence was teaching in Croydon. When Louie Burrows came up for the day, he went to the enlarged Tate with her. And with his knees. At risk of drawing them out of all proportion I must now introduce those knees of his, as they play a major role in the drama of his reaction to late Turner as recorded three years later; upon them his response to 'Norham Castle' hinges.

We hear in Lawrence a good deal about lumbar ganglia, and rather too much about loins. A dotty page or two in *Fantasia* (Ch. 5) presses the claims of the nose as index of character. Knees, however, also recur. 'My very knees are glad,'[6] he says of a book of cosmology that makes him feel 'planted in the universe' and on the earth. And in *Psychoanalysis and the Unconscious* he writes of a child finding its feet in this respect: 'the legs, the little knees that thrust, thrust away, the small feet that curl and tremble upon themselves, ready for the obstinate earth'. That reminds me of Tamsin's baby learning to walk, in *The Return of the Native*.[7] Both writers make much of the way people walk and engage with the obstinate earth – or don't walk but glide, or slide; thus Tess's 'quiescent glide', Little Time's 'steady mechanical creep', Birkin's ghostlike 'drift' and the 'springless lope' of the monks in *Twilight in Italy*. It marks the difference between 'living in the flesh' and on the earth on the one hand and on the other being a disembodied spirit.

I say all this because Lawrence went into the Tate with his knees but nearly didn't come out with them, as he records in his 'Study of Thomas Hardy':

Ever, he sought the consummation in the Spirit, and he reached it at last. Ever, he sought the Light, to make the light transfuse the body, till the body was carried away, a mere bloodstain, became a ruddy stain of red sunlight within white sunlight. This was perfect consummation in Turner, when, the body gone, the ruddy light meets the crystal light in a perfect fusion, the utter dawn, the utter golden sunset, the extreme of all life, where all is One, One being, a perfect glowing One-ness.

... If Turner had ever painted his last picture, it would have been a white, incandescent surface, the same whiteness when he finished as when he began, proceeding from nullity to nullity, through all the range of colour.

Turner is perfect. Such a picture as his 'Norham Castle, Sunrise', where only the faintest shadow of life stains the light, is the last word that can be uttered, before the blazing and timeless silence.[8]

But in the midst of this rapt involvement Lawrence recalls his knees, and they make a hole in the canvas:

But I cannot look at a later Turner picture without abstracting myself, without denying that I have limbs, knees and thighs and breast. If I look at the 'Norham Castle', and remember my own knees and my own breast, then the picture is a nothing to me. I must not know. And if I look at Raphael's 'Madonna degli Ansidei', I am cut off from my future, from aspiration. The gate is shut upon me, I can go no further. The thought of Turner's Sunrise becomes magic and fascinating, it gives the lie to this completed symbol. I know I am the other thing as well.

So that, whenever art or any expression becomes perfect, it becomes a lie. For it is only perfect by reason of abstraction from that context by which and in which it exists as truth.[9]

I quote the passage at some length because it is ignored by Lawrence, Turner and Hardy critics alike. I will discuss later its relevance to a critique of Hardy, but first I want to consider its validity as a comment on Turner.

Two preliminary points. First, the passage is instantly recognizable as Lawrentian, not least in being what Ian Gregor[10] would call 'turbulently involved', violent in its 'flow and recoil of sympathy'.[11] But the flow is itself checked by the repeated, pivotal word 'perfect' – always double-edged in Lawrence, like 'complete' or 'final' or (of Raphael) 'dead certainty' – that betrays the equally characteristic distrust of extremes which prompts the recoil. That distrust leads to the accusation of lies, but its ground note is calm and unassuming: 'I know I am the other thing as well.' A second unease may be about focal length. The passage's power comes from concentrating on effects (Lawrence's body doesn't stand dead as a dustbin) but does it thereby neglect artistic means – technique and texture – in a way that is especially distorting with Turner? At the same time, Lawrence pokes right through the canvas, to psychic origins. He may scorn Clive Bell, as the 'Introduction to These Paintings' professes to scorn Roger Fry, but he no less than Bell in the same year treats art as 'an index to the spiritual condition of an age'[12] and is about to tell us[13] that when a young man 'studies an old master . . . he studies chiefly the State of Soul of the old artist so that he . . . may understand his own soul'. An initial reply to any unease this arouses is that at least Lawrence is not massaging a handful of figures into talismanic polar opposition. My dots in the first excerpt elided for brevity a telling paragraph on Corot, while Raphael, Rembrandt and Michelangelo have already been considered at some length, as has Botticelli who re-enters as balancer in what follows my second excerpt. That said, I now want to show how far Lawrence's view of Turner, 'idiosyncratic' in expression and intensely felt as it is, none the less is tenable, indeed time-honoured and orthodox.

II

Turner and white is the topic to start with. 'If Turner had ever painted his last picture,' says Lawrence, 'it would have been a white, incandescent surface, the same whiteness when he finished as when he began, proceeding from nullity to nullity.' This isn't a purely symbolic remark, an echo of the Bible's 'naked I came into the world, and naked will go hence'. We recall that the perception and technique of Turner's oil paintings were early influenced by his watercolours; that white paper for the latter suggested white wash bases or even top washes for the former; and that, to cries of 'away with the black Masters!', he was greeted as leader of the White School. Although yellow predominated by the 1830s and in 'Norham Castle, Sunrise', this was often, as with that canvas, over a wash of white.

It was equally a commonplace, from a very early stage and even in cool reactions like Hazlitt's, that Turner's subject was light. This, of course, implies no straight and narrow road to 'Norham Castle, Sunrise'. There continue those works in which the struggle of light against dark produces violent contrasts and rhythmic agitation; in which paint textures are thick and vigorously worked-up (witnesses tell of rubbing with breadcrumbs, jabbing with thumb or brush handle, and planting the sun as a raised boss of paint). As for light not pitched against dark but dissolving substance and form, it may be objected that although Turner said 'indistinctness is my forte', we know enough about his grasp of optics, colour theory, meteorology and geology to reinforce Ruskin's point that his 'indistinct' effects come from the very precision of his knowledge. However, even in an otherwise 'distinct' picture like 'Mortlake Terrace' everyone is riveted and disturbed by the section of the parapet eaten away by the light (an effect heightened rather than counterbalanced by the black dog next to it). I say 'disturbed' because one observer sees substance here not just dissolved but 'eroded', another 'devoured'; and that second word (with other, Lawrentian ones like 'annihilated' and 'obliterated') recurs in comment from modern critics as diverse as Lawrence Gowing and Adrian Stokes on later paintings as diverse as 'Norham' and 'The Angel Standing in the Sun'.[14] The same terms might be prompted by *Regulus*, in which the viewer's position is with the hero whose eyelids were removed and who was left to be blinded by the sun; or several Petworth interiors, especially that which seems to include the catafalque of Lord Egremont.

True, it is Stokes above all who stresses that this 'narrow compulsion' was always balanced by Turner's 'contrasting achievements' and that no canvas utterly dissolves and quite forgets 'the world's actuality'.[15] And I imagine that, on the canvas Lawrence selects, a case against him would build on the title word 'Sunrise'. It could be argued that while a picture cannot strictly speaking portray change (it is after all not a film), it can lead the mind's eye forward by its technique and its title (and, with Turner, by appended quotations). We know that after sunrise the sun rises further, mists clear and shapes resolve themselves; so that while the picture captures an hour when substance, light and water merge, this is what Hardy in an equivalent scene calls the 'dim inceptive stage of the day'. And even at that hour, although the cows may be as 'indistinct' as, and smaller than, their watery shadows (contrast the Mortlake dog), the proportions of at least one and its stance – including its knees – are firmly conveyed. But despite this, most people feel all is precariously tenuous, about to dissolve, not resolve, and fear for the future of the cow's knees if not of their own. And as for change through Turner's entire oeuvre, one can trace, parallel with other currents but gaining on them in strength, a steady development to this canvas: it is not a late aberration but a logical destination. In this one can appeal to the long sequence of Norham sketches and pictures (shown together as a 'retrospect' at the big 1974 exhibition) from the watercolours of 1798, through a watercolour of *circa* 1823 entitled 'Norham Castle on the Tweed', to the oil painting 'Sunrise'. The point is reinforced by insisting that, whatever the excuse for not exhibiting it until this century, 'Sunrise' has reached what Turner decided should be its final state: it is not just an elaborated colour-beginning. Even a writer (Robert Melville) who considers it technically incomplete thinks Turner was deliberately finished with it, had stopped because he was 'reluctant to interfere further': 'isn't it possible that he saw the wraiths of landscape features as objects that were disappearing rather than emerging? They look like the victims of an inundation of light.'[16]

Such pictures, Melville goes on, 'are perhaps the records of an exultant brush with nothingness' (compare Lawrence's 'nullity'). Jack Lindsay demurs, yet in tracing the route to Norham through the Turner of the 1820s he appears to echo another word of Lawrence's: 'often the structure appears to exist only in his mind, not on the paper; and yet we feel it dynamically present, glowing, steadily asserting itself yet vanishing at an effort to locate it too definitely – like a music of silence'.[17] But I think the mode of the closing paradox sits uneasily with Lindsay's preceding attempt to be technically analytic. Better the phrase of Lawrence's, frankly as poetic-evocative as Eliot's 'the heart of light, the silence': 'the blazing and timeless silence'.

Yet that synaesthesia leads us into the ultimate stage of Lawrence's case about Turner, the identification of 'light' with 'the spirit': how *could* this be technically analytic, let alone verifiable?

Lawrence himself props up the equation from the rear, historically speaking. The chapter that ends with Turner (I mean both the chapter in 'Study of Thomas Hardy' that discusses Turner and the 'chapter' of Western History that Lawrence says ends with Turner) begins with Jesus, from whose claims the chapter takes its title, 'The Light of the World'. Jesus surely implied an element of opposition: 'I am Light as distinct from the World; I bring light to a benighted worldliness; from another world; or, I come to bring you another world; I bring eternal life.' All this, Lawrence sees, in contradistinction from the Genesis command 'Let there be light': light in this world, coequal with such substances as earth and seas and bodies.

If Jesus is Lawrence's star witness, we can present others for qualified support. Ruskin repeatedly urged, in talking of Turner, that appreciation of physical beauty was conditional on moral and spiritual sensitivity. James, while drawing back from Ruskin, was still typical in suggesting that 'Turner's pigments seem dissolved not in thought but in deep-welling spiritual emotion.'[18]

The reader who fears that, in order to show that even in the most drastic extension of Lawrence's case he is continuous with previous critics, I mean to call a tedious sequence of witnesses, will be relieved that I have only one more in the wings. And – for the second purpose of this article – this is the only one who matters.

This witness supports Lawrence's basic point by remarking that what Turner 'paints chiefly is light as modified by objects' – a startling reversal of what we might expect as the order of priorities, in nature or on canvas (or in a novel). Yet further, the witness supports Lawrence's light-spirit identification if we link remarks from different occasions:

Turner's watercolours: each is a landscape *plus* a man's soul . . . I am no longer interested in the 'simply natural' . . . The exact truth . . . ceases to be of importance in art . . . The much decried, mad, *late-Turner* rendering is now necessary to create my interest . . . the art [of poetry and fiction] lies in making these defects [of Nature] the basis of a hitherto unperceived beauty, by irradiating them with 'the light that never was' on their surface, but is seen to be latent in them by the spiritual eye.

The 'harmony of view' (if not of valuation) between this and Lawrence is strengthened by that between 'I am the light of the world' and 'the light that never was', especially given the latter's context in Wordsworth's 'Peele Castle'. At very least the witness bears out the negative point about Turnerian light, its means of escape from being alive in the too, too solid flesh. And it might have been Turner whom the same witness, in another context, spoke of as knowing 'how to hit to a hair's-breadth that moment of evening when the light and the darkness are so evenly balanced that the constraint of day and the suspense of night neutralize each other, leaving absolute mental liberty. It is then that the plight of being alive becomes attenuated to its least possible dimensions.' The witness is, of course, Hardy.[19] This gives distinguished support to Lawrence's comments on Turner, but also shows their special relevance in a work entitled 'Study of Thomas Hardy'. For Hardy emulated Turner, especially in *Tess of the d'Urbervilles* (from which my second quotation came). Lawrence diagnosed both painter and novelist, in spite of their pagan protestations, as manifestations of terminal Christianity, both conquered by the Pale Galilean. It has to be said that Lawrence leaves these diagnoses side by side: I want to see whether one can knot them together.

III

'After Sue, after Dostoievsky's *Idiot*, after Turner's latest pictures, after the symbolist poetry of Mallarmé and the others, after the music of Debussy, there is no further possible utterance of the peace that passeth all understanding ... There is only silence beyond this.' That comes in the tenth and final chapter of the 'Study of Thomas Hardy'. In the ninth (immediately after the passage on Turner) Lawrence has discussed Sue, and Jude and Arabella, not mentioning Turner but echoing the terms with which he has earlier analysed him and taking his cue from Hardy's admission that 'the book is all contrasts' – Pagan against Christian, flesh against spirit, prayer-book against pizzle.[20] But on *Tess*, a rather brief analysis of which preceded the long one of *Jude the Obscure* in Chapter 9, Lawrence's terms of reference are drawn from a stage in the 'Study' much earlier than the passage on Turner: he returns to the idea of 'the natural aristocrat'. It is odd that he thus misses his own cue, for *Tess* is certainly the most Turnerian novel visually. The connection cries out to be made; or the question asked whether, in the Turnerian scenes, Hardy or his characters are, so to speak, 'terminally Turnerian' in Lawrence's sense – that is, sharing with late Turner that fascination with light and the spirit which

Lawrence sees as characteristic of Christianity in its extreme, terminal stage.

An answer can best be begun by grappling on to the blunt end of this fictional vessel. At the May dance 'ideal and real clashed slightly'; at the Chaseborough dance and its treacly aftermath the clash is no more slight than a slap in the face with a pig's pizzle. To adapt Ian Gregor's painterly phrase for another incident, the episode is done with broad brushstrokes. Hardy, for all his characteristic 'unadjustedness' of fictional modes as of 'philosophical' stances, may have sensed this when he withheld it from the serial and the first edition (claiming to have overlooked it) and further when he gave the title 'Saturday Night in Arcady' to the separately published sketch of which it forms the major part. A subtitle might well have been 'Dancing in Scroff, Wrestling in Treacle'.

The episode flirts with what Hardy had called 'the late-Turner rendering', entertaining it only to undermine it. The light is, first, just before sunset (yellow lights, blue shades; 'the atmosphere itself forms a prospect without aid from more solid objects'), then the 'low-lit mistiness' of moonlight. There is no East Coker stamp of feet, nor do the dancers feel the pull of gravitation or their own 'terrestrial and lumpy' feet and knees. But this comes from relief after a week's 'monotonous attention to the poultry-farm'; from dancing on a pile of dusty straw and in a haze (a 'luminous pillar of cloud') of scroff and vaporized sweat; and from booze. Turner often presses contemporary peasants into the services of classical pastoral or epic myth: the recurrent pattern in this chapter is Hardy bringing his Arcadians down to earth. One moment a couple seem like demigods, the next they 'resolved themselves into the homely personalities of one's neighbours'. A couple feel 'that only emotion was the matter of the universe, and matter but an adventitious intrusion', until gravity and lumpy terrestriality reassert themselves and they fall 'with a dull thump'. On the walk home they feel they are 'soaring along in a supporting medium' (compare the birds in the dawn scene that 'soared into the upper radiance', or Tess's account of how 'our souls can be made to go outside of our bodies') until Car Darch's hair and back (and lower) are trickling with treacle from the basket 'in jeopardized balance' on her head, and she writhes in the grass to rub it off, then leaps up and strips to the waist for a fight.

Now this, artistically speaking too, is rough-and-tumble stuff. Especially elephantine, when we compare their equivalent in the dawn scene, are the allusions to Arcadia or Elysium, syrinxes and nimbuses and Praxitelian beauty. But at least the relation to Turner is that much clearer. Hardy swivels from the late-Turner rendering to 'the mean, unglamoured eye' of the Dutch school (or indeed of Turner's early genre paintings, and of the frequent debris and everyday tasks of his foregrounds). Furthermore, the vocabulary describing this contrast is very much that which, as we've seen, has always dominated discussions of Turner: *irradiation*, *radiance*, *indistinctness* as against matter *resolving* itself. As for Hardy's stance, he rejoices in it (Joyce-like, as in the series of epiphanies and let-downs in *Portrait*), presses the unbeglamoured to the point of what Joyce called scrupulous meanness. Except that there is what Lawrence terms a hesitation, a weakening, at the end, when Hardy appears to give support to the girls' deluded elation.

Am I labouring the obvious as well as the artistically laboured? Not at all, to judge from any of the critics who have touched on this scene with the Hardy–Turner connection in mind. For Richard Swigg it 'sanctifies the country people', Joan Grundy offers it as 'a rustic Renoir', and neither Evelyn Hardy nor J. B. Bullen notices any irony.[21]

I think one can usefully relate that episode to others, or pairs of others, much less savagely sardonic, where the emphatic 'all contrasts' ('of course the book is all contrasts') is toned down to 'flux and reflux – the rhythm of change' – to quote phrases from *Tess* which Ian Gregor[22] says bear on both its manner and matter. Thus Tess's twilight walks are immediately followed by the harvesting that starts at dawn, the sun rising and shining 'like a golden-haired, beaming, mild-eyed, God-like creature'. A further readjustment of the balance comes when Tess, soon after settling at Talbothays, reverts to her dusk mood and unwittingly catches Angel's attention by talk of souls escaping bodies – the contrast is with the farmer whose feet are on the ground and whose knife and form are planted 'like the beginning of a gallows'. But the dawn scene of Chapter 20 – it telescopes a series of dawns – takes us back to the Chaseborough episode.

The pattern is the same, but far more elaborated and delicately balanced. The earlier scene presented ideal and real as distinct opposites; this one throws us into the indivisible Wordsworthian realm of 'what we half-create and what perceive', complicating most irrecoverably Ian Gregor's proposition[23] that Hardy felt 'an obligation to write about the world as he found it' whereas Lawrence could 'make all things new'.

Hardy gives himself up more fully here to the glamour of this 'non-human hour' while also murmuring 'I know I am – or people are – the other thing as well'. He murmurs this not by a succession of banana skins like the treacle-slick, but by tracing a scene of change from dawn's first 'dim inceptive stage of the day', changes of light bringing changes from ethereal to terrestrial and from spirit to substance. 'Spectral, half-compounded, aqueous light', scarcely more distinguishable from sky, water and mist than in Turner's Norham sunrise, gives way to the broad light of common day when Tess 'lost her strange and ethereal beauty'; to the sharp voice of the farmer scolding Deb for dirty hands and to the 'horrible scrape' of the breakfast table.

There is nothing harsh or horrid about the way Hardy here brings us back to obstinate earth, and no doubting his rapt involvement in the Turner rendering, his own phrases of alternately attuned and contrasting words being a powerful linguistic equivalent to paint textures and colour transitions. With him no less than late Turner, 'the eye dwells so completely enthralled on that lucid interval of morning dawn and dewy light' that it 'thinks it a sacrilege to pierce the mystic shell of colour in search of form'. (These are in fact Turner's words, and about Rembrandt.[24]) None the less, the description has not only an overall movement to 'resolution' but constant delicate reminders that life is the other thing as well. Thus 'they seemed to themselves [and Hardy] the first persons up of all the world' suggests the Garden of Eden but, by inserting that little word 'up', keeps in touch with the dairy business. (They were first up, earliest risers, with a job to do: we have already been told that 'it was necessary to rise early, so very early, here'.) Up at a 'preternatural time' – supernatural (a state 'sacrilegious to break') but also 'unnatural' as when we say 'it's unnatural to get up at such an unearthly hour'. It reminds Angel of the Resurrection hour; although 'the Magdalen' stands at his side (this is the scene's only lapse into crude irony – especially in 'he little thought . . .'). Tess looks 'ghostly, as if she were merely a soul at large'; but 'in reality' her face 'had caught the cold gleam of day from the north-east'.

A related touch is that 'he called her Artemis, Demeter . . .', that she responds with 'Call me Tess' – 'and he did'. And this points to a further aspect of the scene, absent from the Chaseborough episode. There, Tess was an uninvolved observer, uninvolved in the elation, concerned only about getting home safely, so that I was able to consider simply the others and Hardy's equally detached mockery of them. Here, the subject is Tess's and Angel's perception of each other. How, then, can we test Lawrence's view that the author, not just his characters, is unsteady in stance?

Not only Lawrence but Ian Gregor thinks Hardy falters with Tess here, failing to 'make the necessary emotional distinctions while maintaining the lyrical intensity. His brush is not fine enough for this sort of shading'; how can Hardy say that Angel 'was god-like in her eyes' when Tess's love for Clare 'is clearly intended to be free of this kind of idealization'.[25] But *is* there such an intention? Ian Gregor himself came to think not when, in *The Great Web*,[26] he dissented from David Lodge's view of the harp scene. Hardy, says Lodge, 'has confused himself and us' by 'the rich possibilities'; Ian Gregor clarifies Hardy's intentions by pointing out a contrast between the two central paragraphs (the first stressing the physical, the second the spiritual and with a specific echo of Tess's speech on souls escaping bodies), the movement between which 'dramatises the fatal dislocation' in Tess, one 'writ large into her whole relationship with Angel Clare'. This dislocation is virtually the one perceived by Lawrence when he sees the novel's 'rhythm of change' as a vicious circle: 'Tess, despising herself in the flesh. . .because Alec had betrayed her very sources, loved Angel Clare who also despised and hated the flesh'.[27]

That is a point in the Study when Lawrence credits Hardy with diagnosing his characters rather than Hardy himself calling for diagnosis as (in my shorthand) terminally Christian. A very different verdict would emerge from considering Angel himself, with whom Hardy is all over the place. Angel is for long 'a complete and substantial male animal – no more, no less' (to adapt Hardy on Arabella!), with a taste for mead and black pudding. There is in his eyes 'nothing ethereal' about Tess who 'sent an *aura* over his flesh' which produces a sneeze clearly intended to suggest another kind of convulsion. Suddenly (Ch. 31) he is 'more spiritual than animal' – 'ethereal', 'Shelleyan'. True, Hardy has him come to his senses in Brazil. But he finally reverts to type; and Hardy stands shoulder to shoulder with him as Angel walks off with Liza Lu, not only the lamented's kid sister but 'a more spiritualized image of Tess'. This is in a sense another very treacly scene. Ian Gregor is reminded of the end of *Paradise Lost*. I think rather of the comic resilience of the ballad hero who lost his beloved in a mining accident (more Lawrentian than Hardy territory, this!): 'so he kissed her / Little sister'.

Tess's little sister is 'tall and budding', 'half girl, half woman'; which *is* very much the territory of the middle-aged Hardy. But not – *revenons à nos moutons*![28] – that of Turner. He liked them mature, preferably widowed and not overspiritual. 'He mated his body easily,' says Lawrence,[29] who linked Turner's art with Shelley's just as Hardy linked Shelley with the ineffectual Angel, but who knew that Turner's life was 'the other thing' as well (or even instead). As it indeed was, to the dismay of Ruskin faced with the erotica, the Margate widow and escapades in the local, er, hostelries: 'While he lived in imagination in ancient Carthage, [he] lived, practically, in modern Margate.'[30]

While they lived in imagination, especially on Saturday evening, in Arcady, Hardy's characters lived, practically, in modern Wessex. The ending apart, I have tried to show that in *Tess of the d'Urbervilles* Hardy, drawn as he is to what Lawrence sees as the ethereal one-sidedness of the late Turner rendering which Hardy strongly admired, none the less always recalls 'the other thing'. In another feet-on-the-ground phrase from the Study, Hardy's novel gives 'fair play all round'.[31]

IV

But it might be retorted that fair play all round hasn't been given by this article which, for one thing, has been virtually confined to one novel: doesn't my case relate to others?

The Return of the Native here and there reminds us directly of Lawrence's remark that Turner 'sought to make the light transfuse the body'; as on the luminous autumn day when Thomasin helps Mrs Yeobright bring down apples from the loft and the sunlight falls 'so directly upon her brown hair and transparent tissues that it almost seemed to shine through her'.[32] But in the main this novel has a more indirect, fundamental and disturbing relation to Turner. I am tempted to call it the 'negative' of Turner, for darkness and solidity here do that work of engulfing which light performs in Turner, and the effect is thereby more darkly pessimistic. This elusive matter can best be stalked via affinities with another painter of light and dark, Rembrandt.

In quoting earlier Turner's praise of Rembrandt, I suggested it could be applied to Turner himself. But both Hardy and Lawrence habitually contrasted the two painters. In the earlier artist Lawrence finds 'the declaration that light is our medium of existence, that where the light falls upon our darkness, there we are', thus making a Genesis-like marriage of equals 'between . . . light and object'.[33] This is not Hardy's idiom but it seems near his impression, to judge from notebook comments and from his own 'study in Rembrandt's intensest manner', the chiaroscuro portrait of Clym is seen by Eustacia at the mumming party.[34]

But Turner's tribute to Rembrandt began with a remark that can lead us back to the 'negative impression' of Turner in this novel. 'He threw a mysterious doubt over the meanest piece of common.' This sentence could be anchored to Egdon by its being a tract of unenclosed common land, if not mean then 'haggard' and 'slighted'; 'mysterious in its swarthy monotony', and conveying 'a protracted and halting dubiousness'. The prevailing relation of heath and sky is not a marriage of opposites but 'black fraternization': Egdon is at the start 'an instalment of night', 'a near relation'. And the principal opposition in the book is of human beings' individuality and independence against that fraternity – especially against the dominant brother, the homogeneous, 'common' mass of earth. Hardy thus projects the idea he found in Herbert Spencer, that evolution consists of 'the transformation of the homogeneous into the heterogeneous'; a thought repeated by another keen reader of Spencer, Lawrence, as he discusses *The Return of the Native*.[35] One can gather many phrases from the novel into a chain: 'piece of common', 'common ground', 'common or undistinguished'. Lawrence saw this and elaborated it with his similar family of terms: 'in common with', 'commonplace', 'the compound', 'the community' and (immediately after a paragraph which has 'community' four times) Clym and other would-be 'singular' people 'cannot separate themselves from the common'. What has this got to do with Turner? One does not need to accept Stokes's Kleinian framework to perceive in Turner's painting an 'engulfing', 'enveloping', even 'obliteration' by 'homogeneity'; and the idea, and the last three terms, are insisted on in *The Return*. In *Tess*, as in those paintings, it is light that threatens to swamp heterogeneity. In *The Return*, the same threat comes from a mass of substance.

So the triangle into which I have drawn my three figures isn't too tight to accommodate a variety of Hardy novels. But the other possible complaint about a lack of fairness or all-roundness in this article could be that, in concentrating on 'Turner and light', I have turned my back on what Stokes, for all his own concentration, repeatedly praises as Turner's 'contrasting achievements'. A fair sample, from later years, would be 'Rain, Steam and Speed', 'Peace – Burial at Sea', 'Agrippina Landing with the Ashes of Germanicus' and 'Snow-Storm – Steam Boat off Harbour's Mouth'. And a reminder not to narrow unduly Hardy's response to Turner comes from the fact that those (with 'Approach to Venice', more obviously assimilable to my preceding approach) are Hardy's own examples.[36] He prefaces the list with the comment that Turner 'said, in his maddest and greatest days: "What pictorial drug can I dose man with, which shall affect his eyes somewhat in the manner of this reality which I cannot carry to him?" – and set to make such strange mixtures as he was tending towards' in those canvases. One can perhaps imagine Hardy asking himself that question, and answering with such strange mixtures as Tess in the stone coffin or next to the Great Western locomotive, or Jude wandering at night through an Oxford as ghostly as the ruined Roman forum. I deliberately extend the range of possible affinities by reaching beyond direct parallels (for instance, the snow storms in Turner and that in *Tess* which Hardy calls 'an achromatic chaos of things'). Of course I thus also make the affinities more remote or speculative. It was, after all, not Turner but Crivelli and Bellini to whom Hardy reached out for support when saying that 'my art is to intensify the expression of things'.[37] And of course each of those Turner paintings can be assigned (with varying degrees of strain) to a genre, while those incidents in Hardy invite discussion in terms of a recognized tradition of the Grotesque.[38] But when the late Hardy wrote in 1906 of his preference for late Turner (and late Wagner) over earlier, 'the idiosyncrasies of each master being more strongly shown in these strains,[39] he surely appeals to us to make a link with what he called the 'idiosyncratic mode of regard'[40] which characterizes his own art.

V

'I would like to add a last perspective,' writes Ian Gregor near the end of *The Great Web*, appending a comparison of Hardy and Lawrence that helped prompt the present article. I in turn would like to add briefly a last perspective. If *Tess* above all is the artistic fruit of Hardy's response to Turner, Lawrence's response comes out most clearly, not in his novels nor his poems, and certainly not in his own paintings, but in *Twilight in Italy*, written a year after the 'Study of Thomas Hardy'. The last pages of 'The Spinner and the Monks' in particular, in its rewritten form, explore the relation of substance to light and flesh to spirit, contrasting their balance and mutual definition with the neutralizing of both – with 'the neutrality of the twilight, of the monks. The flesh neutralising the spirit, the spirit neutralising the flesh.' (This recalls Tess's twilight walks 'when night and day neutralize each other' and 'the plight of being alive is attenuated'). All this is as much a creative meditation on Turner and Hardy as on Italy. And as he traces exquisitely all the 'transitional hours' as the sun wheels over Lake Garda, 'the eye dwelling enthralled' on each transitory stage of light from broad afternoon through dusk to moonlight, Lawrence is surely emulating such scenes in *Tess* and, through that, both recreating and questioning what Hardy called 'the late-Turner rendering'.

NOTES

References are made to chapters, not page numbers, when this gives adequate identification.

1 E. D. McDonald (ed.), *Phoenix: The Posthumous Papers of D. H. Lawrence* (London, Heinemann, 1936), p. 557.

2. R. H. Taylor (ed.), *The Personal Notebooks of Thomas Hardy* (London, Macmillan, 1979), pp. 105, 108–9, 114.
3. M. Millgate (ed.), *The Life and Work of Thomas Hardy, by Thomas Hardy* (London, Macmillan, 1985), p. 192.
4. 'The Wallace Collection', January 1873, reprinted in J. L. Sweeney (ed.), *The Painter's Eye* (London, Rupert Hart-Davis, 1956), p. 72. It is good to see the biter bit: Ian Gregor quotes Graham Greene's comment that James's novels are 'very like the beauty of Turner's late pictures: they are all air and light: you have to look a long while into their glow before you discern the most tenuous outline of their subjects' (Ian Gregor (with Brian Nicholas)), *The Moral and the Story* (London, Faber and Faber, 1962), p. 154).
5. Sweeney (ed.), *The Painter's Eye*, pp. 34, 117, 158–60, 173–4.
6. McDonald (ed.), *Phoenix: The Posthumous Papers of D. H. Lawrence*, p. 294.
7. Thomas Hardy, *The Return of the Native*, New Wessex Edition (London, Macmillan, 1975), Book VI, Ch. 2.
8. D. H. Lawrence, *'Study of Thomas Hardy' and Other Essays*, edited by B. Steele (Cambridge University Press, 1985), Ch. 8.
9. *Ibid.*
10. Ian Gregor, *The Great Web* (London, Faber and Faber, 1974), p. 228.
11. See D. H. Lawrence, *Lady Chatterley's Lover* (Harmondsworth, Penguin Books, 1960), p. 104.
12. Clive Bell, *Art* (London, Chatto and Windus, 1914), p. 215.
13. Lawrence, *'Study of Thomas Hardy' and Other Essays*, Ch. 9.
14. Lawrence Gowing, *Turner: Imagination and Reality* (New York, Museum of Modern Art, 1966), p. 53; Adrian Stokes, *Painting and the Inner World* (London, Faber and Faber, 1963), especially pp. 56, 68, 78.
15. *Ibid.*, pp. 50, 57.
16. Robert Melville, 'Pictures of Nothing', *New Statesman*, 27 November 1964.
17. Jack Lindsay, *Turner: His Life and Work* (London, Panther Books, 1973), p. 223.
18. Sweeney (ed.), *The Painter's Eye*, p. 72.
19. The preceding quotations are from Millgate (ed.), *The Life and Work of Thomas Hardy, by Thomas Hardy*, pp. 225, 192, 118, and Thomas Hardy, *Tess of the d'Urbervilles*, edited by J. Grindle and S. Gattrell (Oxford University Press, 1983), Ch. 13.
20. Letter to Edmund Gosse, 20 November 1895; cf. the novel's Preface.
21. Richard Swigg, *Lawrence, Hardy and American Literature* (Oxford University Press, 1972), p. 17; Joan Grundy, *Hardy and the Sister Arts* (London, Macmillan, 1979), p. 60; Evelyn Hardy, 'Thomas Hardy and Turner – the Painter's Eye', *London Magazine*, new series 15, 2, June–July 1975, pp. 24–5; J. B. Bullen, *The Expressive Eye* (Oxford University Press, 1986), p. 198.
22. Gregor, *The Great Web*, p. 178.
23. *Ibid.*, p. 232.
24. Turner, lecture at the Royal Academy, 1811, reprinted with Introduction by J. Ziff, *Journal of the Warburg and Courtauld Institutes*, 16, 1963, p. 145. See also M. Kitson, 'Turner and Rembrandt', *Turner Studies*, 8, 1, Summer 1988, p. 7.
25. Gregor (with Nicholas), *The Moral and the Story*, pp. 182–3.

26 Gregor, *The Great Web*, pp. 185–8.
27 Lawrence, *'Study of Thomas Hardy' and Other Essays*, Ch. 9.
28 Lawrence borrows the main part of this proverbial phrase for the title of the Study's penultimate chapter when, having surveyed the history of Western art and religion, he returns to Hardy.
29 Lawrence, *'Study of Thomas Hardy' and Other Essays*, p. 86.
30 See G. Wheelan, *Turner* (London and New York, Alpino Fine Arts Collection Ltd, 1981), p. 116.
31 Lawrence, *'Study of Thomas Hardy' and Other Essays*, Ch. 9.
32 Hardy, *The Return of the Native*, Book II, Ch. 1.
33 Lawrence, *'Study of Thomas Hardy' and Other Essays*, Ch. 8.
34 Hardy, *The Return of the Native*, Book II, Ch. 6.
35 *Ibid.*, Chs. 3, 5.
36 Millgate (ed.), *The Life and Work of Thomas Hardy, by Thomas Hardy*, p. 226.
37 *Ibid.*, p. 183.
38 See, for instance, Gregor, *The Great Web*, pp. 60–62.
39 Millgate (ed.), *The Life and Work of Thomas Hardy, by Thomas Hardy*, p. 354.
40 *Ibid.*, p. 235.

9 Present Laughter – Reading Our Contemporaries

Michael Irwin

> *Methinks I see these things with parted eye,*
> *When everything seems double.*
> Midsummer Night's Dream, Act Four, scene 1

> . . . so fat, that when he's playing golf, if he puts the ball where he can see it he can't hit it, and if he puts it where he can hit it he can't see it.
> Old Joke

I

Contemporary fiction is by now a familiar ingredient of school and university English courses. The trend would seem to confirm the easy and natural assumption that the response of intelligent readers to a novel newly published is all of a piece with their response to classics of the genre. This essay will try to show that there cannot be any such direct continuity between immediate reactions and mature assessment. Rather than deriving from first impressions, the later view supplants or distorts them. Reading and rereading contemporary fiction is a distinct, almost a discrete, activity, a subgenre of literary study. Judgements are doubly provisional: a changing reader engages with a changing writer. The individual novel takes on a different aspect as it ceases to be part of a vivid present and becomes an element in a retreating past.

Although the argument may be generally applied, a subsidiary suggestion will be that *British* novels of the past thirty or forty years are perhaps especially apt to turn in the hands of both reader and writer. Partly for that reason the works used for illustrative purposes here date from 1954, the diagrammatic starting-point for 'postwar British fiction', the year in which William Golding, Kingsley Amis and Iris Murdoch published their first novels. All three writers have remained continuously productive, but Amis and Murdoch, at least, are by now very different novelists from their younger selves. And as they change so their earlier work, too, assumes an altered character.

II

Reviewers were quick to detect affinities between *Lucky Jim* and *Under the Net* and to locate the works in an emerging 'school'. In later years these claims have usually been dismissed out of hand: the two novelists had different preoccupations and have manifestly moved in very different directions. But hindsight deceives. There *were* notable correspondences between these first novels, even at the level of detail:

There was nothing I could do for her. 'There is nothing I can do for you,' I said. (UN, p. 180)[1]

The bloody old towser-faced boot-faced totem-pole on a crap reservation, Dixon thought. 'You bloody old towser-faced boot-faced totem-pole on a crap reservation,' he said. (LJ, p. 209)

London passed before me like the life of a drowning man which they say flashes upon him all at once in the final moment. Piccadilly, Shaftesbury Avenue, New Oxford Street, High Holborn. (UN, pp. 239–40)

While he explained, he pronounced the names to himself: Bayswater, Knightsbridge, Notting Hill Gate, Pimlico, Belgrave Square, Wapping, Chelsea. (LJ, p. 250)

Magdalen and I looked at each other like boxers at the beginning of the second round. (UN, p. 13)

... his arms ached like those of a boxer keeping his guard up after fourteen rounds. (LJ, p. 105)

... as the glorious daring and simplicity of the scheme became even plainer to me I capered about the room. (UN, p. 127)

... he threw back his head and gave a long trombone-blast of anarchistic laughter. It was all so wonderful, even if it did go wrong, and it wouldn't. (LJ, p. 103)

'At the moment, quite frankly, she's made me more than a little piqued,' Bertrand said, making a circle of thumb and forefinger to emphasise the last word. (LJ, p. 47)

Almost in despair I nodded, and added to my smile such gestures indicative of total well-being as it is possible to perform in a sitting position with one's back against a door. I shook hands with myself, held up my thumb and index finger in the form of an O, and smiled even more emphatically. (UN, p. 118)

Then suddenly I stiffened and leapt up as if I'd been stabbed . . . (UN, p. 80)

First making his shot-in-the-back face, Dixon stopped and turned. (LJ, p. 27)

I reckoned I had about seventy pounds in the bank. (UN, p. 20)

In the bank he had twenty-eight pounds, but this was a fund he'd started against the chance of being sacked. (LJ, p. 44)

It wouldn't be difficult to lengthen this list of trivial parallels. They aren't accidental, but derive from more substantial similarities in subject-matter, mood and range of observation. Jake and Jim (both christened James) were very distinctly of their time. Early reviewers described Donaghue as 'perhaps the most genuinely contemporary character of recent fiction'[2] and Dixon as an example of an emerging species of hero: 'the intellectual tough, or the tough intellectual'.[3] Both characters, though indeed professionally definable as intellectuals, are déclassé, and make their workaday living to some extent precariously, obliged to count the pounds. Both find the pub a natural place of social resort and from time to time get drunk. Both are supporters – Jim by implication, Jake by direct admission – of the Labour Party. It isn't surprising that they, and the authors who chose to write about them, move in comparable areas of reference and response. In the 1950s it was instantly noticeable that Dixon and Donaghue were far closer in spirit to one another than either of them could have been to the hero of a novel by (say) Waugh, Hartley, Greene or Powell. For all the differences between them – for example, Jake's Francophilia and Jim's Francophobia – they spoke and thought in roughly the same language. The assumption was that the reader, a kindred soul, would speak it too, just as he or she would have faced similar problems or run similar risks. Jake can begin a paragraph 'If you have ever tried to sleep on the Victoria Embankment . . .' In the same spirit readers were expected to share an interest in the business of coping with a hangover, placing a bet or picking a lock with a hairpin.

Both protagonists, and both novels, are inherently cheerful. Not only do Jake and Jim laugh a good deal, they enjoy life in general, its oddities and incongruities:

We stood looking toward St Paul's, each man with a brandy bottle in his pocket. (UN, p. 103)

Dixon grinned to himself at 'Uncle Julius'. How marvellous it was that there should be somebody called that and somebody else to call him that, and that he himself should be present to hear one calling the other that. (LJ, p. 107)

The geniality relates, in either case, to a programmatic unpretentiousness and accessibility, a conscious reaction to the élitist tendencies of Modernism. When Amis does move into a higher style, it is in mock-heroic vein, as in the account of Dixon's hangover at the Welches: 'He lay sprawled, too wicked to move, spewed up like a broken spider-crab on the tarry shingle of the morning.' If Jim recalls an aphorism, it will be vaguely attributed – 'somebody like Aristotle or I. A. Richards'. Behind his crowning insult to Bertrand, quoted above, lies 'a sentence in a book he'd once read: "And with that he picked up the bloody old towser by the scruff of the neck, and, by Jesus, he near throttled him."' Amis doesn't remind the reader that it comes from *Ulysses* any more than he signals, elsewhere in the book, his parodic digs at Greene and Lawrence. The 'learning' behind *Under the Net* isn't worn with quite this resolute lightness, but early readers didn't feel uneasily tempted to take notes on the mythological parallels (Mars, Belfounder and so on). The symbolic properties are unportentous – a dog cage, a film set. The various morals the novel preaches, like those in *Lucky Jim*, are studiously simple. Dixon theorizes that 'nice things are nicer than nasty ones', that 'Doing what you wanted to do was the only training and the only preliminary needed for doing more of what you wanted to do' – both useful precepts for one in his subservient position. Donaghue learns, among other lessons, that 'Some situations can't be unravelled, they just have to be dropped', that 'anyone can love anyone, or prefer anyone to anyone'. Both novelists eschew grandiosity on grounds not merely of decorum but of principle: they are moral empiricists.

It goes without saying that no intelligent reader in 1954 could have failed to recognize that Amis and Murdoch were essentially dissimilar writers. But overall the two first novels, for all their distinctness, seemed to share the degree of consanguinity that might be found among the paintings of a group of artists who constitute a 'movement' and choose to exhibit together. Amis gave *Under the Net* a warm welcome in a *Spectator* review.[4] Certainly, in the year of publication it would have seemed a good bet that the reader who enjoyed one of the two books would also enjoy the other. And a substantial part of that enjoyment would have had to do with the area of intersection: the resemblances were as exciting as the differences. Each novel spoke for its author; both spoke for their time.

What they had in common was itself innovatory. Their popularity revealed a waiting clientele excited to find that their lifestyles, speech styles, tastes, predicaments and opinions were being translated into a fictional medium as for the first time. It's probably only by a conscious effort that those very readers can today recall the peculiar freshness of the two novels when they first appeared. They spoke for an emerging intelligentsia outside traditional class definitions. They colonized disregarded territory. Buses, pubs, cafés, lavatories, newspaper shops, provincial universities suddenly took on enhanced status as potential fictional locales. The dialogue caught up with current practice: Amis was praised for his command of the 'hesitations and nuances of modern speech'.[5] Here were novelists who captured the new flavour of vernacular English, informed by an educated intelligence. Amis had additionally (and retains) an excellent ear for swearing: 'I'll strangle that little sod,' says Dixon of Johns. It is no longer possible to convey the rightness, and the unexpectedness of the rightness, of that locution at that time.

To respond to the novel in this spirit in 1954 was to have the sense that one belonged to a club, the existence of which had hitherto been unsuspected, of like-minded people who spoke a common dialect. It seemed that there were allies about who would recognize, for example, that the *faux-naïf* and *faux-*yobbish aspects of Dixon's behaviour were a natural counterpoise to the academic and artistic affectations of those around him. Various sallies in the novel had almost the quality of a litmus test. The right-thinking would *know* that the phrase 'some skein of untiring facetiousness by filthy Mozart' was directed not against Mozart, but against self-proclaiming Mozartians. To be offended by it was to deserve to be offended by it.

III

The insistence on the here and now that characterized the first novels of Amis and Murdoch has found an echo in many a work written since that time. Curiously, some of those heres and nows have proved more durable than others. Such was the particularity of *The History Man*, for instance, that when it was televised, within a few years of publication, its appeal was already, and designedly, that of a period piece. By contrast, *Lucky Jim* and *Under the Net* seem in many aspects delusively up to date. One can unconsciously transpose the action to a modern Britain of traffic-filled streets, glass office-blocks and universal television, and in so doing misread it. It's easy to forget that these novels belonged to a different world – that Jim had done national service, that Jake's City pub crawl would have led him past bomb sites. Only the occasional detail brings one up short, as when Finn goes to find 'a taxi with a hood' or Dixon alludes to Senator McCarthy and Chiang Kai-shek.

A glance through the *New Statesman* in which *Lucky Jim* was reviewed revives one's sense of the otherness of that time. It welcomes the forthcoming end of butter rationing and reports a breakdown in the Suez negotiations. A theatre review recalls the recent vogue for Anouilh, half a dozen of whose plays had been produced in London within a couple of years – a perspective for the Welches' cultural Francophilia. The correspondence columns feature an outraged response to a 'vulgar' satirical profile of Edith Sitwell, here described as 'the finest female poet since Sappho'. To read these letters, and the article that occasioned them, is to realize how difficult it would be for a schools edition of *Lucky Jim* to provide anything like an adequate gloss for 'making his Edith Sitwell face'. Dame Edith's unique and piquant social-cultural status defies recapitulation. So with Dixon's 'Sex Life in Ancient Rome face': only Amis's contemporaries could recapture the associations of the work that used to stand alongside its companion volume, *Sex Life in Ancient Greece*, in the windows of small, furtive urban shops specializing in contraceptives and orthopaedic appliances. That detail and a hundred others in Amis's text are now coming out the other side of obsolescence.

The general point is, of course, familiar: such is the fate of the topical in fiction. But one of its major implications is rarely discussed. What is lost for later audiences is something that original readers confusingly retain in dwindling and altering form. They have a double perspective, recalling their first reaction but unable fully to retrieve it now that the original context is partly forgotten.

IV

As a novelist acquires enhanced status through a succession of publications, the critical pressure is towards seeing each work in relation to the oeuvre. The later novels are held to elucidate earlier ones that may have been 'misread'. Less obviously, however, the opening of one critical door may mean the closing of another. In *Under the Net* it was only very gradually that Jake, and through him the novel's first readers, came to see that he was trapped in the typical situation of Shakespearean comedy. As Hugo puts it: 'I love Sadie, who's keen on you, and you love Anna, who's keen on me.' Those, however, who come to the book from the later novels will be unsurprised, anticipating from the first the familiar Murdochian sexual daisy chain. There are other such disadvantages. The episode where Jake and his friends go for a drunken swim in the Thames conveyed to the reader of 1954 an impression of pure *joie de vivre*. There *are* hints of a figurative significance, but they could have passed unregarded. This is no longer possible when one has read more widely in Murdoch's novels, and seen how often, how very often, they feature heavily metaphorical swimming in the sea, in swimming pools, in a variety of inland waterways. Anna's removal of her shoes in the Tuileries gardens would again have seemed merely casual to the reader unaware of the long line of footwear to be meaningfully discarded by later characters. To return to *Under the Net* after a reading of the other novels is to return to a more self-conscious book.

As it happens, Murdoch's favourite themes, in *Under the Net* and elsewhere, are such that the reader's acquired readiness to interpret subtracts as it enlarges. It is intrinsic to her work that her characters are set the challenge of coping with a world confusingly clogged with contingent phenomena. But the practised reader is encouraged, by the recurrence of metaphorically loaded patterns of detail, to read meaning into all sorts of apparently contingent activity. Poor old Jake, for example, is retrospectively denied the chance of a random impromptu swim. Thus approached, his adventures seem more significant but less fun. Murdoch's fictional method eventually serves to deny her characters the very freedom of choice she is philosophically concerned to thrust upon them.

But this is a special application of the more general point. Academic appraisal of an emerging fictional oeuvre prises the individual novel away from the context within which it was written and enjoyed and by which it was first defined. Contemporary, or lateral, affinities are neglected in favour of vertical ones. Jim Dixon is set alongside Jake Richardson rather than Jake Donaghue.

V

In *The Black Prince* Murdoch quotes an unattributed claim that 'all contemporary writers are either our friends or our foes'.[6] The comment catches well the personal commitment that one brings to the reading of a living author. To discover an enjoyable novel by a contemporary is akin to making an agreeable new acquaintance. The initial warm response awaits confirmation – in this case through further reading. A unilateral relationship can be established that the novelist's subsequent output may strengthen or weaken. The feelings evoked can be very personal: affection, loyalty, disappointment, irritation.

David Lodge's appreciation of Kingsley Amis suggests the directness of such reactions: '... I constantly experience a strange community of feeling with him, and find that he speaks to me in a way that the great classic novelists do not, in an idiom, a tone of voice, to which I respond with immediate understanding and pleasure and without any conscious exertion of the kind required by critical reading.'[7] Indeed this personal warmth of response conduces to a familiarity that tends to be acritical in its very nature. As it happens both Amis and Murdoch have marked stylistic mannerisms. Amis regularly resorts to a sort of artificialized upper-middle class vernacular: '... what sort of woman does it take to measure what happens to chaps' willies for a living?'[8] Murdoch's characters tend to drift, often inappropriately, into anachronistic girl's public school slang: 'fearfully bad form', 'rather a lark', 'what perfect fun'.⁹ But affectionate contemporary readers may be no more willing, no more *able*, to perceive these foibles than to criticize the ancient tweed suit of a favourite uncle.

Involvement with a novelist's 'contemporary' subject-matter may also preclude critical detachment. Over a period of fifteen or twenty years the pleasures of topicality can be transformed to the pleasure of nostalgia – of a revived sense of what it was like to be a Teddy Boy, or a national serviceman or the head girl of a convent school. The obsolescence of some part or parts of a badly ageing novel can become a source of attachment in its own right, a melancholy enjoyment of a shared transience. We do not necessarily *like* a work of literature the better for thinking it will survive its author's generation, any more than we feel fonder of a friend because he seems bound for the *Dictionary of National Biography*. The academic critic, with good reason, aspires to objectivity, and is therefore wary of the personal aspect of his or her response. But this approach has the disadvantage of being false to the motivating pleasures of reading. The intense empathy that the child, or perhaps still more the adolescent, can feel for certain novels surely shouldn't be seen as an irrelevance or a handicap: it is this very generosity of response that first lends fiction its importance to us.

A year or two back, when Ian Gregor had been rereading *Lucky Jim*, a long-standing favourite of his, for a course we were teaching, I asked whether it had made him laugh again. 'Yes,' he said. 'But I felt that I was laughing with a former self.' The academic critic is always a latter self.

VI

In which Amis novel does the hero, an academic, indulge in private comic by-play, endure an appalling hangover, make a fiasco of a public speech through drink, and have to cope with the suicide attempt of a girlfriend? The answer is – or could be – *Jake's Thing*. It's plainly no accident that this later novel recalls numerous aspects of *Lucky Jim*. Amis is inviting the reader to have second thoughts. This impulse is far from uncommon among his contemporaries. John Fowles published a revised edition of *The Magus*. Evelyn Waugh re-edited *Brideshead Revisited* – while conceding that 'it would be impossible to bring it up to date without totally destroying it'.[10] Amis's most recent novel is a sequel, nearly thirty years on, to *Take a Girl Like You*. In *The Black Prince* Murdoch seems to offer, through her account of the novels of Arnold Baffin, both a critique of, and an apologia for, her own fiction. Hugo Belfounder, who presides over *Under the Net*, dies thirty-two years later in an incidental remark in *The Philosopher's Pupil*. The reflexivity that is a conspicuous feature of so many individual novels of the past twenty years can also be distributed along the length of an oeuvre. Where the later novel is *specifically* a modification of an earlier one, the author is positively soliciting the 'vertical' response.

More generally, Amis and Murdoch resort to cross-reference to scrutinize themselves, implicate themselves – and in so doing implicate regular readers. In *Jake's Thing*, after Kelly has tried to kill herself, Jake's wife Brenda, and the appalling psychiatrist Ed, urge him not to feel guilty: 'It's nothing to do with you except in the sense that she did it to get you involved with her . . .'; 'She's *sick*, Jake, it's not like you've mistreated some normal human being . . .' Surprisingly, the misogynistic Jake refuses exculpation: '. . . there's no such thing as a totally phoney suicide attempt. They all want to be at least a little bit dead for a little while.'

After many a year Amis is reopening the case of Margaret Peel. Did he, did Lucky Jim, did the reader shrug off too glibly her overdose of sleeping pills? The earlier novel is given a fresh charge of provisionality.

VII

It wouldn't do to imply that such recapitulations are unique to the postwar novel. But living writers were selected for discussion here not merely to provide random examples of the problems of contemporaneity, but to hint at the further possibility that today's 'contemporary British fiction' might be different in cast from that of previous generations. There is less of a sense nowadays that the writer's task is to produce a self-sufficient masterpiece (or series of such masterpieces) from which he can stand aloof, paring his fingernails. Of the class of '54 William Golding would seem least susceptible to this diagnosis, but even *Lord of the Flies* resists easy canonization. Its meanings are modified as study guides interpret it for school examinees, as *The*

Coral Island is forgotten, as we move further from Belsen and Hiroshima, as its author writes about other castaways on other kinds of island. Provisionality is enforced and is conceded.

Many a contemporary British novelist in effect purveys a species of sustained discourse to which his or her fiction is only the most notable contribution. Beesley's outburst about university academic standards is an alien insertion into *Lucky Jim*, but Amis takes up the theme directly in his 'more will mean worse' admonitions, and recalls it again in 'Why Lucky Jim Turned Right'. Similarly, any new novel, article, poem or interview is as likely as not to offer some specific further insight into Amis's continuing meditation on the workings of sexual desire, or the differences in temperament between men and women. Admirers will wish not just to read the new novel but to catch up with the latest instalment of his thinking and feelings about such themes. Murdoch is more conceptual in her approach, but otherwise the case is not dissimilar: her directly philosophical work explores and develops the ideas she dramatizes in her fiction. She gives herself an opportunity of providing 'the bite and savour of real thought' – a quality that Bradley Pearson misses in Arnold Baffin's novels. John Fowles, in *The Aristos*, for instance, or in footnotes to his fiction, has offered a version of the same kind of editorial intervention.

Fowles has indeed gone a step further. He, David Lodge and Martin Amis are among the current novelists who have put in Hitchcockian, or Nabokovian, appearances in their own work. One effect of this technique must surely be to suggest that the teller trumps the tale, and cannot be denied the last word. If the superpowers hold off long enough, *London Fields* will be supplemented by some *Guardian* profile giving the author's *latest* reactions to the impending holocaust.

But the fiction still counts most. The lover of novels is not to be weaned away, as by low-alcohol beer, to a diet of periodical essays and didactic interviews. If we seek in contemporary writing less the great novel 'outside time' than the oeuvre that doggedly sustains an engagement, direct or indirect, with the life we have currently to encounter, we are still learning through literature, still caught up in a critical discipline, albeit not of the received academic kind. It is a discipline which has the advantage of taking in that considerable class of novels well worth reading once – and for sound 'literary' reasons – but barely meriting a second read. Through contemporary fiction we compare notes and experiences and modes of seeing. Adolescents, parents, homosexuals, socialists, Catholics, adulterers, solitaries can consult counterparts, imagined or transcribed, and learn from them and from the problems they encounter, imagined or transcribed. If the great novels of the past teach us how to live, contemporary fictions suggest how we should live *now*. That function cannot, by definition, long survive in its original form, but it keeps the genre obdurately alive, continually renewing itself.

NOTES

1. All page references are to the Triad/Granada paperback edition of *Under the Net* and the Penguin edition of *Lucky Jim*.
2. *The Times*, 5 June 1954.
3. Walter Allen, *New Statesman*, 30 January 1954.
4. Kingsley Amis, *Spectator*, 11 June 1954.
5. John Metcalf, *Spectator*, 29 January 1954.
6. Penguin edition, p. 186.
7. David Lodge, *Language of Fiction* (London, Routledge & Kegan Paul, 1966), p. 249.
8. *Jake's Thing*, Penguin edition, p. 88.
9. These examples are from *The Philosopher's Pupil*.
10. Preface to 1982 Penguin revised edition, p. 10.

10 Pinter and Politics:
Re-entering No Man's Land

R. A. Foakes

No Man's Land (written 1974; first produced 1975) had a mixed reception at first, but it has been treated more sympathetically in the 1980s, as the last of the so-called 'memory' plays (*Old Times, Landscape, Silence*) that were in part generated by Pinter's study of Proust for the screenplay he wrote in 1972 based on *A la recherche du temps perdu*. The numerous echoes of earlier plays in *No Man's Land*, the perceived undercurrents of violence and the idea of a battleground suggested by the title have caused the play to be linked still more firmly to a general idea of Pinter's comedies of menace, so that it has been treated mainly as a 'closed' play,[1] on the model of *Waiting for Godot*, as a work that demands acceptance and a suspension of our critical powers. The result is that the play has been interpreted as allegorizing an incontrovertible quasi-metaphysical vision of 'the aimlessness of existence',[2] and Spooner's last speech has been wrenched out of context as if Pinter were making in it a general observation about Man as frozen permanently in a no man's land 'which remains for ever icy and silent'.[3] In fact, Pinter 'roots his characters, with unerring precision, in social and psychological reality',[4] and *No Man's Land*, far from being a closed play, has important social and ideological implications. These implications become clearer if the play is seen as a major reworking of an earlier seminal work, *The Caretaker* (1959), showing how Pinter's imaginative response to his London-centred world changed in the space of fifteen years.

The Caretaker was consciously constructed by Pinter as a full-length three-act play which deliberately departed, none the less, from the tradition of the 'well-made play', concerned with characters in well-defined social roles and energized by conventional motives. Specifically, Pinter distanced himself from the 'angry young men' such as John Osborne and Arnold Wesker, and from their drama, burdened as it was by a weight of social protest, troubled by the sense of a need to care and concerned about political issues like the Suez affair. Pinter creates characters without motives or information, whose experience may seem most acute at the point where the expression of it in language becomes difficult if not impossible. Davies and Aston are inarticulate, and the dramatic style of the play points towards silence, those moments at which dialogue disintegrates, as marked in the numerous stage-directions for a 'Pause' or 'Silence'. There is an absence of conscious explanation or motive for what happens, and Pinter does not attempt to define his characters, who remain ambiguous, even mysterious.

However, if this would seem to nudge the play towards the closed world of, say, *Waiting for Godot*, then some further important distinctions need to be noted. Pinter's characters in fact belong to the ordinary world of city life in England, and the action takes place in a room in a house, apparently a terrace house in a run-down suburb of London, though the location is never made explicit. The characters are recognizably individuals such as we might conceivably pass in a London street, and are to this extent like us, of our world, not, like Beckett's figures, marked off by their costumes as clowns or distanced by their deformities. And, of course, much of the dialogue of *The Caretaker* is realistic in so far as it catches the very rhythms of speech, the repetitiveness and broken syntax of uneducated people who cannot express themselves very well and who, perhaps because of this very inability, come to have great faith in the power of words.

This is especially true of Davies, the central figure, the intruder, rescued from a fight and brought to his room by Aston. Davies recalls from a past fragments he uses to press home his selfish needs and desires. His stories compose a mythology of disasters, from the theft of his tobacco tin to the loss of his 'papers'. His endless tales of woe present us on one level with the whining of a wretched old failure, whose rootlessness and poverty seem to be more due to his own inadequacies than attributable to 'them', the Greeks, blacks, Poles and others on whom he puts the blame for his own failings. From this perspective he is a nasty old man, for all the farcical element in his anecdotes, anxious to claim his 'rights', and by asserting that 'nobody's got more rights than I have',[5] to imply that he is superior to 'them', to everyone else, but especially to foreigners and blacks, the targets of his unthinking prejudices. He has kept himself clean with other people's soap, worn out other people's shoes, and now tries to ingratiate himself with Aston, whose belongings he none the less ransacks as soon as Aston leaves the stage, late in Act One.

At the same time, there is something in the appeal Davies makes to 'rights' and to 'fair play', in his querulous remark, 'Because, you know . . . I mean . . . fair's fair'. If it is possible to appeal to a common sense of fair play or justice, as in the phrase 'fair's fair', then Davies has been badly treated. He enters as a vulnerable figure, having just been beaten up in a fight at a café, and if he is himself feckless, he is also one with whom society cannot cope. 'They', the ubiquitous 'they' who would have him 'in the nick', or who give him mugs he cannot drink from, or who are after his card, can be seen, too, as the faceless bureaucracy of a society all too ready to abandon him; so Davies typifies those who feel lost or isolated in a rootless urban world, even to the point of losing any sense of identity. We have no reason to think that the papers he says are at Sidcup really exist, and his insurance card with a mere four stamps on it is in the name of Jenkins. 'That', he says, 'was before I changed my name', so his identity remains insecure and he drifts in a society that alternately neglects him, oppresses him and physically assaults him.

His entry into Aston's room appears to provide him with the chance to establish an identity as a caretaker and 'look after the place'. Symbolically, too, Davies is a father figure, reminding Mick of his 'uncle's brother', so that the expulsion of Davies from the family group by the two brothers also generates sympathy for him. We know Mick and Aston are brothers, but have little or no sense of how they feel towards one another until the point near the end when they look at each other and smile, formally excluding Davies from their circle. This moment in the action remains enigmatic so far as the relationship of Aston and Mick is concerned, for there seems to be no other bond between them (except that hinted at in the equally enigmatic game they play with Davies's bag). Each has composed for himself a kind of identity. Aston has made his out of collecting bits of junk and lumber, so creating an idea of himself as a workman, a constructor, but his habitual fruitless tinkering with a plug reveals his inability ever to make anything out of the odds and ends he has assembled. Mick has composed his identity as a property-owner and knowledgeable Londoner out of collecting useless bits of information, such as the clauses of an insurance contract or the details of the language of glossy advertisements describing fashionable styles and colours for the home.

The contrast between the brothers, Aston passive and gentle, Mick potentially explosive, adept at tormenting Davies by the games he plays, also contributes to the overall effect of the play, and to the ways in which we respond to it and to Davies. In his attempt to relate to each of the brothers in turn, Davies inadvertently brings out connections of which he is not aware. On one level, Davies can be linked with Aston before the latter suffered the electric shock treatment he describes at the end of Act Two. Davies has not been well: 'I've had a few attacks', he says, attacks by others and attacks of some unspecified illness; and, like Aston, he makes the 'mistake' of talking too much. Perhaps Davies would be better able to 'go out ... and live like the others' if he had treatment. On another level, Davies, like Mick, has a potential for violence, and plays games with people; indeed, Mick's question, 'What's the game?' takes on extraordinary force at the end of Act One in part because of its multiple reference to both him and Davies. But whereas Mick plays his 'game' well in scaring, bullying and eventually tricking Davies into disowning Aston's friendship, Davies plays his 'game' of exploiting the situation for his own benefit badly, lying inadequately about his name, about his relationship with Aston, and then turning on Aston when he thinks Mick wants to employ him.

In all this the play's emphasis is on details. There are numerous references to London suburbs or nearby towns, like Sidcup, Hendon, Shepherd's Bush, Putney, Fulham, Watford and so on, but there is no sense of place. Such details as the 'epic recitals of London's bus routes' with which Mick 'bombards' Davies have been seen as 'instruments of aggression' used to achieve menace,[6] and to some extent this is so, but on a more profound level, such lists, like his catalogue drawn from decorators' advertisements, constitute the only mental world that exists for the characters and so embody for them their sense of reality. This was, and remains, very much in accordance with the social reality of people of limited education whose imaginative space is filled by the tabloid press and television commercials – the details are all-important and compose a comfortable if narrow mental world in which larger and potentially frightening issues can be marginalized or ignored.

The only item among all Aston's junk that might have a larger meaning, the Buddha, is simply a 'very well made' object, that can be casually smashed by Mick to emphasize a point. In contrast to Beckett's plays of the period, like *Waiting for Godot* and *Endgame*, *The Caretaker* rejects metaphysics. Its human dimensions are what matter, the sense it conveys of people who are content with numerous points of reference, but make no connections between them. Aston's collection of junk in his room symbolizes the junk shop that is his mind. Davies lacks even such a frame of reference, and his imaginative horizons are policed by a miscellaneous assortment of authorities and aliens on to whom he can transfer his own inadequacies. Mick's mastery of timetables and advertising jargon enables him to enjoy an ascendancy, a power to torment others, but he has no larger aim; the advertiser's dream of a restyled house will never be realized. So if the play was conceived in rejection of works that manifest a social conscience and have a palpable design on us, it nevertheless registers powerfully a sense of men deprived and isolated in a mode of living which offers no community, no sense of purpose, no meaning beyond the immediate moment. Words are used by the characters to establish a position of leverage, an ascendancy, a form of power. The dialogue continually reinforces this sense of isolation, for language is not used to make conversation or, as in the case of Didi and Gogo, to consolidate their mutual dependency on one another, but rather as a series of manoeuvres in a game, creating and dissolving the alternating friendly and hostile relations between characters, and the alliances of two against one that culminate finally in the exclusion of Davies.

In *No Man's Land*, as in *The Caretaker*, an outsider enters a house in London, attempts in various ways to obtain a place there as confidant or employee, and is eventually expelled, or at any rate excluded. There are more specific links, as when

Spooner, left alone late in Act One, inspects everything in Hirst's room, much as Davies goes through Aston's belongings in Act One of *The Caretaker*; and as Davies finds himself suddenly challenged by the physically threatening figure of Mick, so Foster enters in *No Man's Land* to bring a more subtle verbal menace to bear on Spooner.[7] Perhaps these connections have led critics to want to find in the later play a familiar pattern, and some have been puzzled and frustrated by the radical differences between it and *The Caretaker*. These differences begin with the location, which is much more specific in *No Man's Land* ('A large room in a house in North West London' rather than simply 'A room'), a setting which is more closely identified as Hampstead. The principal characters, like the setting, are middle class; even if Spooner, the parallel figure to Davies, is obviously down on his luck, he is still dressed in a 'suit', however threadbare and soiled.

Pinter's jokiness, even frivolity, in, for instance, naming his characters after well-known cricketers, seems to have led some to think in effect that the play as a whole cannot be serious. This facetiousness is also evident in some of the self-conscious theatrical moments in the play, as when Spooner makes what on one level is an authorial joke in response to Hirst.

HIRST: Tonight . . . my friend . . . you find me in the last lap of a race . . . I had long forgotten to run.
    (*Pause*)
SPOONER: A metaphor. Things are looking up.

This, like Foster's exit at the end of Act One, when he 'turns the light out', both the light of the 'room' in which he is leaving Spooner and the stage lighting, relates to the sense the dialogue conveys that all the characters are performers, presenting changing versions of themselves to suit each occasion. (A similar device is used in *The Birthday Party*, but there its function is to bring to a climax the bullying of Stanley by McCann in Act Two, and no reference is made to stage lighting.) Spooner, the intruder, claims to be a poet, occasionally indulges in bad rhymes, and fantasizes freely, inventing a history for the initially taciturn Hirst in the opening scene. Later on the claims he makes for himself, telling Foster that he has a house in the country, a wife and two daughters may also be fantasy. As Spooner says,

I myself can do any graph of experience you wish, to suit your taste or mine. Child's play. The present will not be distorted.

Only the present, the immediate action we see, will not be distorted; all representations of previous experience may be fabricated, or at least stretch the truth, and, as in *The Caretaker*, the present is composed of a series of experiments or manoeuvres in a complicated game of words.

In Act One Spooner presents himself as a 'staunch friend of the arts', offers himself as a 'friend' to Hirst, and then describes himself to Foster as Hirst's friend. When Hirst returns from a brief sleep late in Act One, he seems not to recognize Spooner and takes him to be a friend of Foster's. In Act Two Hirst greets Spooner as Charles Wetherby, and they appear to have known one another as students many years ago at Oxford. Their anecdotes and accusations revolve around the sexual activities of Hirst, and stories of his seduction of Spooner's wife, Emily; but it is impossible to make sense of all the names and incidents they recall, or to work out their distortions of the past. Spooner, however, seems unable to resist the impulse to rescue from the past a stature to compensate for present inadequacies, and he brings their exchanges to a crisis by adding to his accusations about Hirst's sexual activities an insult to Hirst as a writer, provoking Hirst to turn on him and call him a lout. The effect of this insult is to restore the circle of Hirst, Foster and Briggs: 'We three,' says Hirst, 'never forget, are the oldest of friends'. Spooner's final ploy then, after Hirst gives him another chance by qualifying a verbal attack on him by Briggs with the remark, 'Yes, yes, but he's a good man at heart. I knew him at Oxford', is to offer himself not as a friend but as a secretary and arranger of poetry readings.

Through all the action Spooner has not so much an identity as a series of masks or personae, adapted to each occasion. But these are nevertheless linked by certain characteristics they have in common, which convey the sense of someone who has failed to make a mark and who is 'too old for any kind of expectation'. He is a hanger-on, a 'friend' of the landlord of the Bull's Head, one who collects beer mugs from the tables, a would-be poet, whose repeated allusions to T. S. Eliot's 'The Lovesong of J. Alfred Prufrock' in speeches beginning each time with the phrase 'I have known this before' suggest that Spooner, like Prufrock, has a pointless, repetitive existence:

> For I have known them all already, known them all,
> Have known the evenings, mornings, afternoons,
> I have measured out my life with coffee-spoons . . .

Like Prufrock, he is 'an attendant lord',

> Deferential, glad to be of use,
> Politic, cautious and meticulous,
> Full of high sentence, but a bit obtuse.
> At times, indeed, almost ridiculous,
> Almost, at times, the Fool.

He is a bit obtuse in quarrelling with Hirst, and nowhere nearer appearing the Fool than when he offers himself as Hirst's companion and secretary; here, as if by a self-generating momentum, Spooner seems drawn to inflate his potential role in Hirst's life until it topples into the absurd double image of a medieval knight taking on all comers in defence of his lord and a homosexual lover offering himself as a partner in bed:

I will accept death's challenge on your behalf. I shall meet it, for your sake, boldly, whether it be in the field or in the bedchamber. I am your Chevalier. I had rather bury myself in a tomb of honour than permit your dignity to be sullied by domestic enemy or foreign foe.

Spooner's reference to the 'bedchamber' here is absurd in relation to his earlier accusation that Hirst 'betrayed Stella Winstanley with Emily Spooner, my own wife, throughout a long and soiled summer'; and the comic gap between this speech and the offer he next makes, to organize poetry readings for Hirst in a public house, is characteristic of the way Spooner oscillates between pretentiousness and servility, even if here the slightly hysterical dignity of this final plea to Hirst suggests the desperation of a last shot by someone who knows he has lost.

If Spooner owes something to Prufrock, Hirst owes something to Hamm in Beckett's *Endgame*. He has a chair in which he sits centrestage, facing the audience, in a visual link with Hamm. In Act One he speaks of being 'in the last lap of a race', and towards the end says, 'Today I shall come to a conclusion', as if he too is playing an endgame. He drinks continually, and his inexhaustible supply of alcohol contrasts with Hamm's rapidly used-up stock of painkillers. He has the curtains drawn against the world and daylight in Act One, and after Briggs opens them in Act Two, Hirst orders them drawn again, recalling the by-play with the two small curtained windows in *Endgame*. Above all, Hirst is a figure who takes his power for granted, but as Hamm is dependent on Clov, so Hirst is dependent on Foster and Briggs. So his power and success, if, as Foster says, Hirst is a creative man, an artist, seem now sterile. It would appear that by his drinking, and his preference for having 'the shutters closed', he seeks to close off the outside world. He cannot bear being alone. At one point he says to Foster and Briggs:

How nice to have company. Can you imagine waking up, finding no-one here, just furniture, staring at you? Most unpleasant. I've known that condition, I've been through that period – cheers – I came round to human beings in the end. Like yourselves.

He has come round to them only in the sense of needing them to minister to him, and they treat him alternately with respect and contempt, but not with affection.

They have no identity for Hirst. Just as Spooner becomes Charles Wetherby for him, so he calls Briggs 'Denson' and later 'Albert'. Hirst seems essentially lonely; the mutual dependency which holds him, Briggs and Foster together has no emotional content, in spite of their repeated play with the term 'friend'. It appears in Act One that Hirst's emotional life is locked away in the Proustian photograph album he cannot find, which recalls his youth; then 'What was it informed the scene? A tenderness towards our fellows, perhaps'. In speaking nostalgically of the 'true friends' of his youth, who look out at him from the lost photographs, he thinks of them as 'transformed by light', in contrast to the darkness he now prefers. The image of the album returns towards the end of Act Two, but this time Hirst's nostalgia is focused on figures who are no longer made living by the present tense in which 'My true friends look out at me from my album', but are distanced as dead in his remark to Spooner: 'I say to you, tender the dead, as you would yourself be tendered, now, in what you would describe as your life'.

The album is never produced, and may itself be a fiction; but something of that past which meant an emotional life for Hirst is possibly dramatized in the exchanges between him and Spooner in Act Two. What Hirst recalls, however, is not tenderness, but seduction, betrayal and corruption, focusing especially on Emily, Spooner's wife, to whom Spooner says, Hirst 'behaved unnaturally and scandalously'. The period the album and their recollections refer to is that of the late 1930s; and the Second World War, in which Spooner says he served in torpedo boats, presumably as a seaman, while Hirst claims to have been in military intelligence, implying that he was an officer, marks a cut-off point. The years since the war remain an enigma; all we know is that Hirst has done well as a man of letters and Spooner has fared badly. It is as if whatever of importance happened for Hirst took place when he was young, and now he is elderly and alone (his wife, if he had one, is dead, according to Spooner); he introduces the image of no man's land, unchanging, an image that perhaps embodies the way he chooses to see his condition since the war, as if nothing has mattered much since then. Originally the term 'no man's land', first recorded in the fourteenth century, meant a piece of waste or unowned land, and only during the First World War did it become more strongly associated with the unoccupied, waste and dangerous territory between opposing forces. For Hirst it seems to signify a waste zone of time, perhaps between the opposing forces of life and death.

Something, nevertheless, has changed for him by the end of the play. Hirst's 'depressing' dream or nightmare of someone drowning is transformed at the end into an exciting dream, full of birdsong, and the drowning figure has gone. The exclusion of Spooner leaves Hirst with Briggs and Foster, who in fact insist that the subject has been changed for ever, to winter (or death) so that 'nothing else will happen forever', as Foster says, and it will always be night. This is how Briggs and Foster want it to be, since the dependency of Hirst on them would then be permanently guaranteed. Hirst changed the subject, however, in response to Spooner's last plea to be taken on as his secretary, so effectively rejecting Spooner, who has his minor revenge in joining with Briggs and Foster at the end to insist that Hirst is 'in no man's land'. Hirst's last line, 'I'll drink to that', may well be ironic, for the coming of Spooner has brought a kind of release to Hirst from his nightmare of a drowning man, perhaps

Spooner as his alter ego; the nightmare turns into a pleasurable reverie, recapturing birdsongs as they sounded when he was young, and perhaps recalling the image of birdsong in T. S. Eliot's 'Burnt Norton', which is associated with children, laughter, and the transcendent experience that remains:

> Quick now, here, now, always –
> Ridiculous the waste sad time
> Stretching before and after.

The arrival of Spooner triggered in Hirst memories of youth which turn out to be very different from the images of charm, 'tenderness' and grace embodied in the photograph album; Spooner transforms these into anecdotes of what he calls Hirst's 'insane and corrosive sexual absolutism'; so Spooner would shatter Hirst's nostalgia for tendering the dead, his 'love of the good ghost', and Hirst naturally rejects his offer to carry out a 'proper exhumation' of the faces in his album. Briggs, too, pours scorn on these images, a scorn focused in this unexpected use of the word 'mate' in addressing his employer, Hirst: 'They're blank, mate, blank. The blank dead'. Briggs and Foster, like Spooner, seek to cut Hirst away from his album, his memories, but fail to do so; Spooner, indeed, seems unintentionally to rid Hirst of his nightmare, so that at the end he has recaptured a vision of excitement and innocence.

The ending of the play is thus equivocal. Spooner, Foster and Briggs would lock Hirst into an icy and silent no man's land, an emotional wasteland, which is what they inhabit, but Hirst has a vision denied to them, and has finally lost the shadow that has been haunting his dreams. Spooner accepts from the start that he won't stay long, and takes comfort from eliciting 'a common and constant level of indifference'. His final, absurd, pedantic appeal to be hired as Hirst's secretary-cook-companion-defender-lover marks his acceptance of defeat, though, at the same time, its very extravagance also expresses Spooner's buoyancy, a zest for fantasizing, or creating ever-new variations on the themes he plays on his instrument, the English language. If he is excluded from Hirst and his group, he will find other 'friends', like the landlord of the 'particular public house ... who happens to be a friend of mine'; and this leaves him finally superior to Hirst and the others, to the extent that he is physically still a 'free man' and can return to hanging about on Hampstead Heath.

As to Foster and Briggs, they too play games with words, and it is never clear what their functions are as attendants on their master, though their names may be suggestive of their dual nature as caring for Hirst (fostering) and confining him (as a 'brig' is a prison in common American usage). Foster, for example, at first says he is Hirst's son, then has to clean the house in Act One and make the breakfast; but in Act Two he claims to be Hirst's secretary and then his chauffeur, housekeeper and amanuensis. They can take on any role in Hirst's household and all their routines in relation to Spooner seem to be designed for self-protection. They have a kind of homosexual bond as 'pretty boy and tough guy',[8] and in the end they act together ('We share all burdens, Jack and myself') to preserve the security of their position in relation to Hirst, on whom they depend, even as they assert a kind of power over him in lines like Foster's 'We'll be with you, Briggs and me'. Briggs and Foster are distinguished one from another, as Briggs is a Londoner while Foster refers several times to an exotic background, has links with Australia; (Foster's lager is a famous Australian brew) and indeed claims to have been in Bali when sent for to become Hirst's assistant. Foster's talk of the Siamese girls he misses leads to Briggs turning on him with insults that appear to be part of their familiar way of talk, perhaps containing a hint of admiration for his sexual prowess: 'Unspeakable ponce. He prefers the Malay straits, where they give you hot toddy in a fourposter. He's nothing but a vagabond cock'. Such insults are possible between 'friends':

BRIGGS: (To Foster) The best time to drink champagne is before lunch, you cunt.
FOSTER: Don't call me a cunt.
HIRST: We three, never forget, are the oldest of friends.
BRIGGS: That's why I called him a cunt.

The playful abuse of Foster by Briggs marks their intimacy, and the two join forces against Spooner to keep him out of their group and prevent him from driving 'a wedge into a happy household'. At the end of the play Briggs and Foster speak approvingly of one another before Briggs turns on Spooner for the last time, calling him with contempt a 'pisshole collector', a 'shithouse operator', a 'jamrag vendor', and so on. This abuse has a quite different weight from Briggs's remarks to Foster, and effectively dismisses Spooner, putting up, as it were, a 'keep out' sign. Briggs and Foster settle for the security and emptiness of no man's land, while Spooner will presumably drift on to seek other 'friends'.

Apart from the images of no man's land, the photograph album and the drowning man, two other extended images have prominence in the play. One is the strange picture Spooner 'decided to paint' but never did, of a joyous scene in Amsterdam, a fisherman catching a fish, a girl laughing, lovers kissing. The 'man whistling under his breath, sitting very still, almost rigid', suggests Hirst, like Spooner, a voyeur, both excluded as watchers from the joy of the scene; but as the key figure, the enigmatic whistler has some inner pleasure (in memories?) that prompt him to make music. Another important image is created in Briggs's aria on Bolsover Street (the play here on 'balls over', the suggestions of sterility, and the links with other sexual images in the play have drawn a good deal of commentary[9]). This fictitious story of how he met Foster ('he'll deny this account'), turns directions for a journey along streets of London into a maze of despair, a place from which there is no escape; Briggs's story is entitled 'Life at a Dead End' (in deliberate contrast to Spooner's title 'The Whistler'); if Spooner's title suggests him as voyeur, ignored by others but able to sing, the title of Briggs's story suggests the condition of existence in no man's land, and indeed his narrative, a splendid bravura piece of writing, seems in performance to constitute a kind of parody of the main situation explored in the play. Although this speech, like much of the dialogue, is very funny, it also encapsulates the bleakness of the whole. Where *The Caretaker* registered the deprivation and isolation of working-class characters (Davies, Aston), unable to cope in a world without care or concern for them, *No Man's Land* takes us into a middle- or upper-middle-class ambience, in which success (Hirst) proves empty and the characters play games and create fictions as a way of existing in a spiritual dead end. The interval of fifteen years between the plays marks a considerable shift in Pinter's attitudes. The earlier play now seems almost optimistic when studied in relation to the reworking of 1974-5.

The links with *Endgame*, Proust and T. S. Eliot have encouraged metaphysical readings of the play, and the insistence with which Foster, Briggs and Spooner try to close off Hirst 'forever' in no man's land has led to interpretations of the play in terms of universals, as concerned with 'Man's need not to remember his pain and guilt [which] becomes the root of an even greater isolation – isolation from life itself,[10] or 'the dynamics of modern man's struggle with life and his retreat from living it fully'.[11] I have stressed the ironies of the ending to show that what Spooner or Foster says should not be taken as the 'message' of the play. The Bolsover speech especially brings out another aspect of *No Man's Land* that helps to guard against merely allegorizing the play into a general statement about Man's relation to life or death. Bolsover Street is a real street in London, and, like so much of the text, this speech is specific in detail about actual places, even if Briggs's directions cannot be followed. The named locations, Hampstead, Chalk Farm, Jack Straw's Castle, the Ritz Hotel, Balliol College, and so on, give the play a social context that is more distinct than that of the other memory plays like *Old Times*, and differentiates it from *The Caretaker*. Whereas in *The Caretaker* there is no sense of place other than Aston's room, and the details of names and objects make up the mental world of the characters, *No Man's Land* keeps reminding us of a named suburb of London, and the references to actual places compose a social setting and frame of reference enabling Hirst and Spooner to relate in terms of their recollections of Oxford in the 1930s or service in the Second World War. When these two first share their nostalgia for country cottages with tea on the lawn, Spooner tries to out-manoeuvre Hirst by inviting him to speak about 'the socio-politico-economic structure of the environment in which you attained to the age of reason'. Hirst, of course, ignores this request, but I suspect Pinter was writing the play in an awareness of the socio-politico-economic structure of England, and perhaps the world, in the early 1970s.

An important author's comments tend in print to acquire a special authority, as though what was said impromptu or in self-protection in an interview can be taken as representing his views for all time. So some remarks Pinter made early in his career have been much cited as evidence of a fixed attitude to social and political issues. In 1961, for example, he was asked whether politics interested him and replied, 'I find most political thinking and terminology suspect, deficient'.[12] In a later interview, in 1970, responding to the question whether it had ever occurred to him to express political opinions through his characters, he commented, 'No. Ultimately, politics do bore me.[13] Such statements have been used by critics to fence Pinter's plays off from political issues, and the dramatist for a long period seemed to sanction such treatment. Yet it now seems that his remarks were made to turn aside any probing as to his beliefs or commitment, and they mark his dislike of 'agit-prop'.[14] In the 1970 interview with Bensky, Pinter went on to say, 'I don't care about political structures – they don't alarm me, but they cause a great deal of suffering to millions of people'; and his anger at this suffering broke through in his desire to 'burst through the screen with a flame-thrower' and burn politicians he saw talking about the Vietnam war on television.[15]

Pinter may not be committed to some party line, but he does care; moreover, as long ago as 1961, he said, 'as far as I'm concerned, my characters and I inhabit the same world ... I think we're all in the same boat',[16] so that he recognized the reference to social reality in his work. Recently he has engaged directly with political issues, and his play *One for the Road* (1984) arose out of his concern at the treatment of political prisoners in Turkey. In conversation he remarked on his earlier 'detached contempt' for politicians and political structures, but in the context of another comment, 'I wouldn't say that my political awareness during those years was dead. Far from it.' At the beginning of this conversation he also observed that the 'political metaphor' in the questioning of authority in *The Dumb Waiter* (1960) was obvious to the cast and the director, even if the critics missed it[17] – Pinter also spoke of *The Birthday Party* (1957) and *The Hothouse* (written 1958; published 1980) as concerned with 'the abuse of authority'. In seeming to deny that his plays had a political content, Pinter was also protecting himself as a dramatist, for his growing overt concern with issues relating to what he calls 'the nuclear bureaucracy', or the harsh treatment of political prisoners in many countries, has now for him made it 'very difficult to write *anything*'.[18]

It is time we noticed that a political awareness informs the major plays of a dramatist who for years let it be thought that he was not interested in politics. In *No Man's Land* his characters may not talk much about the subject, but they inhabit a world affected, however obliquely, by political issues, and it is therefore appropriate to set the play in a political context. The most obvious meaning of the title relates it to the First World War, but also to war generally. Beginning with the symbolic closing off of East from West with the erection of the Berlin Wall in 1961, and the enormous escalation in the building of nuclear arsenals in the East and the West after the Cuban missile crisis of 1962, a deepening pessimism may be sensed in Britain about the future of the world and the continuing possibility of peace. The years immediately before Pinter wrote *No Man's Land* were marked by the mindless horrors of the war in Vietnam. The last American troops left in March 1973, but the Americans went on funding the South Vietnam government; the play opened in London one week before the North Vietnamese captured Saigon in April 1975. In 1974 President Nixon was threatened with impeachment, and he resigned as a consequence of the Watergate affair. In 1974 also Turkey invaded Cyprus, and the British government imposed direct rule on Northern Ireland. Nearer home, there was a major oil crisis in 1973, and a crippling miners' strike, and the years 1970 to 1975 brought record inflation, huge international payment deficits, and a decline in the standard of living to Britain. *No Man's Land* may be seen in the context of these events, as well as in relation to Pinter's own changing social status.

The play concerns two older men, writers in their sixties, whose lives once had a richness and purpose now lost. Spooner, the drifting 'betwixt twig peeper', imagines himself incongruously as a gentleman of culture, adept at French cuisine, and possessing 'piety, prudence, liberality and goodness'. Hirst, like him, was 'one of the golden' of his generation, and clutches on to his vision of a happier world in the photograph album of his memory, closing the curtains to shut out the present and devoting himself to the bottle. The younger men, Foster and Briggs, in their thirties, are by contrast unscrupulous con men, who lie, say anything, to maintain their apparently easy positions as companions in relation to Hirst, like scroungers living off the welfare state, and contemptuous of it (as when Foster says, 'I don't have to waste my time looking after a pisshound'). So *No Man's Land* may be seen as a bitterly comic expression of a writer's disillusion with the state of affairs in Britain and the world. If *The Caretaker* crystallized an image of the socially deprived living in the tattered fringes of a society that didn't want to know, and seemed vaguely left-wing, the later play appears by contrast to be essentially conservative in its nostalgia for a past that had meaning. If the play may be regarded in some sense as Pinter's *Endgame* in which 'Hirst has achieved Hamm's goal, and there will be no more change of subject: story itself is ended and with it, life',[19] *No Man's Land* is nevertheless not a 'closed' play but invites question, and is less a commentary on 'the aimlessness of existence' than a portrayal of disenchantment with a society trapped in economic decline, caught up in useless wars, and increasingly dedicated to greed. Perhaps it is more than coincidence that in the year it was first staged, 1975, Margaret Thatcher was elected leader of the Conservative Party in Britain.

NOTES

1. John Peter, *Vladimir's Carrot. Modern Drama and the Modern Imagination* (London, André Deutsch, 1987), pp. 18–19.
2. David T. Thompson, *Pinter the Player's Playwright* (London, Macmillan, 1985), p. 53.
3. *Ibid.*, p. 95.
4. Peter, *Vladimir's Carrot. Modern Drama and the Modern Imagination*, p. 319.
5. Harold Pinter, *The Caretaker* (second, revised edition, London, Eyre Methuen, 1962). All references are to this edition.
6. A. R. Braunmuller, 'Harold Pinter: The Metamorphosis of Memory', in *Essays on Contemporary British Drama* edited by Hedwig Bock and Albert Wertheim, (Munich, 1981), p. 157.
7. Harold Pinter, *No Man's Land* (revised edition, London, Eyre Methuen, 1975). All references are to this edition.
8. Kristin Morrison, *Canters and Chronicles. The Use of Narrative in the Plays of Samuel Beckett and Harold Pinter* (University of Chicago Press, 1986), p. 211.
9. See, for instance, Elin Diamond, *Pinter's Comic Play* (Lewisburg, Pennsylvania, Bucknell University Press, 1985), pp. 189–90.
10. Lucina Paquet Gabbard, *The Dream Structure of Pinter's Plays* (Rutherford, New Jersey, Fairleigh Dickinson, 1977), p. 271.
11. Katherine H. Burkman, 'Death and the Double in Three Plays by Harold Pinter', in Alan Bold, *Harold Pinter: You Never Heard Such Silence* (London, Vision Press, 1984), p. 143.
12. 'Harold Pinter Replies', *New Theatre Magazine* II, January 1961, p. 9.

13 Lawrence M. Bensky, 'Harold Pinter: An Interview', in Arthur Ganz (ed.), *Pinter: Twentieth Century Views* (Englewood Cliffs, New Jersey, Prentice Hall, 1972), p. 27.
14 Harold Pinter, *One for the Road*, with production photos by Ivan Kyncl and an interview on the play and its politics (London, Methuen, 1985), p. 18.
15 Bensky, 'Harold Pinter: An Interview', p. 27.
16 'Harold Pinter Replies', p. 9
17 Pinter, *One for the Road*, pp. 7, 12.
18 *Ibid.*, pp. 18–19.
19 Morrison, *Canters and Chronicles. The Use of Narrative in the Plays of Samuel Beckett and Harold Pinter*, p. 213.

11 Fact and Fiction in the Novel: An Author's Note

David Lodge

And here I solemnly protest, I have no intention to vilify or asperse anyone; for although everything is copied from the book of nature, and scarce a character or action produced which I have not taken from my own observations and experience; yet I have used the utmost care to obscure the persons by such different circumstances, degrees and colours, that it will be impossible to guess at them with any degree of certainty; and if it ever happens otherwise, it is only where the failure characterized is so minute, that it is a foible only, which the party himself may laugh at as well as any other.
Henry Fielding, Preface to Joseph Andrews (1742)

Is it possible for an ordinary person to climb over the area railings of no. 7 Eccles St., either from the path or from the steps, lower himself from the lowest part of the railings till his feet are within 2 feet or 3 of the ground and drop unhurt? I saw it done myself but by a man of rather athletic build. I require this information in detail in order to determine the wording of a paragraph.
James Joyce, letter to Mrs William Murray, 2 November 1921

'Hey,' I said. 'When you, do you sort of make it up, or is it just, you know, like what happens?'
'Neither.'
Martin Amis, Money (1984)

I

There is a passage in my novel *Small World* (1984) which affords a convenient, if somewhat ribald, introduction to this complex subject. The situation is that Professor Morris Zapp, of Euphoric State University, USA, en route from a conference in Rummidge, England, to the Rockefeller Study Centre at Bellagio, on Lake Como, is delayed in Milan by a public services strike, and is offered hospitality for the night by Fulvia Morgana, a rich Marxist professor of cultural studies whom he met on the plane from London. Her interest in him had quickened when she realized that his ex-wife, Désirée, was the famous author of a best-selling feminist novel in the style of Erica Jong or Marilyn French, called *Difficult Days*. Was it autobiographical, Fulvia inquired. In part, he replied. Now, in Fulvia Morgana's palatial house just off the Via Napoleone, after partaking of a delicious dinner for two, Morris Zapp becomes uneasily aware that Fulvia has plans to seduce him.

'Don't let us talk any more about books,' she said, floating across the dimly lit room with a brandy glass like a huge bubble in her hand. 'Or about chairs and conferences.' She stood very close to him and rubbed the back of her free hand over his crotch. 'Is it really twenty-five centimetres?' she murmured.

'What gives you that idea?' he said hoarsely.

'Your wife's book . . .'

'You don't want to believe everything you read in books, Fulvia,' said Morris, grabbing the glass of cognac and draining it in a single gulp. He coughed and his eyes filled with tears. 'A professional critic like you should know better than that. Novelists exaggerate.'

'But 'ow much do they exaggerate, Morris?' she said. 'I would like to see for myself.'

'Like, practical criticism?' he quipped.

Fulvia did not laugh. 'Didn't you make your wife measure it with her tape measure?' she persisted.

'Of course I didn't! That's just feminist propaganda. Like the whole book.'

He lurched towards one of the deep armchairs, puffing clouds of cigar smoke like a retreating battleship, but Fulvia steered him firmly towards the sofa, and sat down beside him, pressing her thigh against his. She undid a button of his shirt and slid a cool hand inside. He flinched as the gems on one of her rings snagged in his chest hair.

'Lots of 'air,' Fulvia purred. '*That* is in the book.'

'I'm not saying the book is entirely fictitious,' said Morris. 'Some of the minor details are taken from life –'

"Airy as a beast . . . You were a beast to your wife, I think.'

'Ow!' exclaimed Morris, for Fulvia had dug her long lacquered nails into his flesh for emphasis.

"Ow? Well, for example, tying 'er up with leather straps and doing all those degrading things to 'er.'

'Lies, all lies!' said Morris desperately.

FACT AND FICTION IN THE NOVEL

'You can do those things to me, if you like, *caro*,' Fulvia whispered into his ear, pinching his nipple painfully at the same time.

'I don't want to do anything to anybody, I never did,' Morris groaned. 'The only time we ever fooled around with that S/M stuff, it was Désirée's idea, not mine.'

'I don't believe you, Morris.'

'It's true. Novelists are terrible liars. They make things up. They change things around. Black becomes white, white black. They are totally unethical beings. Ouch!' Fulvia had nibbled his earlobe hard enough to draw blood.[1]

Fulvia Morgana is making an elementary mistake here about the relationship of fiction to reality. Because the fiction corresponds to historical fact in some respects (for example, the male character's chest hair), she assumes that it does in every respect. Most novelists are familiar with this reaction from readers, even quite sophisticated readers, whom they meet face to face. The physical presence of the writer, with his or her personal history available for interrogation, seems to push aside the willing suspension of disbelief, the aesthetic appreciation of elegant narrative structure, the ludic delight in the proliferation of meaning, in favour of a beady-eyed curiosity about the 'true story' behind the fiction. Spouses of novelists, or other relatives and close acquaintances, are apt to suffer this curiosity in a particularly trying form, as Morris Zapp discovers.

For the record, this episode in *Small World* has no source in my own experience, but was generated entirely by the needs and possibilities of the narrative. Admittedly I was once resident at the Rockefeller Study Centre at Bellagio – but *after* writing the novel, not before (a circumstance that has a story of its own attached to it). I certainly met no one like Fulvia Morgana on the way to anywhere. *Small World* is subtitled 'an academic romance', a designation that plays on the recognized genre-term 'academic novel' and also indicates what kind of romance is invoked – not the Mills and Boon kind, but the kind studied and loved by academics: Heliodorus, the stories of King Arthur, the *Faerie Queene*, *Orlando Furioso*, the late plays of Shakespeare, and so on. As one of the characters says, 'Real romance is a prenovelistic kind of narrative. It's full of adventure and coincidence and surprises and marvels, and has lots of characters who are lost or enchanted or wandering about looking for each other, or for the Grail, or something like that' (p. 258). *Small World* in this way claims the licence to be highly fictive, as the epigraph from Hawthorne says: 'When a writer calls his work a Romance, it need hardly be observed that he wishes to claim a certain latitude, which he would not have felt himself entitled to assume had he professed to be writing a novel.'

But of course *Small World is* a novel, a comic novel. The passage between Morris Zapp and Fulvia Morgana is designed to contribute both to the romance theme and the comic effect. Morris Zapp is re-enacting the situation of the errant knight lured into an enchanted castle and trapped in the toils of a seductive sorceress. The name Fulvia Morgana echoes that of Morgan Le Fay in Arthurian legend. In her mirrored bedroom Fulvia snaps handcuffs on to Morris Zapp's wrists and removes his underpants, rendering him powerless to escape. Travesty turns into farce as the terrified Zapp hears Fulvia's husband, Ernesto, letting himself into the house and climbing the stairs. In a reversal of the outraged-husband stereotype, Ernesto greets Morris Zapp genially and prepares to join him and Fulvia between the crimson sheets of the circular bed. Reversal is indeed the keynote of the whole episode. There is a reversal of normal seduction roles in Fulvia's hot pursuit of the reluctant Morris. There is a reversal of 'normal' sado-masochistic roles in that Fulvia, while inviting Morris to hurt her, actually hurts him. Thus in the very process of trying to re-enact *Difficult Days*, to force reality to fit the fiction, she is in fact reversing the fiction, just as Morris claims Désirée reversed the facts.

It is important to note, however, that the reader does not know whether Morris Zapp is telling the truth, *and neither do I*. I know nothing more about Désirée's novel, or the sexual side of their marriage, than is fragmentarily revealed in the pages of *Changing Places* and *Small World*, and for my purposes as a novelist it was not necessary to determine how accurate an account of the Zapp marriage is given in *Difficult Days* or by Morris Zapp in his conversation with Fulvia Morgana. In short, there is no source for this episode, either fictional or factual, against which its truth could be checked.

This does not, however, mean that there are no factual sources for other episodes in *Small World*, or that the whole novel is not full of discrete facts culled from my observation of the real world. Of course there are and of course it is.

II

It has long been recognized by historians and theorists of the novel that, in this kind of writing, 'fiction' is bound, in a peculiar and complex way, to the world of 'facts'. In his classic study, *The Rise of the Novel*, Ian Watt stressed the referential or pseudo-referential character of the language of the earliest major English novelists, Defoe and Richardson, who presented their invented stories as real documents – letters, confessions, and so on – of which they posed as the editors. These stories were fictional, but formally indistinguishable from 'true stories'. The telling of them is full of facts of the kind that constitute reality for an empirically minded culture. The novel, according to Watt, rose in response to: 'that vast transformation of Western civilization since the Renaissance which has replaced the unified world picture of the Middle Ages with another very different one – one which presents us, essentially, with a developing but unplanned aggregate of particular individuals having particular experiences at particular times and particular places.'[2]

More recent, Foucauldian attempts to locate the origins of the novel in the Renaissance episteme have focused on the same problematic. Robert Weimann, for instance, has argued that, whereas the medieval narrative writer was a quasi-anonymous mediator of stories authorized by tradition ('I fynde no more written in bokis that bene auctorized,' Malory says on winding up the *Morte D'Arthur*), the Renaissance writer saw himself as the maker or begetter of an original discourse put together from heterogeneous sources and models, entailing a fusion or confusion of fiction and history. 'The "fained image" of the *fabula* was rendered in terms of that different type of discourse which, as *historia*, was "bound to tell things as they were".'[3]

In his *Factual Fictions: The Origins of the English Novel* (1983), Lennard J. Davis argues that the novel emerged out of a new kind of narrative writing, the precursor of modern journalism, which he calls 'news/novels discourse' – the reporting of recent or current events in broadsides, pamphlets, ballads, criminal confessions, and so on, made possible by the invention of the printing press. The characteristic feature of this discourse is that it foreshortens or collapses the distance between language and reality, and thus between the audience and the matter of narrative. Whereas medieval narrative presented a story for the sake of its moral, which had to be allegorically interpreted, in news/novels discourse the medium is the message, the words efface themselves as signifiers and strive to coincide with the events they signify, the human interest of which is taken for granted, like the contents of a newspaper. Novelists perceived that by imitating the form of this new kind of documentary writing they could exert an exciting new power over their readers, giving to fictitious characters and events an unprecedented illusion of reality.

This theory of the rise of the novel, like Watt's, seems to apply more readily to Defoe and Richardson than to their great contemporary Henry Fielding who mocked the technique of pseudo-factual writing in *Joseph Andrews* ('He accordingly eat either a rabbit or a fowl, I never could with any tolerable certainty discover which'),[4] and himself employed an ostentatiously literary style full of echoes of and allusions to classical mythology and scripture. However, as Davis points out, Fielding was a journalist before he was a novelist, and he integrated the facts of a real event (the Jacobite Rising of 1845), as it unfolded, into his fictional *History of Tom Jones* and made adjustments to his original design to accommodate them. He thus established a precedent that was followed and developed by later novelists such as Scott, Thackeray and George Eliot. (Compare the Porteus riots in *Heart of Midlothian*, the Battle of Waterloo in *Vanity Fair* and the Reform Election in *Middlemarch*.) And although Fielding's characters may seem to us like stock types, to his contemporaries they were often recognizable portraits of real people, in spite of the precautions he claims to have taken in his Preface to *Joseph Andrews* (see the first epigraph to this essay).

The ambivalent and contradictory relationship between fact and fiction in the early novel persists into its classical and modern phases. Novelists are and always have been split between, on the one hand, a desire to claim an imaginative and representative truth for their stories and, on the other hand, a conviction that the best way to secure and guarantee that truthfulness is by a scrupulous respect for empirical fact. Why else did James Joyce take such pains to establish whether his fictional character

FACT AND FICTION IN THE NOVEL

Leopold Bloom could plausibly drop down into the basement area of no. 7 Eccles Street?

Novels burn facts as engines burn fuel, and the facts can come only from the novelist's own experience or acquired knowledge. Not uncommonly, a novelist begins by drawing mainly on facts of the former kind and, when these are 'used up', becomes more reliant on the latter. Joyce's progress from the realistic and autobiographical *Dubliners* and *A Portrait* to the increasingly encyclopaedic *Ulysses* and *Finnegans Wake* is an example. So is the career of George Eliot, who began with *Scenes of Clerical Life*, so closely based on the Nuneaton of her childhood that 'keys' to 'Janet's Repentance' were soon in circulation in the town, and ended with the massively researched *Daniel Deronda*.

Inasmuch as fact and fiction are opposites, one could say that the novel as a literary form is founded upon contradiction, upon the reconciliation of the irreconcilable, something novelists have endeavoured to conceal by various kinds of diversionary mystification: framing narratives, parody and other kinds of intertextuality, and metafictional devices such as Martin Amis's introduction of himself into his own fiction, to be questioned about his writing by his own character. The question John Self asks 'Martin Amis' (see my third epigraph) is the question Fulvia Morgana asks Morris Zapp about his wife's novel. It is the question readers always ask novelists, and his answer is the one they always give. I gave it, anticipating the question, in the Author's Note that prefaces *Small World*.

Like *Changing Places*, to which it is a sequel, *Small World* resembles what is sometimes called the real world, without corresponding exactly to it, and is peopled by figments of the imagination. Rummidge is not Birmingham, though it owes something to popular prejudices about that city. There really is an underground chapel at Heathrow and a James Joyce pub in Zurich, but no universities in Limerick or Darlington; nor, as far as I know, was there ever a British Council representative in Genoa. The MLA Convention of 1979 did not take place in New York, though I have drawn on the programme for the 1978 one, which did. And so on.

At first glance this looks like a familiar defensive manoeuvre to disclaim any representation of real people and institutions that might take offence. But the Note also informs readers that some components of the book they might suppose to be invented are in fact 'real'. I wanted my readers to know, for instance, that the panel discussions at the MLA Convention in Part V, on 'Lesbian-feminist Teaching and Learning' and 'Problems of Cultural Distortion in Translating Expletives in the Work of Cortazar, Sender, Baudelaire and Flaubert' were not parodies but the real thing. I wanted them to know that the Dublin pub painstakingly dismantled and re-erected in Zurich in memory of James Joyce, who wrote most of *Ulysses* in that city, was not some strained conceit of mine but a fact: a fact that says much about the curious intertwining of high culture and popular culture in our epoch, about the reification of literary reputations and the deification of dead writers, a process in which the academic literary profession is deeply implicated.

If *Small World* had a single point of origin, it was the James Joyce Symposium of 1979, held in Zurich, which I attended, and where I first made acquaintance with that pub, thronged with Joyceans from every corner of the globe, knocking back tumblers of draught Guinness and discussing textual cruces in *Finnegans Wake* at the tops of their voices, while outside on Pelikanstrasse the burghers of Zurich went decorously about the serious business of making money, and across the river in the redlight district, where my hotel (chosen at random) was situated, squeaky-clean prostitutes stood on the well-swept street corners, one per corner in the methodical Swiss way. What strange conjunctions and piquant contrasts the lives of modern academics encompassed, it struck me, as they toted their conference papers and lightweight luggage around the global campus. There might be a novel in it.

From Zurich I flew direct to another conference in Israel, an experience that provided much of the local colour for the conference organized by Morris Zapp in Part IV of *Small World* (p. 298):

Now it is mid-August, and Morris Zapp's conference on the Future of Criticism is in full swing. Almost everybody involved agrees that it is the best conference they have ever attended. Morris is smug. The secret of his success is very simple: the formal proceedings of the conference are kept to a bare minimum. There is just one paper a day actually delivered by its author, early in the morning. All the other papers are circulated in Xeroxed form, and the remainder of the day is allocated to 'unstructured discussion' of the issues raised in these documents, or, in other words, to swimming and sunbathing at the Hilton pool, sightseeing in the Old City, shopping in the bazaar, eating out in ethnic restaurants, and making expeditions to Jericho, the Jordan valley, and Galilee.

I always feel a twinge of guilt when I reread this passage, for those who hosted and attended the conference that was its 'source' know that it was in fact an extraordinarily hard-working affair, and that the sightseeing and other hedonistic diversions mentioned in the passage from *Small World* were indulged in only after we had been released from long days in smoke-filled seminar rooms, or during an optional four-day tour of Israel after the conference had disbanded. But for the purposes of the novel this conference had to be the one in which the institution of the international conference would demonstrate most spectacularly its 'way of converting work into play, combining professionalism with tourism, and all at someone else's expense' (p. 231). I suppose this is what Morris Zapp means when he says that novelists are totally unethical beings: when the truth of fact and the needs of fiction conflict, the novelist will always favour the latter.

But, broadly speaking, the academic-comedy-of-manners level of *Small World* is derived from the world of 'fact', while the interlaced plots (of quest and adventure and love and mysterious origins and identities) are derived from the world of fiction. The challenge, the 'game' of writing the novel, was to nudge and fiddle these two planes into a near-perfect fit with each other, and the Chapel of St George at Heathrow was invaluable for this purpose because it is both a real and a romantic place. I discovered it (not without difficulty, for few people at the airport can direct you to it) one Sunday morning in November 1981 while I was waiting for a flight to Warsaw, where I was to attend (what else?) a conference. I had already started work on *Small World*, and the underground chapel, secreted amid the labyrinthine ways of Heathrow, with its chivalric patron saint and its low roof curved like the passenger cabin of a wide-bodied jet, immediately offered itself as a location for my story. Although it was a non-denominational chapel, the Catholics seemed to have taken it over, making it a congenial place for my young Irish hero, Persse McGarrigle. There was a statue of Our Lady against the wall, and a red sanctuary lamp burning on a side altar. As I sat there, a priest clothed in vestments came in. I said, 'Is this going to be a Catholic mass?' He said, 'Yes, d'you want communion?' I said, 'How long will it take?' He said, 'As quick as I can make it.' Perhaps he had a plane to catch too. His rapid recitation of the liturgy was punctuated with burps from indigestion. I did not use this incident in *Small World*, but I did take note of the petition board at the back of the chapel, especially a poignant, scribbled prayer from what sounded like an Irish girl in trouble. Only slightly modified, it found its way into *Small World* and gave rise to Persse's meeting with his cousin Bernadette. The petition board also became an important property in the story of Persse's pursuit of Angelica. When Howard Schuman adapted *Small World* for Granada TV's six-part serial, he framed the whole narrative with Persse's tape-recorded 'confession' in the chapel of St George, and these sequences were actually shot there.

When you are working on a book, everything that happens to you is considered for possible exploitation in the work-in-progress. After my visit to Poland I introduced a Polish character into *Small World*, Wanda Kedrzejkiewicelska, a young lecturer at the University of Lodz, specializing in British absurdist drama, which she finds not at all funny but a sombrely realistic analogue of life in Poland. I wrote a scene or two for her, one in which she is shown queueing for sausage for her husband's dinner and reading *The Birthday Party*, shoving before her with her foot a capacious bag equally handy for carrying books and foraging for food, dreaming longingly of a projected visit to a British Council Summer School at Oxford that would bring her into the plot. Later I decided that the trip to Oxford would never materialize, that Wanda would spend the entire novel travelling about Lodz by tram, getting off to join any likely-looking queue, poignantly excluded from the plot and the fun the other characters were having. But the character of Wanda herself obstinately refused to come alive, and it became obvious to me that the plight of the Polish academics I had met, and of the Polish nation at large, was too grim for incorporation into my light-hearted satire on the global campus; so I cut her out of the novel.

III

'Rummidge is not Birmingham, though it owes something to popular prejudices about that city.'

Fictitious place names are, of course, one of the novelist's most transparent devices for incorporating fact into fiction. The elaborately coded topography of Hardy's Wessex, for instance, or Arnold Bennett's Five Towns, is not designed to deceive anybody as to the real locations of their novels, but to avoid the logical contradiction, and perhaps legal risks, of putting fictional characters in places that at a given time were occupied by historical individuals. The implied rules governing this matter cast an interesting though indeterminate light on the relations of fact to fiction in the novel. You can invent an imaginary London street, but you cannot have a capital of England that is not London. You can have an imaginary Oxford or Cambridge college, but it would seem awkward, to say the least, to have an ancient English university that was not Oxford or Cambridge. You can site a university in a city that doesn't actually have one (though there are risks entailed in this practice; I understand that the Institute of Higher Education in Limerick, of whose existence I was unaware when I wrote *Small World*, is at present seeking university status, and that there have been high-level discussions in Ireland about what to call it in view of the rather prejudicial image of my fictitious University College Limerick.) You can, it seems, have a provincial city or town with a fictional name (Middlemarch, Casterbridge, Rummidge) occupying the same geographical space as an actual city or town, and closely resembling the original in every respect except inhabitants.

In January 1969 I took leave of absence from the University of Birmingham to take up the post of visiting associate professor at the University of California, Berkeley. At that time, both campuses, like most campuses, were in the throes of the student revolution; but whereas Birmingham's 'occupation' had been a relatively mild-mannered and good-humoured affair, in Berkeley there was something like civil war in progress, with police chasing demonstrators through the streets with shotguns and clouds of teargas drifting across the campus. And if Birmingham was timidly responding to the vibrations emanating from Swinging London, Berkeley was at the leading edge of the Permissive Society, the Counter-Culture, Flower Power and all the rest of the 1960s baggage. Out of this experience I constructed a comic novel, *Changing Places: A Tale of Two Campuses*, centring on an exchange between two university teachers of English Literature at that particular moment in history: Philip Swallow, an undistinguished lecturer at the University of Rummidge in the damp and grey English Midlands, and dynamic, abrasive Professor Morris Zapp from Euphoric State University, on the sunny west coast of America, who end up swapping wives as well as jobs. The plot was a narrative transformation of the thematic material and the socio-cultural similarities and differences I had perceived between Birmingham and Berkeley. I did not go to Berkeley on an exchange scheme and, unlike my main characters, I took my wife and family with me across the Atlantic. (When I explain this to people like Fulvia Morgana I detect on their faces a look of surprise mingled with disappointment, even resentment, as if they feel they have been conned.) The plot is completely fictional, though the background events of student protest and civil disturbance are closely based on actual events which I observed. Several of the 'quotations' which make up Chapter 4 of the novel, entitled 'Reading', were transcribed from real journals and documents.

Changing Places also has its carefully worded Author's Note:

> Although some of the locations and public events portrayed in this novel bear a certain resemblance to actual locations and events, the characters, considered either as individuals or as members of institutions, are entirely imaginary. Rummidge and Euphoria are places on the map of a comic world which resembles the one we are standing on without corresponding exactly to it, and which is peopled by figments of the imagination.[5]

The fictitious and jokey place names licensed me, I hoped, to exaggerate and deform reality for literary purposes. Rummidge is more dourly provincial, Euphoria more 'far out' than their respective models. The University of Rummidge in particular is a much smaller and dimmer place than the University of Birmingham, and its undistinguished English Department, which seems never to have had more than one professorial chair in its entire history, could not conceivably be confused with the large and flourishing School of English (rated in the country's top six by the UGC in 1986, and the only one outside Oxbridge to achieve top marks for research in a recent UFC survey) in which I have had the privilege of working for most of my professional life.

At the time of writing *Changing Places*, I had no plans for a sequel, but when, about ten years later, I conceived the idea of a 'global campus' novel, it seemed an obvious move to incorporate some of the characters from the earlier book, and to throw the wilder shores of the international conference circuit into relief by starting the story at a rather depressed and depressing conference at Rummidge. For this opening sequence I drew on memories of several comfortless gatherings in halls of residence belonging to various British universities. (The unseasonable snow that exacerbates the privations of the Rummidge conferees was suggested by the experience of returning from a blossom-laden Washington in late April 1981 to an England totally immobilized by a freak snowstorm – it took us longer to travel from Heathrow to Birmingham than from Washington to London.)

When I began work on a novel about the impact of Thatcherism on universities and industry, intertextually related to the so-called Industrial Novels of the nineteenth century, Rummidge offered itself once more as the setting with a certain inevitability. What point would there be in creating another fictitious Midland industrial city with a university in it? But *Nice Work* is a more sober and realistic novel than its carnivalesque precursors, and the physical setting became less of a caricature and more of a likeness of Birmingham in its composition. The membrane between fact and fiction, between 'Birmingham' and 'Rummidge', has undoubtedly become thinner and more transparent with the passing of time, and I was concerned that it might be actually ruptured by the recent television serialization (which I scripted) because it was filmed entirely on location in Birmingham, including the campus of the University. This was a great bonus for the production team, but I was slightly surprised that the University agreed to it, and so, I think, were some of my former colleagues. The administration evidently decided that the PR advantages of displaying its impressive campus on television would outweigh any negative feedback from the satirical elements in the story and, having seen the finished product, I think they were probably right.[6]

Watching *Nice Work* being filmed (strictly speaking, one

should say 'recorded', since it was made on videotape, but the distinction hardly matters to the layman) was a fascinating but at times disorienting experience, for I was seeing many scenes that I had invented being returned to the 'real' locations which had given rise to them – not only on the academic side of the story, but also on the industrial side. Most of the foundry sequences in Episode One, for instance, were shot in the very first foundry I visited while researching the novel (in which my own awed and appalled reactions are transferred to Robyn Penrose). One Sunday morning in March 1989 I drove from my house in Edgbaston to the main entrance of the University, and there, like a dream or hallucination, was a traffic jam I had invented three years earlier: an articulated lorry was drawn up across the road, blocking the passage of other vehicles, while placard-waving pickets of the Association of University Teachers engaged the driver in earnest discussion of their grievances. A girl student rushed up beside me. 'Oh dear!' she cried. 'Is the University closed?' She hadn't taken in the signboard, with its fake heraldic shield, that read: *University of Rummidge*. 'It's only a TV film,' I reassured her. I didn't tell her that I had written the script.

IV

I doubt whether I could have countenanced the use of the Birmingham campus as a location for the filming of *Nice Work* if I hadn't retired from my post there a couple of years previously. The paradoxes and contradictions of my position had been acute enough while 'Rummidge' was just a verbal construct, confined and consumed within the covers of a book, or books. To have collaborated in a re-creation of the fictional place that would be visually indistinguishable from its real-life model while performing a professional role in the latter would, I think, have placed an intolerable strain on the distinction I always tried to preserve, however artificially, between my life as an academic and my life as a novelist. The writer who works in an institutional environment on which he draws for material and inspiration is peculiarly sensitive to the conflicting imperatives and interests of the world of fact and of the world of fiction. Crossing and recrossing the frontier between the two worlds, one is apt to feel like a double agent, always vulnerable to the accusation of treachery, always fearful of being 'exposed'. I will conclude these ruminations with a personal anecdote, not entirely creditable to myself, but illustrative of the point.

It will be recalled that in the passage from *Small World* with which I began, Morris Zapp is on his way to the Rockefeller Study Centre at the Villa Serbelloni in Bellagio, on Lake Como. Since there is no reference to this place in the Author's Note, readers might be forgiven for supposing that it is an invention of mine. It is in fact a real institution, which offers hospitality for periods of about a month's duration, mainly to scholars, but also to writers, artists, musicians and so on, and their spouses, in surroundings of great luxury, elegance and outstanding natural beauty, in order that they can work on some suitable project, with no more distraction then the occasional walk or game of tennis, and civilized social intercourse over meals and after dinner. Several friends and acquaintances of mine who had stayed there had spoken highly of its attractions and urged me to apply. At some time early in the 1980s I did so, in my capacity as a novelist. I had just started *Small World*, and it seemed to me that the Villa Serbelloni would be a very appropriate place to work on this book. In the event, I was too late with my application to be accepted for the coming year, but the Rockefeller Foundation in New York encouraged me to reapply in the future. This I did, but in the meantime two things had happened. First, I had nearly finished *Small World*. Second, I had incorporated the Villa Serbelloni into it. For the more I had discovered and thought about the place in connection with my original application, the more irresistible it had become as a setting for part of my story, and I accordingly sent Morris Zapp to stay there (p. 151):

Morris was shown into a well-appointed suite on the second floor, and stepped out on to his balcony to inhale the air, scented with the perfume of various spring blossoms, and to enjoy the prospect. Down on the terrace, the other resident scholars were gathering for the pre-lunch aperitif – he had glimpsed the table laid for lunch in the dining-room on his way up: starched white napery, crystal glass, menu cards. He surveyed the scene with complacency. He felt sure he was going to enjoy his stay here. Not the least of its attractions was that it was entirely free. All you had to do, to come and stay in this idyllic retreat, pampered by servants and lavishly provided with food and drink, given every facility for reflection and creation, was to apply.

Of course, you had to be distinguished – by, for instance, having applied successfully for other, similar handouts, grants, fellowships and so on, in the past. That was the beauty of the academic life, as Morris saw it. To those that had, more would be given.

As readers of the novel will know, a punishment awaits Morris's hubristic enjoyment of this ultimate academic freebie: later in the story he is kidnapped by Italian political extremists while jogging in the grounds of the Villa and held to ransom.

Since I knew I would have finished the book before I got to Bellagio, I could not make it the project of my second application. Accordingly, I applied this time in my capacity as academic literary critic, proposing to work on an article on the form of Jane Austen's novels, commissioned for inclusion in *The Jane Austen Companion*, edited by J. David Grey, A. Walton Litz and Brian Southam (published by Macmillan in 1986).

The two sides of my schizophrenic existence were now set on a collision course, though I did not know it. I vaguely supposed that my novel would either be published well before my arrival at the Villa Serbelloni, in which case I would have to grin and bear the amusement and/or disapproval of my hosts and fellow guests, in a manner to which I was accustomed; or (preferably) it would appear after my departure, in which case nothing need be said about it. A better plot-maker than I, however, contrived that the novel was published on 19 March 1984, just a couple of weeks before I set off to spend my appointed month at Bellagio. I flew straight from a hectic fortnight of interviews, bookshop promotions and anxious scrutiny of the review pages to the peace and beauty of the Italian Lakes.

The Villa Serbelloni, I was glad to discover, corresponded in every particular to my description of it in the novel, based on data obtained from various informants. But professional satisfaction at this achievement was qualified by a certain unease about my own position there. The charming and gracious Italian administrators of the Villa knew nothing of *Small World*; neither did my fellow-guests, most of whom had flown direct from North America and were not aficionados of contemporary fiction. Indeed, nobody knew even that I was a novelist, for I appeared on the current list of residents, supplied by the Foundation in New York, as a Professor of English Literature, working on Jane

Austen. (There was a nice additional irony here, since Morris Zapp was also a Jane Austen man – in his own words, *'the* Jane Austen man' – before he converted to deconstruction). What was I to do? It has never been my style to invite discussion of my fiction. I certainly didn't feel like volunteering the information that I had just published a satirical novel about academic globe-trotters in which one of the chief characters was kidnapped while jogging in the grounds of the Villa Serbelloni. So I said nothing about it; and of course the more time that passed, the more difficult it became to say anything.

The time passed very agreeably. Villa life was as comfortable and civilized as it was reputed to be. The sun shone; the company was agreeable. A jolly professor of nursing from Winnipeg proposed that we all collaborated on writing a thriller to be called *Murder at the Villa Serbelloni*, and was disappointed by my lack of enthusiasm for the project. My wife, freed from her teaching job by the Easter holidays, arrived to share the last two weeks of my stay. She has her own very good reasons for not advertising the fact that she is married to a novelist (*vide* the conversation between Fulvia Morgana and Morris Zapp, above), and was only too pleased to preserve my 'cover', but I suffered from a lingering sense of guilt, or bad faith, and occasional spasms of longing to confess. It seemed to me that it was only a matter of time before I was found out.

One day a fellow guest who had gone to Milan to meet his wife returned without her (her flight had been delayed) but with a Penguin copy of *Ginger You're Barmy*, which he had picked up from the airport bookstall. He confronted me with it and genially accused me of hiding my light under a bushel. My cover was partly blown, but still nobody seemed to have heard of *Small World*. The Study Centre is also used for short, select international conferences, and on two occasions during April about thirty people flew in from various parts of the world, including Britain, for this purpose, and joined us at meals. I was sure one of them would have a copy of *Small World* in their luggage, or at least a newspaper cutting, for the book had been widely reviewed in England; but this never happened. The Villa itself did not subscribe to British newspapers, but it did take the *London Review of Books* and it seemed to me that this was the most likely medium through which news of *Small World* would travel to Bellagio. No review had appeared in the pages of that journal, however, by the time my period of residence came to an end. I shook hands with our hosts and fellow guests with my guilty secret still intact, resolving that as soon as I got home I would write a letter to the chief administrator, confessing all and donating a copy of *Small World* to the Villa's library.

This I did, and in due course both letter and book were received and acknowledged with great good humour. But amongst the heap of mail that awaited me on our return home was the latest issue of the *London Review of Books*, containing a review by Frank Kermode of *Small World*, which must have arrived in the library of the Villa Serbelloni shortly after I left. It was, I am glad to say, a very favourable review, but that wasn't what struck me most forcibly about it. It was entitled – by whom, I do not know, nor upon what whim, or with what telepathic insight, for it was not the most obvious of headings – 'Jogging in Bellagio'.

NOTES

1 David Lodge, *Small World: An Academic Romance* (London, Secker & Warburg, 1984) pp. 134–5. All page references are to this edition.
2 Ian Watt, *The Rise of the Novel* (Harmondsworth, Penguin Books, 1963) p. 32.
3 Robert Weimann, 'Appropriation and Modern History in Renaissance Prose Narrative,' *New Literary History*, XIV, 1983, p. 478.
4 Henry Fielding, *Joseph Andrews* (1742), Ch. XV.
5 *Changing Places: A Tale of Two Campuses* (London, Secker & Warburg, 1975).
6 Since this was written, the University announced the result of a MORI poll it commissioned into the effect of the series on viewers' perception of Birmingham University. 61 per cent of viewers apparently felt 'that the campus featured in the programme is attractive'. And even though the story is about a lecturer at 'the University of Rummidge', a majority of all viewers mentioned spontaneously that the programme was filmed at Birmingham.

12 Word and World

Laurence Lerner

I

One of the most famous moments in English poetry occurred when Wordsworth walked from Hawkshead to Ambleside around 1784. The moment, he tells us, 'was important in my poetical history' – and not only his: 'for I date from it consciousness of the infinite variety of natural appearances which had been unnoticed by the poets of any age or country, so far as I was acquainted with them; and I made a resolution to supply, in some degree, the deficiency'.[1]

A century and a half later John Crowe Ransom published *The World's Body*, a critical manifesto which claimed that the aim of true poetry is 'only to realise the world' – that is, the full 'body and solid substance of the world'. This gives us a form of knowledge which is not the abstract knowledge of science but an attempt to make up for the abstractions of science by offering us the physical world 'rendered richly and wastefully'. The aim of art is to 'reconstitute the world of perceptions'. Plato could see no sense in the artist's imitation of natural objects, but not only is that a valuable task, 'I suggest that the artist is not necessarily doing anything else'.[2]

It is not difficult to see the resemblance between these two statements, made by such very different poets and in very different circumstances. For both of them, the proper task of poetry is the rendering of the physical world in all its particularities: the world's body is its infinite variety of natural appearances. Whether or not Wordsworth was right that this had hitherto been unnoticed by any age or country, it certainly fills the century and a half that follows. As Charles Kingsley urged: 'Study the forms and colours of leaves and flowers, and the growth and habits of plants; not to classify them, but to admire them and to adore God. Study the sky! Study water! Study trees! Study the sounds and scents of nature!'

Elizabeth Gaskell's delightful anecdote in *Cranford* makes the point beautifully. The narrator is being taken for a walk through the fields by Mr Holbrook, elderly bachelor and enthusiastic gardener, and is a little discomposed by his eccentric habit of quoting poetry to himself:

We came upon an old cedar-tree, which stood at one end of the house;
> The cedar spreads his dark-green layers of shade

'Capital term – "layers!" Wonderful man!' I did not know whether he was speaking to me or not; but I put in an assenting 'wonderful', although I knew nothing about it; just because I was tired of being forgotten, and of being consequently silent.

He turned sharp round. 'Aye! you may say "wonderful". Why, when I saw the review of his poems in "Blackwood", I set off within an hour, and walked seven miles to Misselton (for the horses were not in the way) and ordered them. Now what colour are ash-buds in March?'

Is the man going mad? thought I. He is very like Don Quixote.

'What colour are they, I say?' repeated he vehemently.

'I am sure I don't know, sir,' said I, with the meekness of ignorance.

'I knew you didn't. No more did I – an old fool that I am! till this young man comes and tells me. Black as ash-buds in March. And I've lived all my life in the country; more shame for me not to know. Black: they are jet-black, madam.'[3]

A gardener is clearly someone aware of the physical world in all its particularities, so the poet who can teach the gardener his own business is a triumphant example of the Wordsworth/ Ransom theory. Tennyson's rich and wasteful rendering of the physical world can be found everywhere in his work:

> He clasps the crag with crooked hands.
> Close to the sun in lonely lands,
> Ringed with the azure world he stands.
>
> The wrinkled sea beneath him crawls.
> He watches from his mountain walls.
> And like a thunderbolt he falls.[4]

This could claim to be a poem of pure description: the aim of each line is to make us *see*. We see the sea from above, like the eagle; we see the eagle from below, like the human watcher; we see his claws as a close-up, like (it is tempting to say) the television viewer.

Tennyson never went to the tropics, but tropical landscapes are common in his work – in 'Enoch Arden', in 'Locksley Hall', in 'The Lotos-Eaters':

> 'Courage!' he said, and pointed toward the land,
> 'This mounting wave will roll us shoreward soon.'
> In the afternoon they came unto a land
> In which it seemed always afternoon.
> All round the coast the languid air did swoon,
> Breathing like one that hath a weary dream.
> Full-faced above the valley stood the moon;
> And like a downward smoke, the slender stream
> Along the cliff to fall and pause and fall did seem.[5]

Because we tend to see the unfamiliar more vividly than the familiar, the exotic setting can be seen as a device to concentrate our attention; but because we can describe only what we have seen, the details must come from observation, so it is not surprising to learn that the last two lines were 'taken from the waterfall at Gavarnie, in the Pyrenees, when I was 20 or 21' – that is, not long before he wrote the poem.

Hopkins is perhaps an even better example than Tennyson. I take as example the first quatrain of 'Duns Scotus's Oxford':

Towery city and branchy between towers;
Cuckoo-echoing, bell-swarmed, lark-charmed, rook-racked, river-rounded;
The dapple-eared lily below thee; that country and town did
Once encounter in, here coped and poised powers . . .[6]

The poem says (as its title announces) that he lives in the same town as Duns Scotus, yet neither that trite observation nor the lines devoted to Duns have much interest. It is this opening description that gives the poem its distinction; the contrast of textures in the first line, the series of sense impressions in the second, reconstitute for us the world of perception.

It is not surprising, then, to find Hopkins writing in a letter, 'I have particular periods of admiration for particular things in nature; for a certain time I am astonished at the beauty of a tree, shape, effect, etc., then when the passion, so to speak, has subsided, it is consigned to my treasury of explored beauty'; or to find one of his greatest modern admirers, himself a poet, writing: 'to know this poet, one does not need dictionaries alone...: one must also have, or must also cultivate, some equivalence of pure sensation, some of Hopkins' own accurate emphatic cognition of the plants, trees, fruit, ... activities, perfumes, of all the phenomena at which he stared or to which he opened his senses...[7]

Hopkins, Tennyson – and Wordsworth? Although I have cited Wordsworth as the one who formulated this poetic programme, I must now add that it is largely absent from his poetry.[8] The Fermor note from which we began is attached to the following passage in 'An Evening Walk':

> Now, while the solemn evening shadows sail
> On slowly-waving pinions, down the vale;
> And, fronting the bright west, yon oak entwines
> Its darkening boughs and leaves, in stronger lines.
> 'Tis pleasant near the tranquil lake to stray
> Where, winding on along some secret bay,
> The swan uplifts his chest, and backward flings
> His neck, a varying arch, between his towering wings:
> The eye that marks the gliding creatures sees
> How graceful pride can be, and how majestic, ease...
> Long may they float upon this flood serene;
> Theirs be these holms untrodden, still, and green,
> Where leafy shades fence off the blustering gale,
> And breathes in peace the lily of the vale!...
> Thence issuing often with unwieldy stalk,
> They crush with broad black feet their flowery walk.[9]

That the passage is offered primarily as description is clear from the connecting phrases that hold it together: "'Tis pleasant...', 'Long may they...', which can be regarded as the verbal equivalents of pointing and murmuring with pleasure. But the description has a good deal of eighteenth-century clutter about it (evening is 'solemn', the swan illustrates human qualities, pride and ease), as well as eighteenth-century poetic diction ('flood serene') and conventional touches to provide the topos of the *locus ameonus* (the leafy shades provide shelter from 'the blustering gale'). Such writing would have seemed unsurprising and even old-fashioned in 1793: only two details seem directly to confront the infinite variety of natural appearances.

One is the second couplet, which Wordsworth himself singles out in his note, saying, 'This is feebly and imperfectly expressed, but I recollect distinctly the very spot where this first struck me. It was in the way between Hawkshead and Ambleside, and gave me extreme pleasure.' The couplet has some resemblance to the first line of 'Duns Scotus's Oxford', and the comparison is surely to Hopkins's advantage. Both poets have looked at branches against the sky, but only Hopkins has thought of a contrast of textures. Less carefully accurate than Wordsworth's conscientious couplet, his line does more for the world's body. I wish instead of this 'feeble and imperfect' couplet Wordsworth had singled out the last line above: to notice that swans' feet are black may not require as keen an eye as to notice the colour of ash buds, but to mention it as part of the rendering of the birds' ungainly walk, and to describe that in a number of clumping monosyllables (poetic diction leans always to the polysyllabic) is to prefer pure observation over conventional poetic expectations.

But this is after all Wordsworth's juvenilia, and long before he apologized for it in his note he had already apologized for the whole poem in a letter of 1801, in terms which contain exactly the same mixture of satisfaction and disparagement: 'they are juvenile productions, inflated and obscure, but they contain many new images and vigorous lines'. In fairness, we ought to turn to his mature work; and when we do so, we do not find that he has improved in the rendering of the infinite variety of natural appearances, but rather the contrary. This is how the physical world appears to the later Wordsworth:

> Magnificent
> The morning rose, in memorable pomp,
> Glorious as e'er I had beheld – in front,
> The sea lay laughing at a distance; near,
> The solid mountains shone, bright as the clouds,
> Grain-tinctured, drenched in empyrean light;
> And in the meadows and the lower grounds
> Was all the sweetness of a common dawn –
> Dews, vapours, and the melody of birds,
> And labourers going forth to till the fields.[10]

These wonderful lines describe Wordsworth's moment of dedication to poetry ('I made no vows, but vows / Were then made for me'), arising out of a moment of heightened awareness and communion with Nature. They are like Adam opening his eyes and seeing the splendour; their force lies in the feeling that the world is now being seen for the first time. Of course, it is not the first time, and the passage must therefore register the copresence of newness and familiarity: hence the line 'Was all the sweetness of a common dawn', where the slight emphasis that the rhythm lays on 'all' and 'common' renders the awe with which the ordinary has been transfigured, while remaining ordinary. There is empyrean light, but there must then be everyday details, representative, familiar and suddenly *seen*; there must be a list that the voice can tell off in delighted surprise, a list in which no item surprises. These lines have more important matters to deal with than the infinite variety of natural appearances.

One could probably make a similar case for Ransom, whose poetry does not show great interest in rich and wasteful rendering of the world's body. But we read poet/critics for what they preach as well as for what they practise, and there is little doubt that the view I have been describing was both practised and preached all through the nineteenth century. Here, to round things off, is a poem that does both:

> When the present has latched its postern behind my tremulous stay,
>   And the May month flaps its glad green leaves like wings,
> Delicate-filmed as new-spun silk, will the neighbours say,
>   'He was a man who used to notice such things'?
>
> If it be in the dusk when, like an eyelid's soundless blink,
>   The dewfall-hawk comes crossing the shades to alight
> Upon the wind-warped upland thorn, a gazer may think,
>   'To him this must have been a familiar sight'. . . .[11]

The poem preaches the Wordsworth/Ransom doctrine: as the speaker hopes that he will be remembered for his awareness of the infinite variety of natural appearances; and it practises what it preaches, as we see in the meticulous description of leaves in a spring breeze, or of the silent landing of the hawk on a branch. If the poem derived its details from the expected topos, the bird would be a raven, bird of death, but instead of that it comes from the next field, and flies off into the lines with the unfussy familiarity of a real, unsymbolic hawk. The poem both claims and demonstrates that a poet is a man who notices such things.

II

It is now time to say that the relation between language and the world which this discussion has so far assumed could be considered naïve. If language is a window, the relation between words and the world is unproblematic, and in looking at the referent we do not think about the sign: as long as the window is clean and unflawed, we see the object. But if things were as unproblematic as that, there would be no need for semiotics. The opposite view of language is that which sees it as a self-contained system, in which linguistic elements can refer only to other linguistic elements, since it is not possible to break completely out of the system of text. Poetry can be seen as the extreme example of such a view of language, especially if we stress its elements of verbal play. Poetry does not invite us to push aside the sign in order to arrive at the referent, but to linger on the behaviour of the signs themselves, delighting in the dance they perform, not in order to tell us something, but for the sake of the dance. The image of the dance comes from Valéry, who compared prose to walking and poetry to dancing, the aim of the former being to arrive somewhere (as the function of a window is to enable you to arrive at the sight of something outside), the aim of the latter being contained within itself.[12] The image of the game says something very similar, since a game is not a means of communication, not a transitive activity whose purpose is to achieve an objective outside itself. We watch or take part in a game in order to admire or exercise the skill required to play it well.

It is not difficult, in modern criticism, to find examples of such a view of poetry. Michael Riffaterre believes that we misread poems because of the referential fallacy, the belief 'that words mean by referring to a reality without the pale of language', whereas 'the very core of the literary experience is that perceiving mode known as intertextuality. The text refers not to objects outside of itself, but to an intertext. The words of the text signify not by referring to things, but by presupposing other texts.'[13] This concept of intertextuality draws together a number of traditional critical practices: the intertext may be a particular poem, in which case we are dealing with allusion or influence; it may be a kind of poem, in which case we are dealing with genre; or it may be a set of verbal practices that conjoin in poems when a particular subject crops up, in which case we are dealing with a topos.

Perhaps the most influential proponent of the view that poetry is not a window is Roman Jakobson, and for a convenient and trenchant statement we can turn to one of his early essays: 'Poeticity is present when the word is felt as a word and not a mere representation of the object being named or an outburst of emotion, when words and their composition, their meaning, their external and inner form acquire a weight and value of their own instead of referring indifferently to reality.'[14]

Let us therefore set against the Wordsworth/Ransom view of poetry what I will call the Valéry/Jakobson view, which focuses on the poet as the manipulator of language, the skilful player, the inventor of new dance steps, inviting us to delight in his verbal dexterity and not to move outside the universe of language. Let us, that is, turn from world to word, and look for illustrations of that theory.

And this is where the shock comes. There is no need to replace the examples we have already discussed by other, contrasting poems. The same ones will do. They will do particularly well.

Before we turn to the examples, it is necessary to clear up one apparent ambiguity. Is skill displayed in the flawless execution of existing steps or the invention of new ones? To take the example of metre, is supreme craftsmanship shown in Pope's mastery of the heroic couplet (which all his contemporaries used) or in Donne's brilliant invention of new stanza forms? These seem to be two very different concepts of what we mean by 'feeling the word as a word', by attending to the medium not the referent.

But it may be that the difference is more apparent than real. The skilful chess player does not, obviously, change the rules of chess; what he does is invent new combinations or unexpected variations within familiar patterns. Pope's mastery of the couplet does not simply consist in causing the stress to fall with unerring accuracy on the second, fourth, sixth, eighth and tenth syllables; any minor eighteenth-century poet can do that. It consists in varying the place of the caesura, or in inserting an occasional trochee or spondee, or (more important) in playing speech rhythm against metrical pattern so that we can hear both, or (more important still) in playing semantic against metrical patterns. And Donne's new stanzas are not created *ex nihilo*: they are new combinations of familiar line lengths, and of the two basic rhyming patterns, successive and alternating. Unless we could recognize the competent handling of these elements, we would not admire the newness of the combination. The emphasis may vary, but craftsmanship is always a mixture of new and old, though since it tends to be the new which strikes us, it is that, rather than the old, which is likely to be mentioned in descriptions of a poet's technical skill.

As we can see if we turn to 'The Eagle'. This seems very conventional in its technique, yet it can also be seen as innovative (that remark applies to most of Tennyson!). It has three alliterations in the first line, prominently placed, calling attention to themselves; once the line is over, there is no more alliteration. It is like an opening display of skill, that need not be repeated. Why three? Enough to be prominent no doubt, and more would begin to look grotesque; but there may be another reason. The poem is in a rather unusual three-line stanza, and the three alliterations may draw attention to the unit of three – as does the prominent and unusual rhyme-scheme, aaa bbb. None of this has anything to do with the eagle, yet readers do not wish it away. It is a bravura element, announcing that this is a poem to attend to; and so announces that its description is likely to be worth attending to as well.

'*The Lotos-Eaters*' is more ingenious in its artistry. Tennyson remarked of the first three lines, '"The strand" was, I think, my first reading, but the no rhyme of "land" and "land" was lazier.' The laziness of the subject-matter has been transposed into the verbal behaviour, so that we are invited to admire the (unlazy) skill which has caused the stanza to behave with such apparent laziness. Such skill pervades the stanza, in the assonance of 'weary dream' (to slow us down), the alliteration of 'smoke . . . slender . . . stream', and the assonance that chose the same vowel for the succession of verbs and pauses in the last line.

We can discuss the Hopkins in a similarly technical way. Much of the effect of the first line derives from the adjectival form chosen. English adjectives ending in y often have the feel of nonce words: they attribute, with a kind of vague gesture, a not very clearly defined quality to the person or place or scene. They have a semantic quality that is something like the feathery scatter of small branches against the sky, so that 'branchy' is a perfect example of Jakobson's formula of equivalence: the word as word is equivalent to the word as sign. But the line contains two adjectives ending in y, and a tower has, visually, just the opposite qualities. To speak of 'towery city', then, is to defy equivalence on one level, while on another to suggest that the towers have lost their firmness of outline, that the watcher is looking at them with unfocused gaze.

The second line is certainly a bravura performance: five compound adjectives, each made up of noun and past participle, has lost all link with natural speech: the words do not walk, they perform. The participle derives, in each case, from what the noun does, so that the list of very miscellaneous sense impressions is held in a recurring semantic pattern. To this a few extra flourishes are added: the eye-rhyme of 'swarmed/charmed', the contrast between the harsh monosyllabic 'rook-racked' and the softer 'river-rounded', with its voice consonants, along with the shared alliteration.

As for Hardy's 'Afterwards', is there any semantic reason why the Present latches a 'postern' behind him, and not simply a gate – apart from the alliteration with 'Present'? Has the alliteration in 'May month' and 'glad green' (as well as 'wind-warped') anything to do with the exact rendering of Nature, or is it pure decoration? On 'postern' there may be an answer: the speaker is not an important enough person to have been shown out by the main door, and so is hinting to us that his poem is going to be minor, or quaint – an unofficial variation on the solemn poems about death. The man who used to notice such things, then, is not a poet with his singing robes on, his lips touched by the Muse, but a simple countryman who uses the back entrance; just as it is not the critics, or the writers of obituaries, to whom he appeals for remembrance, but the neighbours. All this constitutes a self-regarding point, in which the poem tells us what kind of poem it is. We can also see 'tremulous stay' as an example of equivalence, in contrast to the firm monosyllable of 'stay', ending the line like a door stop, 'tremulous' sounds a tremulous word, and makes the speaker even less at home, even more likely to slip out through the postern.

The bird in the second stanza does not come from the iconography of death, but the diction does cause it to cross not the shadows (the normal word in this case) but the 'shades', which clearly come to the poem from Greek mythology, and introduce the death topos. This topos appears again in the final stanza:

> And will any say when my bell of quittance is heard in the gloom,
>   And a crossing breeze cuts a pause in its outrollings,
> Till they rise again, as they were a new bell's boom,
>   'He hears it not now, but he used to notice such things'?

The sense impression so carefully recorded here has nothing to do with the meaning of the bell, which could be announcing Sunday morning service instead of being his bell of quittance, and still be cut off by the crossing breeze. But the fact that it is a funeral bell belongs closely with 'he hears it not now', for the bell is announcing that he is no longer there to hear anything. The poem itself is a bell of quittance; it tells its readers not only that Hardy cannot hear the bell any longer but also that he cannot read the poem either. Yet the poem he cannot read contains his own awareness that he cannot read it, or see the spring leaves; and also contains the spring leaves themselves in all their vividness. We seem to be faced with an Escher picture, in which a hand draws itself, and the poem becomes a self-consuming artefact.

III

Here, then, is a paradox: two contrasting, even opposed theories of poetry, and the passages that best illustrate the one turn out to be the very passages that best illustrate the other. To resolve it, I suggest we need the notion of stereotypes.

We can make sense of the booming, buzzing confusion we live in only by imposing patterns on it: language itself is the main instrument for doing this, and words can be seen as devices for showing similarities between our experiences – that is, for assimilating them to stereotypes. But since a vivid awareness of any sense experience is likely to emphasize its uniqueness, the organization of experience by means of language will be unjust to each particular moment. If the variety of natural appearances is infinite, their uniqueness cannot be represented by ordinary language, where the number of words is limited and the number usually deployed very limited indeed. White curtains, coloured women, red wheelbarrow are phrases which suppress particularity. But communication is only possible through language, and therefore to convey our awareness of particularity we need to use language against language, we need to prise off the smoothing clutch of words by using other, sharper words.

Words are sharpened by linguistic inventiveness: by departing from stereotypes, words can free perception from their constricting hold. Inventiveness can also be practised for its own sake, as a game: this does not prevent it from serving this other, contrasting function, as bodily organs (the mouth, the nose, the penis, the hand) can have several functions that do not interfere with each other. We can call this overdetermination, or plurality of function, and it enables us to answer Riffaterre. He is a perceptive and at times a brilliant reader of poetry, able to show us exactly how words or phrases operate to create meaning. Their operation includes drawing on intertextual significance, and by teasing out what the language of Rimbaud's 'Le loup criait' owes to the code of hunger, he makes a puzzling poem totally coherent and powerful. But this teasing-out was preceded by the assertion that the text 'refers *not* to objects outside of itself, *but* to an intertext' (my italics). Why must we be faced with these incompatible alternatives? That the poem draws on an intertext no more prevents it from referring to the infinite variety of natural appearances than the fact that the mouth is used for eating prevents it from speaking, or vice versa. But whereas in the case of the mouth we merely want to say that the one function does not interfere with the other, in the case of poetry I am proposing that the intertextual reference actually aids the mimetic function.

In a small way the title of this essay can, I hope, claim to illustrate its argument. What is the point of the sound echo in 'word' and 'world'? I could, after all, have called the essay 'Language and Experience': that would have been as accurate but less fun, and also less distinctive (there must be lots of essays with that title). Partly, the point is to play a game: the fact that 'word' and 'world' have no etymological connection makes the wordplay arbitrary, and their conjunction merely entertaining. But it also invites us to wonder if these two unconnected vocables will turn out after all to have something in common, if amusing ourselves with the crooked hands of linguistic enjoyment will help us to clasp the crag which is the world's body.

NOTES

1. Fermor note to 'An Evening Walk', Wordsworth's *Poetical Works*, edited by De Selincourt (Oxford, 1940), Vol. 1, p. 318.
2. John Crowe Ransom, *The World's Body* (New York, Scribners, 1938).
3. Elizabeth Gaskell, *Cranford* (1853), Ch. 4.
4. Alfred, Lord Tennyson, 'The Eagle' Fragment, 1851, in C. Ricks (ed.), *The Poems of Tennyson*, (Longmans, 1969), p. 495.
5. Tennyson, 'The Lotos-Eaters', 1832, ll. 1–9, in Ricks (ed.), *The Poems of Tennyson*, p. 430.
6. Gerard Manley Hopkins, 'Duns Scotus's Oxford', 1879, ll. 1–4, in Gardner (ed.), *Poems of Gerard Manley Hopkins* (Oxford, 1948), p. 84.
7. Geoffrey Grigson, *Gerard Manley Hopkins* (London, British Council, 1955), p. 8.
8. One critic who has noticed this is Donald Davie; see *Articulate Energy* (London, Routledge, 1955), p. 107: 'Wordsworth's world is not pre-eminently a world of "things". His language has not, in St-John Perse's sense, "weight and mass".'
9. William Wordsworth, 'An Evening Walk', ll. 212–21, 232–5, 242–3, in *Poetical Works*, edited by De Selincourt, p. 23.
10. Wordsworth, *The Prelude*, 1850, IV 324–32, *ibid.*, Vol. IV, p. 127.
11. Thomas Hardy, 'Afterwards', 1917, ll. 1–8, in Hardy's *Collected Poems* (London, Macmillan, 1962), p. 521.
12. See, for instance, '*Au sujet de cimetière marin*', *Variété* III (Paris, Gallimard, 1936), especially p. 67.
13. Michael Riffaterre, 'Interpretation and Undecidability', *New Literary History*, Winter 1981, Vol. 12, p. 227ff.; see also 'Interpretation and Descriptive Poetry', *New Literary History*, Vol. 4, p. 229ff. The latter article shows, insistently, that everything we get from the poem comes from attending to the language: the more we attend, the more we get. It is difficult to imagine any serious critic denying this, and it does not show that the language is non-referential.
14. Roman Jakobson, 'What is Poetry?' *Selected Papers*, Vol. 3, p. 750.

13 From Ascesis to Conversion: René Girard and the Idea of Vocation in Modernist Writing

Stephen Bann

Criticism and biography have tended to keep their distances in the study of Modernist literature. At the height of the Romantic period, it was possible for a critic like Prosper de Barante to cause a certain stir by proclaiming that he would 'investigate the relationships which the works of Schiller have with the character, the situation and the opinions of the author, and with the circumstances which surrounded him'. As a close friend and disciple of Madame de Stael, Barante had gradually worked himself round to the view that classical conventions should be jettisoned in favour of a contextual and historical approach. By contrast, Modernism – in the guise of its critical fellow traveller, the New Criticism – has worked heroically to expel the shadows of history from the celebration of literature. At a recent exhibition of the manuscripts and editions of Pound's *Cantos* it was recalled that the poet was awarded the Bollingen Prize in February 1949, just four years after his arraignment for treason in liberated Italy. Controversy was undoubtedly provoked by the award, but the very decision to make it reflected 'the growing hegemony of the New Criticism', and their advocacy of 'the radical separation of literary works from their historical contexts'.

Of course, such an opposition is apt to seem far more absolute when it acquires a fixed and mythic form, than when it is tracked through the labyrinth of a sophisticated and many-layered critical position. Roland Barthes is well known for having published, in 1968, a brief and incisive text on 'The Death of the Author'. This deliberately paradoxical title is apt to make us forget that Barthes is above all interested in conjuring up the possibility of a creative role for the reader ('the birth of the reader must be at the cost of the death of the Author'). It is also liable to obscure the fact that Barthes was entirely ready, at a decade's distance, to advocate an author-friendly criticism. An 'affectionate criticism' was what he commended in his review of Phillippe Sollers's *H*, which would enable one to 'include in the reading of a text the knowledge that we might have its author'. Admittedly, this eavesdropping of the author's life was not to be its own justification, but, once again, an enlargement of the creative prerogative of the reader: if we read '*over the shoulder* of the one who writes', it is as if 'we were writing at the same time as he'.

But what if the Modernist author refuses to offer his shoulder to the prying critic? At least as significant as the critic's tendency to proclaim the liquidation of history, and the author's death, is the devilish ability of the author himself to evade capture. There are indeed a number of Modernist, and pre-Modernist, authors who appear to have conceived their life's work as a strategy for disappearing into the text. Readers of Proust were generally excited, a quarter of a century ago, when George Painter began to publish his exceptionally detailed biographical study. Few can fail to have been disillusioned, after a short time, as the pasteboard figures of the Belle Epoque succeeded one another in his pages, scantily justifying their existence by the hypothesis that they had lent a trait, here and there, to a Duchesse de Guermantes or a Swann. A lesson might have been learned perhaps from the first (and still most circumstantial) biography of Proust's admired precursor, Walter Pater, where the unfortunate author, Thomas Wright, turns in desperation to composing the 'imaginary portrait' of one of Pater's self-proclaimed friends, the egregious Richard Jackson.[1] At least in this way Wright succeeds in writing, in spite of himself, a legitimate tribute to Pater, where the most recent biographer, Michael Levey, loses himself in the amateurish attempt to find psychosexual constants in the mythic texture of Pater's prose.[2]

All I can hope to have shown, up to this point, is that there is a type of critical strategy which maintains, as a necessary fiction, the idea of the 'Death of the Author', and that there is a type of biographical approach which trivializes (to the point of completely disregarding) the subtle interrelations between the text and the author's life. But what if the modern critic chose to take his stand upon an issue which belongs neither to the world of the text, conceived as an autonomous linguistic entity, nor to the social world, conceived as a concrete historical milieu: the idea of an artistic vocation? André Green, the French psychoanalytic critic, has devised the attractive term 'the text of the life' to account for the fact that the lives of some writers are indeed written out in filigree in some of their works, though this is not the social 'life' that the writer experienced: it is a 'figure in the carpet', visible only to the extent that the person in question succeeded in concretizing their obsessions in an intelligible form. The idea of a vocation seems a similarly problematic one, neither a textual effect nor a biographical fact, but a structure whose implications are to be registered across the whole field of experience. What kind of evidence should we take for the existence of a vocation? How are we to judge if it was genuine or false? Indeed, does this distinction have any meaning at all? Is there any reason to suppose that the sense of having been 'called' to be an artist affects, in any intelligible way, the achievement of what we still persist in terming a 'life's work'?

The contemporary figure who has provided the most forthright answers to this chorus of sceptical questions is, without any doubt, Jean-Paul Sartre. In his biographical studies of Genet, Baudelaire and Flaubert, and indeed in his writer's autobiography, *Words*, Sartre has persistently maintained that the decision to become an artist is a psychological event of extraordinary interest and complexity. We choose to commit ourselves to the world of 'words', but we do so within the grip of social and especially familial circumstances which help to explain the bizarre significance of our 'choice of the unreal'. In *Words* Sartre makes use of the happy abundance of information on his own biographical circumstances to frame a far-reaching diagnosis. Not only he but his family (or at least its male members) possessed a vocation. Charles, his grandfather, exercised it by dedicating himself to 'an attenuated form of spirituality, a priesthood . . .' – that is to say, he became a teacher. Yet he impressed the ambition for a nobler form of self-renunciation upon his grandson, who even as a child developed the yearning to set himself up 'above worldly possessions, of which [he] had none, and . . . would have found [his] vocation without difficulty in [his] comfortable penury'. The outcome of this process was, of course, Sartre's definitive commitment of himself to the ideal of being a writer, a choice which, even by the strenuous exorcism of *Words*, he is quite incapable of reversing. 'I have renounced my vocation, but I have not unfrocked myself. I still write. What else can I do?'

A special fascination comes through, in this account of a misapplied youth, whenever the name of Gustave Flaubert is mentioned, since Flaubert is, for Sartre, the type of the Modernist author, and the one whose 'choice of the unreal' has acquired the status of a triumphant myth. Sartre's monumental biography of Flaubert, *The Family Idiot*, which began publication in 1971 and was his last substantial work, is therefore a vehicle for his own personal investment, at the same time as it seeks to tease out the infinitely subtle ramifications of the writer's early experiences:

> We are saying that in order to resolve his inner conflicts, Gustave *made himself* into a writer. Yet from his earliest correspondence we learn that he wants to write. Was he then constituted as a *writer*? No, but little by little the meaning of that term becomes more precise and enriched: we raise ourselves from one revolution to the next on the totalizing spiral. I *will be* a writer ... Now we must reconstitute in all its phases the dialectical movement by which Flaubert progressively made himself into 'the-author-of-*Madame Bovary*.'

Sartre indeed pluralizes to an astonishing degree the notion of 'vocation', pointing out that Flaubert had to incorporate in his self-awareness the early experience of a calling for the stage. 'Why did he abandon the stage for literature, and what remained of his first "vocation" in his second?' Yet the ultimate significance of this whole drama of self-constitution is reduced, as we have seen, to a sobering conclusion. Flaubert has 'chosen the unreal'. 'Sensible children dream of the future: they will plant the flag in the new territory, they will save their fellow citizens by the thousands during a cholera epidemic, they will be rich, powerful, honoured.' Even though Sartre chooses to present the alternative ironically, the delusive character of the artist's vocation cannot be gainsaid.

A crucial factor underlies the apparently paradoxical character of Sartre's view of the artist's vocation. This is the link which he invariably detects between the very notion of vocation, in the artistic sense, and the religious commitment to which such a notion was, in the former history of the Western world, irretrievably linked. For Sartre, the artist's vocation is, as it were, doubly unreal: not only does it accept unreality in place of 'being' but it also derives its structure from a system of belief in which its practitioners no longer have any stake. Thus we have the painful image of the writer Gustave, for ever going over his manuscripts not (as his vulgar contemporaries thought) to obtain *'le mot juste'*, but to merit the gift of grace which he knows he will never, in fact, receive!

It is as if Sartre felt there to be no point in castigating religious belief as such (who, after all, would now spring to defend it?), and determined to assault the bad faith of the artistic vocation, conscious at the same time that his own practice as a writer was perversely contaminated with the same bad faith. But for René Girard, Sartre has chosen a more formidable adversary than he knows when he singles out the writer for his duplicitous attack:

In the eyes of the novelist, modern man suffers, not because he refuses to become fully and totally aware of his autonomy, but because that awareness, whether real or illusory, is for him intolerable. The need for transcendency seeks satisfaction in the human world and leads the hero into all kinds of madness. Stendhal and Proust, even though they are unbelievers, part company at this point with Sartre and Hegel to rejoin Cervantes and Dostoevsky. Promethean philosophy sees in the Christian religion only a humanism which is still too timid for complete self-assertion. The novelist, regardless of whether he is a Christian, sees in the so-called modern humanism a subterranean metaphysics which is incapable of recognising its own nature.

Girard wrote these words in 1961 – that is to say, three years before the first publication of *Words*, and ten years before *The Family Idiot*. And in his subsequent writings, as we shall see, he has considerably refined his idea of 'vocation' in the light of his intensive study of the Judaeo-Christian tradition. But already in *Deceit, Desire and the Novel*, as this extract testifies, he was able to formulate a critical strategy which credited the novelist with a self-knowledge incomparably superior to that of the anxiety-ridden philosopher. For him, Flaubert had not chosen the unreal, but, on the contrary, learned to confront the delusory creations of the Romantic mentality: 'When Flaubert cries, "Mme Bovary, c'est moi", he is not trying to say that Mme Bovary has become one of those flattering doubles with whom romantic writers love to surround themselves. He means that 'the Self and the Other have become one in the miracle of the novel.' In other words, Girard does not for a moment deny that the writer can be committed to a world of unreality in which the creatures of imagination simply serve to enhance and protect his own narcissism. But he holds at the same time that it is the writer, and perhaps particularly the novelist, who can learn how to defeat these blandishments and make a present of his self-knowledge to the reading public. The nineteenth-century novelist – and here Girard concentrates especially, as in his subsequent critical work, on Stendhal, Proust and Dostoevsky – has made us a present of the incomparably useful notion of the triangularity of desire. He has taught us that there is no desire for the other without a mediator, and thus desire springs not from the full subjectivity caressed by the Romantic artist, but from the capacity for imitation, or mimesis. Proust's narrator has already decided to give up Albertine when he learns of her possible infidelity, and immediately his obsession is reinforced. For Girard, this interposition of a third party is a decisive clarification of the very nature of desire.

Here we already have an estimate of the novelist's art which is diametrically opposed to that of Sartre. Where Sartre cannot get over the sense that the decision to write springs from a radical weakness in character, Girard shows the writer to be pre-eminently lucid: only he has the insight which will enable us to identify our own desire, and so compensate for the devastating effects of unchecked mimesis in the social sphere. Moreover, this striking difference is directly registered in the way in which Girard considers the idea of vocation. He does not for a moment deny that the artist's vocation is capable of being, as it is for Sartre's Flaubert, a 'choice of the unreal'. But he introduces a crucial distinction between the delusive and the real vocation which turns, as does everything in Girard's analysis, on their relative degrees of lucidity as regards the law of mimetic desire. '*Ascesis* in the service of desire', as it might be termed, is a self-denying discipline which merely endorses the reality of the triangular desire which engenders it. The true idea of vocation cannot simply be based on ascetic self-denial, but requires, in some form or other, the experience of conversion.

I am aware at this point that Girard seems to equivocate

between the idea of a vocation as it is lived by the artist and the fictional presentation of such lives as they occur in the novelist's writings. One of the examples which he gives for *'ascesis* in the service of desire' is Don Quixote doing amorous penance in honour of the Lady Dulcinea. But this apparent confusion is not inadvertent. It is immediately after these two citations that Girard accuses Hegel and Sartre of 'an inability to relinquish religious patterns of desire when history has outgrown them'. For him, it must be an essential part of the self-knowledge of the great novelist that he should detect, and expose in his writings, the fallacious notions of self-fulfilment that Western culture has generated, in its gradual replacement of a religious by a secular ethic. Don Quixote and Marcel are there to warn us, in their different ways, of how a misunderstanding of the law of mimetic desire can lead us astray, whether we be love-sick old gentlemen, apprentice writers or great philosophers.

Yet this *carte blanche* which is handed to the novelist does, at the final stages of *Deceit, Desire and the Novel*, come to appear remarkably generous, if not permissive. Girard states that: 'All novelistic conclusions are conversions.' In context, this statement is not a mere endorsement of the technical device of closure, but requires, once again, that we pay attention to the idea of vocation which can be unpacked from the overall structure, and development, of the narrative. Julien Sorel, having experienced the delusions of mimetic desire and having also practised the self-denying *ascesis*, comes to realize, when he is condemned to death, the slavery to which he has been bound and triumphs in the very experience of defeat. He is 'converted'. According to this logic, Proust defines the type of all novels (or all that fall into Girard's highest category) when he caps the narrator's career of enslavement to love, society and the false notion of artistic vocation with a final book in which self-renunciation is accompanied by the newfound ability to write. In this way, as Girard puts it: 'Every novelistic conclusion is a *Past Recaptured*.' Every such conclusion revolves around the moment of final lucidity, which is, in a real sense, the metaphor of the artist's 'panoramic vision'.

No doubt it is possible to be puzzled at the claims which are being made for the novelist's art in *Deceit, Desire and the Novel*. The high price which is being set on the capacity to detect the effects of 'mimetic desire' is connected implicitly to the assumption that such a principle is the dominant force in our modern culture. And yet little is done, at this stage, to persuade us of the fact. Girard had to make an immense detour, through the literature of the ancient world and also through the fields of anthropology and psychology, before he could present in full the cultural diagnosis of which mimetic desire was the most salient feature, and the one most accessible to the novelist's act of demystification. In particular, he had to compose the summa of his cultural investigations, *Things Hidden since the Foundation of the World* (1987), where Proust and Dostoevsky reappear once again, as touchstones of the knowledge which can be offered by the artist, but do so in a context which has become infinitely more suggestive in its ramifications.

The very magnitude of the scope of *Things Hidden* prevents me from giving more than a token reference to its major thesis in this essay. But a brief account must be given, if only because it helps to establish the credentials on which Girard ventures to dispute with Sartre, and the other *maîtres à penser* of the contemporary world. Girard reaches back into the history of the world before the emergence of man and detects mimesis, or imitative behaviour, as the primitive root of sociality. But what is it that allows 'hominisation' – the passage from the higher mammal to the human state – to take place? For Girard, it is the development of the 'scapegoat mechanism', which, in ensuring the unanimity of the group in the act of murdering the chosen victim, creates the definitive bond which expresses itself in human society. Girard freely acknowledges the insight of Freud in relation to this hypothesis: after all, Freud argued in *Totem and Taboo* that human society derived from the collective guilt of the sons who had murdered the aboriginal father. Yet, for Girard, Freud's explanation, though revealing, is inadequate. On the one hand, the Oedipal cast given to the founding murder is misleading: nothing but the fact of the escalation of mimetic desire is required to explain the motive for the choice of an exemplary victim since the imitation of the 'disciple' inevitably ends by provoking the hostility of the 'master'. On the other hand, Girard is far from accepting that the founding murder takes place once and for all: it must in fact be re-enacted, through the establishment of a sacrificial system, since the contagious effects of mimesis are always liable to precipitate a crisis and this remains the only way of resolving it.

Yet there is one solution to the problem of mimetic desire, which is writ large in the experience of modern society (according to Girard) precisely because the sacrificial systems used to conjure it away have lost their former efficacy. This is the unique power of demystification offered by the text of the Judaeo-Christian scriptures. Girard insists that the Crucifixion of Christ, anticipated in the Old Testament and described in the Gospels, is not simply a repetition of the sacrificial principle which has been built into human society from the very moment when it constituted itself as human. It is the utterly effective unmasking and repudiation of that principle. From the time of the Crucifixion – and even though it has taken two millennia to realize this in its full implications – it has been open to us to read a transparently clear message. Violence comes from man and not from God. It is indeed the precondition of human society, and hence the need to disavow its presence is a particularly strong one. This is what Christ means when he says: 'I will utter what has been hidden since the foundation of the world' (Matthew, 13, 35).

Obviously, Girard's overarching hypothesis (of which the foregoing account offers a necessarily schematic picture) does not alter his conviction that writers, also, can offer special kinds of illumination. But it adds a much higher degree of specificity to the experience which he has already identified as 'conversion'. In *Deceit, Desire and the Novel* he was content to observe that novelists like Stendhal and Proust, 'though they are unbelievers', conduct a kind of negative critique of 'modern humanism'. But the detailed demonstration of the links between mimetic desire, the sacrificial system and the demystificatory power of the Judaeo-Christian scriptures allows him to speak more positively and confidently. The hypothesis pursued so exhaustively in *Things Hidden* enables him to explain, not only the religious context of the unmasking of mimetic desire but also the reasons why such an identification had to be treated with considerable caution at the earlier stage. As Girard points out, the sacrificial mentality – which is capable of extending the status of a scapegoat to any and every human or cultural corpus – has in our own times taken as its victim the Judaeo-Christian tradition in itself, which it censors and relegates to nullity even if it cannot dismiss it altogether. Hence Guy Lefort (one of Girard's two interlocutors in *Things Hidden*) thinks it reasonable to remark, after Girard has spoken of the 'fall' which is necessary to turn a person into a great writer: 'Argue that such a form of experience really exists and is similar to what has always been called religious experience, and most of our contemporaries will see red. Something makes the very thought of it intolerable – something that must be bound up with the almost universal hostility toward Judaeo-Christian ideas.'

Since *Deceit, Desire and the Novel* Girard has added to his stock of novelists whose career demonstrates the effects of a 'fall' or conversion. He has, for example, written illuminatingly about the process in relation to Albert Camus's *La chute* and *L'étranger*. But his prime example, revived with a considerable amount of additional detail in *Things Hidden*, remains the work of Proust. It is Proust who is used to demonstrate the finest perceptions of the working of the law of mimetic desire, when he anatomizes the respective movements of the 'little band' of girls, disporting themselves on the promenade at Balbec to the pleasure and mortification of the timid narrator. It is also Proust who is invoked as the most telling example of an artist who has abandoned his former self and acquired self-knowledge: the subsection which introduces this theme is called, quite simply, *Proust's Conversion*. In *Deceit, Desire and the Novel* Girard pointed to a recondite but fascinating text in order to characterize Proust's attainment of the artist's lucidity. In the strange article, 'The Filial Sentiments of a Parricide', published in *Le Figaro* by the young writer in 1907, reference is made to a double tragedy which had occurred to a family which the Prousts slightly knew: Henri Van Blarenberghe had killed himself after murdering his mother. The source of Proust's interest in this sad story is exactly conveyed, as Girard relates, by the supposition that the parricide, even he, is accessible to remorse and conversion. Proust refers to 'that belated moment of lucidity which may occur even in lives completely obsessed by illusions', and he then leaves us in no doubt that he is already thinking in terms of the self-knowledge of a *fictional* character when he adds, 'since it happened even to Don Quixote'.

We can see that there is no reason for Girard to posit a strictly biographical origin for Proust's 'conversion'. Unlike Sartre, he does not need to commit himself to explaining, indeed to over-explaining, the significance of a supposedly crucial juncture like Flaubert's accident in the carriage, driving back from Deauville, on a dark evening in January 1844. For Girard, the crisis of mimetic desire, and the strategies for overcoming it, are already so irretrievably programmed into the writings of our culture that there is hardly any need to localize the moment of the artist's decision. All that we need to know is that, at one point, a particular writer was performing under the handicap of a misguided vocation – possibly the misconceived ascesis which Girard attributes to the young Marcel. At a later stage, however, he displays all the evidence of having experienced a change of heart. In *Deceit, Desire and the Novel* Girard relates that change of heart to the 'belated moment of lucidity' with which the parricide reviews his wasted life, implying that what for Van Blarenberghe became a motive for suicide could, for the artist, be an acceptance of the magnitude of the self-renunciation necessary for literary work. In *Things Hidden* he relates it to a new, and perhaps more far-reaching example: the radical change in the conception of the 'hero' which strikes us if we compare the early novel *Jean Santeuil* with the mature achievement of *A la recherche*. *Jean Santeuil* is, for Girard, 'like a working model of the theory of narcissism'. That is to say, it represents a hero whose boundless egoism reflects 'the Romantic and Symbolist aesthetic at its most banal'. By contrast, the Proustian narrator in *A la recherche* is recognizable specifically because he has withdrawn his desire from the delusions of society and no longer feels the need to establish a model of subjectivity upon which all other desires converge: 'The late Proust knows that narcissism has no existence *in itself*: he knows that to represent desire in a convincing manner, you must represent it from outside the Guermantes' box, unable to gain access. Desire should not attempt to make us believe that it is in control of the situation.'

For Girard, therefore, it is ultimately unnecessary to search the artist's biography for the evidence of his 'conversion', since the process is infallibly registered in the different strategies for mastering desire which he manifests in his 'early' and 'late' works. *Jean Santeuil* reflects the dominant aesthetic of Proust's youth, in presenting us with a hero who attracts the attention of the most distinguished members of society to his effulgent person. But *A la recherche*, by contrast, shows virtually the same milieu from a radically different perspective. It is precisely its function to expose the narcissistic investment of the would-be author and subject him to a long process of apprenticeship, at the end of which he is genuinely capable of the disinterested activity of creating a work of art. As Girard puts it concisely: 'The mediocrity of *Jean Santeuil* arises from the fact that the work still reflects back the image of himself that Proust, as a man and a writer, wanted to convey to others. By contrast, *A La Recherche* exposes this image and concentrates upon the why and wherefore of this strategy.'

Even if we have followed Girard's argument up to this point, and accepted its remarkable pertinence to the case of Proust, there remain at least two questions to be asked. The first bears on the specificity of literary creation within the context which Girard has sketched out. If we accept that 'conversion' is, in the last resort, a religious experience, how can we define the special role of writers who have had that experience as opposed to the numerous other categories of person who are presumably just as capable of having it? My first answer to this question, admittedly a quibble, is that visual artists also manifest the process of 'conversion' across the full extent of a career. In particular Cézanne, with his exemplary dedication to the 'priesthood' of art, can be shown to have undertaken a similar process of withdrawal from narcissistic investment as Girard indicates in the case of Proust.[3] But, as to the wider question of whether creative artists in general are specially vested with the lucidity which comes from 'conversion', the Girard of *Things Hidden* has a categorically negative answer. Such an experience is far from being reserved for them; indeed, it may well be that they are less prone to it than other people. Even if they have had it, it will not necessarily result in a flowering of late work. It may result in the simple decision not to write any more.

Such a conclusion is, no doubt, inevitable. In *Deceit, Desire and the Novel* Girard was still disposed to present the great novelists of his choice as exemplary in their unmasking of the laws of desire. But he was less sure about the historical and cultural context within which such a 'Christian', or at least anti-humanist, strategy acquired its meaning. Now that he has achieved, in *Things Hidden*, an incomparably greater mastery of the anthropological data and the scriptural texts, the role of writers like Proust is inevitably somewhat diminished. They may know more than Freud about the fundamental issues of psychology, but they are inevitably cast into the shade by the blinding light emitted by the Judaeo-Christian scriptures, as they fulfil their unique demystificatory role. 'No salvation outside Proust', would be a senseless slogan.

This brings us to the second question which must be addressed to Girard's work. Given that he has found a novel way of integrating the 'life' of an author with our critical judgement of his achievement, given that he has reinvigorated the tired concept of 'vocation' and suggested how we might learn to take it much more seriously, then how might his ideas help to illuminate our general awareness of the development of Modernist writing – for example, in the field of poetry, which he hardly touches at all in his critical work? In my own view, the most precious contribution which he has made is to focus on the notion that a 'vocation' can be true or false, according to whether it merely disavows or actually comprehends the investment of desire which is its inevitable component. Sartre, in his life of Flaubert and also in his autobiographical *Words*, cannot get away from the idea that a writer's vocation is inauthentic, a 'choice of the unreal'. Consequently, the entire proliferating edifice of his own writing on Flaubert, with its unremitting attention to the way in which the young man *'made himself'* into an artist, rests on the implausible presupposition that, for an authentic vocation, Flaubert would have done better to follow in his father's footsteps and become a surgeon. Girard has a term for the inauthentic vocation: it is *'ascesis* in the service of desire'. But he confronts and contrasts it with the idea of the authentic vocation, which can be discovered only as a result of the process of conversion.

I can provide just a few examples of how this distinction might illuminate our knowledge of the development of Modernism. First of all, it is important to recognize how important a part is played by the theme of 'ascesis' in defining the specially self-conscious dedication of the artist in the later nineteenth century (or, as Girard might put it, the Symbolist period). For

Swinburne and for Pater (whom I treat in this context as an honorary poet, since he is certainly not a conventional novelist), the idea of the ascetic youth, dedicated to an ideal higher than mere physical fulfilment, exerts a fascination which is undoubtedly connected to its significance as a surrogate for artistic activity. In Pater we have Marius the Epicurean and Gaston de Latour, on the broadest scale, but also the subjects of the many 'imaginary portraits' which shows purposive, vocational activity close to, though not identical with, the pursuit of art: Duke Carl of Rosenmold, Sebastian van Storck, the Hippolytus of 'Hippolytus veiled'. In Swinburne perhaps the most memorable example is Meleager, in *Atalanta in Calydon*, whose sexless dedication to the huntress Atalanta, and implicitly to the goddess Artemis, brings as an inevitable consequence his own destruction at the hands of earthier gods.

If we accept that ascesis is thus a privileged point of reference for these two writers, the next question follows strictly Girardian lines. How far does the presentation of the ascetic hero also involve an unmasking of the processes of desire which have been disavowed in the pursuit of a vocation, and to what extent does a process of conversion supervene? Obviously there is only space here for the merest suggestions of a type of reading that might prove productive.

To begin with, Swinburne might appear to be a fully fledged adherent of Girard's 'Promethean philosophy [which] sees in the Christian religion only a humanism which is still too timid for complete self-assertion'. Yet on closer inspection, it can be seen that his 'Promethean' commitment is no more self-assertive than the debased contemporary Christianity which he polemically tries to subvert. Swinburne is not Shelley, and one need only compare his elegy for Baudelaire, 'Ave atque vale', with Shelley's 'Adonais' to see that he utterly rejects the religion of nature with which the Romantic poet fuels his celebration of the immortal Keats.

Indeed, as Morse Peckham has argued, there is considerable significance in the way that Swinburne rejects the preoccupation with external (capitalized) Nature which characterized the Romantic poets, and turns to consider nature in its personalized, psychological sense. The author of *Poems and Ballads* offers us a complex analysis of the nullity of human desire, in the harsh light of which his artistic achievement could appear equally precarious. 'The Triumph of Time' describes the hypothetical union of the poet and his mistress in terms of a kind of ascesis *à deux*: 'I had grown pure as the dawn and the dew, / You had grown strong as the sun or the sea'. But the price of knowing the impossibility of this outcome is a bleak negation of the blandishments of art, which of course asserts its own special kind of artistry in the process.

Perhaps for a truly Girardian progression we should turn from 'The Triumph of Time' to a very different work, the neo-classical tragedy *Atalanta in Calydon*, which Swinburne began in the same year (1863), and completed in September 1864. Not only does the huntsman Meleager enact, in his pursuit of the wild boar and his love for the virgin huntress, an exemplary pattern of ascesis, but his final death, at the hands of his own mother, is accompanied by the searing self-revelation of man's psychological bondage. 'For there is nothing terribler to men / Than the sweet face of mothers, and the might.' This is Meleager's first intuition, which is compounded at the moment of death:

> Mother, I dying with unforgetful tongue
> Hail thee as holy and worship thee as just
> Who art unjust and unholy.

If Proust's 'conversion' (according to Girard's first analysis) can be linked with the odd 'Filial Sentiments of a Parricide', perhaps Meleager's dying words are also significant. Morse Peckham, at any rate, sees precisely this avowal as evidence for Swinburne's pre-Freudian awareness 'that in the familial relationship is rooted all that is most terrible in human nature'. Meleager acquires a final lucidity about the 'cognitive corruption of man' and accepts death in that knowledge, just as Henri Van Blarenberghe acknowledges his parricide and takes his own life. In both cases, it hardly needs to be said, the question is how these decisions are filtered through the consciousness of the artist, Proust or Swinburne.

In the works of Walter Pater we do not have to look far to find the idea of vocation, which could indeed be said to be the governing motif of his fiction. Marius the Epicurean is only the most elaborately characterized of a series of Paterian heroes who repeat (on the vulgar biographical level) Pater's own experience of finding his call to the Church barred in the period of early manhood. Of Marius, it can be stated: 'That first, early boyish ideal of priesthood, the sense of dedication, survived through all the distractions of the world, when all thought of such vocation had finally passed from him, as a ministry, in spirit at least, towards a sort of hieratic beauty and orderliness in the conduct of life.'

Is this simply the religion of art – that is to say, a religion which can only deplore its own lack of transcendence? The case is more complicated than that. In a study which still remains unique in its comprehensive understanding of Pater, Gerald Monsman emphasizes the consistency of Pater's idea of vocation, from the early stages represented by his poem 'Chant of the Celestial Sailors' to the final drafts of the unfinished Gaston de Latour, which Pater's friend Shadwell described as the 'spiritual development of a refined and cultivated mind'. But at no stage does the writer, in Monsman's view, abandon the possibility of an authentic religious experience or, to quote from Pater's own letters, 'a . . . sort of religious phase possible for the modern mind'. The question to be asked, in Girard's terms, is simply this: Does the Paterian ascesis allow for a form of transcendence that exists apart from the transcendence embodied in the work of art?

It does so, surely, in the sense that Pater does not precisely describe the lives, and vocations, of artists. Almost exclusively, he re-enacts lives that must be over and done with before the artistic flowering, the 'renaissance', can take place. Hippolytus, spiritual kinsman of Swinburne's Meleager, dies as a result of his determined chastity, but then he is resurrected, in the form of the lost play by Euripides which bears the same title as Pater's essay, 'Hippolytus veiled'. Duke Carl of Rosenmold, prince of a petty German state, arranges for his own symbolic funeral in order to facilitate a 'humanistic pilgrimage to the sources of culture'; his burial place is finally marked with the purposive inscription '*Resurgam*', and Pater marvellously transmutes his resurrected self into the spectacle of the young Goethe, skating on the ice. As Monsman puts it, Pater's heroes are not 'exiles without a goal', but 'pilgrims – those who will eventually find the lost form of the center after travelling the circumference'. A

Girardian interpretation would extend this distinction somewhat further. Pater does not confuse an artistic vocation with a strictly religious vocation, let alone see the latter as a surrogate for the former. If he is able to figure conversion only through the recurrent motif of death and resurrection, this is none the less an infallible sign of his dedication to a religious quest.

To extend this line of inquiry into the twentieth century is to take it outside the well-known context of the Victorian 'crisis of faith'. None the less, it may well be appropriate to look at Modernist writers in these terms, just as Girard looks at Camus. It is not difficult to see the idea of artistic vocation represented by a figure like Ezra Pound as, initially at any rate, fulfilling the imperatives of a narcissistic self-absorption. Pound's preoccupation with Sigismondo Malatesta, as a type of the 'New Man', testifies to an extraordinarily aggrandized sense of the artist's ego, with the condottiere's ascesis in the building of the Templo Malatestiano replacing the immediate desire of his love for Isotta. Yet, after his imprisonment and confinement to a mental hospital, Pound invests the Cantos with a new note of humility:

> 'Master thyself, then others shall thee beare'
>   Pull down thy vanity
> Thou art a beaten dog beneath the hail . . .

Certainly it would be consistent with Girard's hypothesis (in *Things Hidden*, at any rate) if the distressing experiences through which Pound purged his pride resulted in mere indications in his poetic work, and ultimately in a total disenchantment with his own vocation. But there is a more positive note to be struck if we look, finally, at one of the poets who was closest to Pound, at the early stages of her life, and yet produced a life's work with a more satisfying, cumulative shape to it.

H.D. is, in many respects, uncannily close to Swinburne and Pater in her conception of the idea of vocation, mediated as it is by the type of the 'intellectualised, crystalline youth'. I am not referring to the H.D. of the Imagist period, who still regarded Pound as her mentor, but to the H.D. of the following decades who published *Hedylus* in 1928, and engaged in her own effective tribute to the Greek sources of such a type when she composed *Hippolytus Temporizes* (1927) and *Ion* (1937) as versions of Euripides. H.D.'s Hippolytus is a fervent follower of

Artemis, who is tricked into the experience of human passion by the designing Phaedra. The Paterian epiphany, as a quintessentially artistic form of experience, is supplanted by a troublesome and ultimately fatal experience of human desire.

If *Hippolytus Temporizes* is the tormented questioning of ascesis, *Ion* was undoubtedly taken by H.D. as a sign of the consolidation of her artistic vocation. Ion, the young priest of Apollo, avoids the threatened fate of being murdered by his mother (Meleager's doom at the hands of Althaea, and indeed that of Hippolytus at the hands of his father's wife, Phaedra), and becomes King of Athens, thus giving his name to the civilizing mission of the Greeks as it begins to spread throughout the Mediterranean world – Ionian. It is after the first publication of this work that H.D. finds it possible to write: 'I am, I am, I AM a Poet'.

Yet H.D.'s period of intensified self-knowledge came, like that of Pound, after the war, and in a period of confinement to hospital: in her case, it was the breaking of her hip, in 1956, and the long period of convalescence spent on Lake Zurich, throughout 1957, that initiated a crucial change in her work. From this stage were to come her greatest poems: *Sagesse* (composed summer–winter 1957), *Hermetic Definition*, the *Trilogy* and *Helen in Egypt*. To attempt a summary of their significance at this stage would be pointless. But it is worth asking, as a final interrogation of the process 'from ascesis to conversion', whether its signs are present in the transition from H.D.'s excited sense of vocation to her sober presentation of how the poet appears to a curious world, like 'a white-faced Scops owl' in captivity:

> they will laugh and linger and some child may shudder,
>
> touched by the majesty, the lifted wings,
> the white mask and the eyes that seem to see,
>
> like God, everything and like God, see nothing . . .
>
> A white-faced Scops, a captive and in prison,
> but noble and priest and soldier, scribe and king
>
> will hail you, sacrosanct while frail women
> bend and sway between the temple pillars,

till torches flicker and fail,
and there is only faint light from the braziers

and the ghostly trail of incense, and cries of recognition
and of gladness in the fragrant air.

Swinburne's 'Sonnet (with a copy of Mademoiselle de Maupin)', dedicated to Théophile Gautier as the veritable priest of *'L'Art pour l'Art'*, presents a similar scenario of the temple in which art's rites are celebrated. But H.D.'s vision is anticipated by an image of the artist as victim, despised and rejected: *Sagesse* indeed.

NOTES

1 The relationship between Pater and Richard Jackson is not documented in any existing correspondence. But neither is the relationship between Pater and Charles Shadwell, the dedicatee of *The Renaissance*, apart from a single brief note. Wright's informant cannot be dismissed out of hand in his claim to have had a special place in Pater's life.
2 See my article, 'The Case for Stokes (and Pater)', *Poetry Nation Review*, 9, 1979, pp. 6–9.
3 See Stephen Bann, *The True Vine – On Visual Representation and the Western Tradition* (New York, Cambridge University Press, 1989), pp. 171–81.

BIBLIOGRAPHY

Prosper de Barante, *Mélanges historiques et littéraires* (Paris, 1835), Vol. III.
Roland Barthes, *Image-Music-Text*, translated by Stephen Heath (London, Fontana, 1977).
Roland Barthes, *Sollers écrivain* (Paris, Le Seuil, 1979).
H.D., *Hermetic Definition* (Oxford, Carcanet Press, 1972).
H.D., *Hippolytus Temporizes* (Reading Ridge, Conn., Black Swan, 1985).
H.D., *Ion*, with Afterword by John Walsh (Redding Ridge, Conn., Black Swan, 1986).
Freud, *Totem and Taboo*, in *The Origins of Religion* (Harmondsworth, Penguin Books, 1985).
René Girard, *Deceit, Desire and the Novel*, translated by Yvonne Freccero (Baltimore, John Hopkins Press, 1965).
René Girard, *Critiques dans un souterrain* (Paris, Grasset, 1976).
René Girard, *Things Hidden since the Foundation of the World*, translated by Stephen Bann and Michael Metteer (London, Athlone Press, 1987).
Gerald Monsman, *Pater's Portraits* (Baltimore, John Hopkins Press, 1967).
Ezra Pound, *Selected Poems* (London, Faber & Faber, 1975).

Lawrence S. Rainey, *A Poem Including History – The Cantos of Ezra Pound* (Yale University: The Beinecke Rare Book and Manuscript Library, 1989).

Jean-Paul Sartre, *Words*, translated by Irene Clephane (Harmondsworth, Penguin Books, 1967).

Jean-Paul Sartre, *The Family Idiot – Gustave Flaubert 1821–1857*, translated by Carol Cosman (Chicago, University of Chicago, 1987).

Algernon Charles Swinburne, *Poems and Ballads – Atalanta in Calydon*, edited by Morse Peckham (New York, Bobbs-Merrill, 1970).

14 Glimpses of 'Gregor'

Mark Kinkead-Weekes

There are many Professors of Modern English Literature, a growing number of ex-Pro-Vice-Chancellors, quite a few good critics; so why a volume in honour of this one? Who is 'Gregor', what is he, that all these so commend him? The answer would lie only partially in an account of his writings (though we append a bibliography) or any memoir in the past tense, since his is very much the present. It would need – to say the least – to wear its seriousness lightly.

In conversation – his best medium – he remarks of one of Eliot's last poems which he thinks too merely and nakedly autobiographical that seeing Eliot without his objective correlative is like seeing a house guest at breakfast without a dressing-gown. He also thinks that Arnold's voice carries across the years as a voice sometimes carries across a room, because it is pitched low. How much of him is caught in those two glimpses ... Present him, then, in glimpses, by his friends?

This will also inevitably be a portrait of a critic of a certain age, a period piece! No worse for that, perhaps; especially for non-aquaintances, who may yet be interested in meeting an endangered species embodying in his whole mode of living and teaching a style that is going or has gone.

A Man at Work, then

Writing

Critics go about their business in very different ways. One friend of Ian's prepares to write by washing hands and face and carefully polishing his shoes, to feel immaculately neat before sitting at his desk. Another used to meditate in the lotus position, or stand on his head against a wall for a few minutes (very disconcerting if one happened to come in). A third clears his desk of everything but a single sheet of paper and a lamp – and then covers the floor with scrumpled discards. Each says something of the critic's view of criticism, of how it is hoped to overcome chaos or emptiness. Ian's desk and floor are bestrewn with critical books and texts, open at book-marked places (though he never writes in them). Criticism becomes visibly the common pursuit. Originality must take off from what has been well (or improvably) said. He used to cover pages in a neat italic hand, manufactured by will and practice from his original handwriting. Often words are left out, however, as the mind travels ahead of the pen. And he is quite useless as a proofreader of his own work. 'Arabella seeds Jude,' said the critic, to the delight of the friends who read. Ian didn't notice ... for him it was 'needs'; the rest was mechanical.

He would never use a typewriter; regards his word-processor (now that writing is physically difficult) with the darkest suspicion, like all machines. He says his father beat him once for offering sixpence to the smaller boy next door to mend a puncture for him. He does not seem to be a follower of Samuel Smiles ...

Lecturing

The notes are notes, not twenty pages of script. But the lecture is usable again – after (he says) one has replaced the jokes about rationing – but only if it is re-rehearsed at some length; for a great part has to be 'live', particularly the rendering of carefully chosen passages or poems with prac-crit commentary. So something spontaneous plays within and against the carefully deliberated. He always has hand-outs, so that everyone shall carry *something* away! Having a text in your hand (he says) helps to regulate the timing; and it is true, he never has to gabble at the finish. Other people drink water (in the days when there was a carafe) to moisten the throat; he does it when he wants his audience to stop and think, or as he is about to change direction or gear. He likes to do this twice in the hour if possible, but always at least once. The lecture has a strong and clear structure, aimed to stay in a listener's mind afterwards. There are always jokes, though the old pro doesn't let them seem stuck in (as against the tyro – his tale – who agonized all lecture long because he knew he was going to end with, 'And so, like Lady Godiva, I come to my close', and then walk out amidst groans, through the pickled foetuses in the lobby of the old gynaecology lecture theatre, in the 'Athens of the North'; 'Shall I compare thee to a summer's day?' had a different resonance, as the lecturer's eye caught some anatomical diagram, everywhere he looked....

His lecturing began at King's College London, but was fine-tuned in Edinburgh, where traditions were still mediaeval – a rowdy reception to begin with, then attention if you were held to be at least trying hard, then a noisy verdict which left you in no doubt how you had done, one way or the other. 'English' also operated in a converted church, through a microphone, with an old Servitor at the controls, so that lecturers were never quite in charge of their own voices. Then they built new lecture theatres, which were soundproof until the fire chief demanded connecting doors. Do not lecture in such circumstances when Ian is next door – gales of laughter will make both your audience and you want to pack up and get in there. ('It's Doctor Greyger,' she said in guid Fife tones, wiping her eyes untragically. 'Ah canny wait for Leeear next week.' He'd been debunking romantic views and performances of *Othello*.)

He identifies the two or three most intelligent listeners in different parts of the room and talks to them, to keep himself alert. This can be disappointing. He was once mesmerized by the most intelligent listener of all, a face the most delicately responsive, who came up afterwards – not of course at once, for the most sensitive always hang back – to ask, in strong mittel-European accent, 'Zis Middlemarch, vot books he has written?' (It is a pleasure in Gregorian anecdote that so many alternative versions exist, all equally characteristic. Another is to watch the stories grow as the weeks pass.)

On the Teaching and Learning Committee

A scientist, attending for the first time, steels himself for the inevitable statement of the obvious, the jargon, the fashionable rhetoric, on the subject of small-group teaching. Ian is the first speaker, but himself has nothing to say. He spends his time analysing how he has heard academics talk casually to one another in common rooms about classes and students. He uncovers, in tone and vocabulary, the underlying attitudes to teaching and the kinds of teaching faults that might follow. This is only a serious (and funny) application of his zestful, yet affectionate, mockery of his friends. He will seize on some revealing remark to caricature, in wild amplification and distortion, yet never lose the initial accuracy. Laughter is delight, unease, education. All Ian's friends learn to live on terms with caricatures of themselves, laughed into self-knowledge.

The Small-Group Teacher

Students clearly get the other side of his tongue if they have not read the book, or prepared the page of notes in answer to the questions he put at the end of the previous meeting. He can be supercilious, sarcastic. Colleagues in adjacent offices learn to have a box of tissues handy (when the snuffles become audible in the corridor) and some sympathy – but not too much, and directed towards the difference that doing some work will make to the tutorial relationship. He does not practise himself, though he respects in able practitioners, the quaker-like use of silence, or the idea that the teacher's primary function is to draw out the student's own ideas. His seminars have a programme of questions, and his questions presuppose certain kinds of answer; but he can nevertheless enjoy the student good enough to take the group up another road, if it leads somewhere. And when students show that they have ideas, he will take much time and trouble to foster them. Authoritarian? Schoolmasterish? – he started as a schoolmaster. Old-fashioned? Perhaps. He is still in frequent touch with pupils from thirty years back (by no means only the most brilliant ones) – who have all learned something of his bantering.

Provincial, Redbrick, Oxford, London, Scottish University, New University

He holds the 'nap' hand.

A Geordie

In the centre of the mantelpiece are two photographs. One is an aerial view of Newcastle upon Tyne. The other is a slum street in that city, in which urchins are playing cricket, with a dustbin by way of stumps. (The mantelpiece is half a mile from Canterbury cathedral and opposite the Kent cricket ground. Ian is a member of the second but not the first.) Into the photo frames are stuck, for convenience, the latest postcards from friends all over the world. Each will be worth inspection, albeit for a variety of reasons. One may be the latest move in a generic and competitive sequence: old Hollywood, the ultimate in boring, the horrors of golf, Victoriana. Others will be reproductions of unusual paintings or landscapes. All will have been carefully chosen to please or amuse a sophisticated eye. They sit incongruously against their background ... obvious tensions and transitions there! Yet Tyneside is (simply) basis, not background, where he 'lives' still, by himself in the family home, only not as many months as he lives in Canterbury; and where he moves in a group of friends he has known from childhood.

A Northerner who never imagines that what is important is necessarily in London. A voice which, if it gives little away, nevertheless clearly still has the Geordie flat 'a' and several other locutions; and can do 'The Lambton Warm' on occasion. An ingrained supporter of Newcastle United, who goes to St James's Park regularly and, like most of its inhabitants now, is given to melancholy and reminiscence. (Do not, incidentally, accept bets which involve identifying grounds, or naming strips, or Cup Final results. In fact, as a rule, do not accept bets, however little. Nine times out of ten he wins, and the tenth he is liable oddly to forget.)

He is shaped by Oxford (where he studied for his doctorate under Humphrey House – on Arnold, of course, hence the first date on our title-page – but took the degree itself, like his BA, in Newcastle); and by London (where he held his first university post). But he is a regional man, a provincial, and much of the literature he most cares for is the same. He has also known, twice, his comfortable background split open. As a child evacuee with a label round his neck he waited to be 'chosen' – every child's deep fear when teams are picked – and was among the last to be taken away ... to a home whose living-conditions are indelibly etched into his memory, and whence he was fairly quickly removed with a skin ailment. And because of the last three numbers on his call-up card he went to the coalmine as a 'Bevan Boy', 'down pit' though never of it, and never afterwards unaware. He still keeps his miner's lamp in the hall. Middle class he may be, apostle of Arnoldian culture even today, politically middle of the road, admirer of Jane Austen and Virginia Woolf as well as of Hardy, Lawrence and Joyce; but one of the things he will show a visitor to Geordieland is T. Dan Smith's Byker Wall, as an example of slum clearance without destruction of community, and he has not forgotten Richard Hoggart's *Uses of Literacy*. Perhaps Austen and Woolf are what they are to him because in their 'rooms', too, is one patch of darker and less comfortable awareness that is not merely picturesque, but changes the tonality of everything else – though it is everything else that mostly holds the eye, the animation, the essential action.

The Bevan Boy

What strange creatures such middle-class youths, drafted into the coalmines, must have seemed – and suddenly felt themselves to be. Ian, after his 'training' – which consisted of watching old films of coalmining in America – cycled to his mine, a few miles out of town. There was an interview with an undermanager. What did Ian imagine he might do? Well, said the budding intellectual, who had spent one term at university and had thought about the question himself, perhaps he could be useful if he learned to be a surveyor? There was a pause; a weary sigh. How many men did he imagine worked this coalfield, how many thousands, laddie? They had so far managed to get along somehow with two surveyors, each with a lifetime's expertise. Did he see that man over there, pushing wagons to the pithead? Go and be his assistant. So he was, for the next three years, except that he got promoted to pushing the wagons at the bottom of the shaft instead of at the top.

What did he chat about at snap-time? The Pools, mostly, after the football talk. But the 'On-Setter' in charge of the cage lift was a music lover, with an ambition Ian couldn't grasp at first. It was to be a 'conasser', a 'real conasser'. Is that a funny story . . . ?

Ex-Servicemen at Newcastle University

Frank Kermode remembers them as 'tough. They had no time to waste and wanted attention, so they nagged us relentlessly. And you must remember that we were tyros, I in particular still covered with the rust of 5½ years' naval idleness, with little substantial reading. Ian sensibly attached himself to Peter Ure rather than anyone else.' (In fact the influence of John Butt and Kermode himself was no less strong.) Since there were only six staff 'and since there was an enormous programme of lectures and seminars, we were worked almost to death, not least by I. G. and his veteran pals, who were not that much younger than I was, and in some cases better educated. There was never again a time like it, for within a couple of years all the fresh (wo)men were eighteen again, and we were almost thirty.'

A University Teacher, in London

He asks whether you have ever kissed a piece of paper? He has, twice. One was an unexpected Cup Final ticket. The other was the letter to say he had a temporary assistantship at King's.

The wheel has come full circle in universities now, when tenure has been abolished for new appointments and it is almost impossible to get into the profession in Humanities. The assistantship at London and in the Scottish universities in the 1950s was a stop-ended three-year appointment, no matter how good you were or how much your professorial head of department wished to keep you. But after travelling the length and breadth of Britain with a (subsequently distinguished) circus of rivals, no success ever after seemed so sweet.

Assistants taught what they were told and developed a secular catholicity. Ian boasts of being the only don still active who has lectured to a second-year audience on *The Magnetic Lady*.

Edinburgh (seen, and reseen, by a new assistant lecturer)

Edinburgh English seems to be led and energized by John Butt and three 'principal lieutenants'. Ian is a sharp contrast with the other two. A Geordie – though the measured voice gives little away – not at all athletic-looking, almost plump, with pale-blue eyes that really can twinkle. He seems to have nothing to do with either toughness or intensity; what he seems 'about' is ease, manner, wit, relaxation, sociability. But closer acquaintance modifies as well as confirms: the relaxed urbanity can be deceptive, the mind behind the large domed forehead is sharp, colleagues and students need to be on their toes – yet the manner, like the polished prose, is the man, who has made civility into a fine art. He is an entrepreneur, but of human relationships. It is thanks to him that Edinburgh in the early 1960s remains a benchmark of what a sharing, communal, academic experience can be. It was he who recognized that ideas, values, energies, require a social context to flourish in; he who led in the creation of an 'Edinburgh' kind, out of what lay to hand, in Scottish ingredients. (A quick association test: Ian Gregor? Seven out of ten people will say 'malt whisky'. The three will say 'gin and tonic'. It is a matter of timing.) So the 'English Department' itself became one of the good things in life, and achieved an extraordinary degree of unity of purpose which had nothing to do with any intellectual unanimity, but a great deal with a sense of how a 'department' should exist collectively. (Kent colleagues will recognize the affinity.) This 'society' had to include its students outside the classroom: the lively literary-society meetings, with food and drink as good as could be searched out and afforded; the reading-parties at the country house open to the Scottish universities; the end-of-year 'theme' parties, where the students provided the wine and cheese (financial contributions gratefully accepted); the staff provided the cabaret – much of it now legendary – and the period costumes were, to say the least, imaginative. Invariably Ian made things happen, his qualities became all our qualities . . . a university experience that was more than clever talk in academic surroundings or at high tables.

A New University

Kent is an opportunity, as 'founding father', to help re-create the Edinburgh sense of community both in the English Board and in two Colleges in turn, and add the 'new university' dimension of the common pursuit – the Newmanesque idea that each discipline is seen truly only when it is closely related to those it adjoins. Copies of *The Idea of the University* are in evidence at the first faculty meetings. The first-year course is to be run by the faculty as a whole and is to culminate in 'topics' taught jointly by colleagues from different disciplines. Ian comes into his own in 'Education and the Idea of Culture (English, History, Modern Languages) and Exploring Reality (Literature, Philosophy, Science, Theology).' He is a pleasure to teach with, always casting himself in a role that plays deliberately off the others, and teaching well with quite opposite kinds of colleague. He also labels himself Professor of Modern English Literature now – no more magnetic ladies; indeed a 'bit of a gap' between Shakespeare and Crabbe, though Donne still figures. As Chairman, he also develops habits of mediation. 'Is there not,' he will say, 'a sense in which . . .?'

He has to administer at higher levels later – and, characteristically, produces creative results as Pro-Vice-Chancellor by being a master of delegation. Chief of these is the Kent Society – another insistence that community is the essence of the university experience and must not be allowed simply to vanish after the degree ceremony. Moreover, it is not only for former students but for local friends of the university as well – and that is characteristic too.

Hyphenations

A friend says Gregor is a funny man, a serious man, a kind man, a brave man . . . and all these things are true – especially in hyphenation. He is fond of that himself, like those central critical metaphors of his . . . the titles with 'and' in them, like a bridge which both links and calls attention to the gap; the idea of looking for the 'fissure' in the texture of a work which will reveal both the opposing stresses and pressures within it, and the degree of the unifying force that tries to hold it together; and the net or web, which can 'catch' and hold all sorts of fugitive things, but only if it is strong and close-textured enough, despite its holes.

Funny/Serious, then

Nothing could be more serious to Ian than his Catholicism. As a student, he became editor of the periodical *Crux*; he is in touch with Catholic intellectuals from Cardinal Hume to Herbert McCabe, and with several who have left the Church but not their faith. His one temptation to forsake university life was the headship of a Catholic college. He is seriously ecumenical (the son of a Catholic mother and a father who remained a lifetime presbyterian; one uncle an Elder of the Kirk, a cousin a minister, an aunt who forsook one congregation because she thought the altar wine too strong) – but in this he has tended to be travelling ahead of his bishop. One of his first activities in Kent was to organize a series of ecumenical seminars to discuss the liturgy and the meaning of the Eucharist, to be followed by an actual Eucharist in which all the denominations would worship together, as far as could be allowed on a special occasion. (This was 1966, long before the Joint Commission report.) The Roman Catholic bishop, however, ruled that Catholics could take part only if they were physically separated after the Ministry of the Word. Fortunately, the church which the university had been lent as a chapel had a partly glassed aisle, used for coffee after services. Thither the Romans had to march off, with the Anglicans (of course) staying in the centre aisle, and the Methodists and Nonconformists moving to the far one . . . all still in earshot of one another, all taking part in services which were audibly identical. It was one of the most educative, shaming and moving of experiences . . . a living image of the 'church', formed by intelligent people who had put their minds and Arnoldian best selves to understanding why it was so, and therefore were together, separately, as never before.

But it is not by accident that a funny writer, also a Catholic, should have dedicated a book to him (David Lodge's *How Far Can You Go*). Ian was, for once, somewhat disconcerted by an angry 'father of daughters' who attacked *him* because Lodge had 'gone too far'; but it ought not to be misunderstood, either, when some Gregor anecdotes show that his God is a laughing one. Cautiously raising the aerial on his new Renault, and as it reaches only a quarter up from the horizontal on the roof, he murmurs, 'I think that's high enough for a Catholic.' At a pot-luck party for staff and graduate students a beautiful Moroccan woman approaches and asks, most politely, 'Professor Gregor, would you care to try a little of my cous-cous?' He makes his neighing sound, instantly followed by, 'I'll have to ask my parish priest.' (One of his favourite parish priests spent much of his time on the golf course, and advised him once – following a good scriptural precedent about serpents and doves – to run his ball out of a bunker with a putter, over a bare patch about six inches wide. Ian's golf was always . . . interesting . . . and often a spiritual exercise rather than 'sport'. Wasn't golf, after all, invented by puritans, for whom pleasure was inherently sinful?)

He created also an informal discussion group of religious people, with a simple agenda: the theological dimension of anything its members found interesting. There were university people from all three faculties, the Dean of Canterbury and perhaps the most distinguished and certainly the most literary of the canons, the university chaplains, the head of the Canterbury School of Ministry, and a floating population of visitors. Would those who know Ian care to try guessing its title? It was called, and it was, 'Theologywine'.

Yet here, too, there is a sense of darkness in the world. He is no Jansenist, but his admiration of writers like Greene and Mauriac is significant; as of course is the devotion of a religious man to Thomas Hardy. Like all comedians, also, there is an always-potential melancholy and aloneness in him . . . against which the sociability, the humour, the extraordinary talent for friendship, the hedonism, play. The melancholy isn't merely temperamental, it is also theological; but it goes with a spectrum of tough-mindedness. Leaning on one side of his mantelpiece one might imagine the Beerbohm caricature of Arnold (funny *because* it so distorts the author of 'Dover Beach'). On the other side, of course, stands Hardy. But the picture would be incomplete without the Newman both of the *Apologia* and *The Idea of the University*. 'The Dream of Gerontius' is on the shelf and the record player.

One of his best roles is Eeyore, in a variety of guises. It gets laughs because he plays it from the inside.

The 'Modern Movement' seminar goes for a weekend to Paris, dines (some of them) *chez* Allard, the rest where recommended. At the exceptionally small and cheap hotel on the Left Bank the chief memory (and Gregorian imitation afterwards) is the appearance with the breakfast tray of what seems to be a blind waiter, in the blackest of dark glasses. At the gruff cry, '*Messieurs*', all precipitate themselves from bed to stop the offerings falling to the floor. Hurry up, please, it's time.

Is there a Hyphenation of 'Kind'?

He is endlessly and gracefully companionable; never forgets birthdays or Christmas cards (always lamenting their number and vowing to cut them to ten); takes pains to keep in touch with a huge variety of friends. He will go to considerable trouble to help and encourage talented people in unrewarding situations, as well (of course) as his students past and present. He is also, tellingly, dear to the wives of his friends, though not always at first.

So what hyphenates? Nothing unkindly. Perhaps, that if there is a Purgatory – speaking ecumenically – Ian will have road maps to all its destinations, good food and pub guides to its best spots, and friends carefully positioned at convenient driving distances, and others ready to do odd jobs.

And there are the practical jokes, not malicious exactly, yet necessarily humbling – especially since the Gregorian kind always depend for their success on acute perception of the character of the victim. (Always the educator!) Another tradition he has perpetrated at Kent is that no elected Chairman of English must leave office without having one of these played on him or her – and since they are now expected, they have to be more and more cleverly disguised. A proposal for a particularly time-wasting kind of collaboration with a neighbouring institution, or a UGC letter asking (in tabulated form) for the exact distribution of staff members' time in an average working day, or a proposed new topic on 'Socialist Women in Gissing'; depended for their success not only on the careful forgery of letterheads and subornation of registry personnel, but on the excessive diplomacy of one Chairman, the sheer conscientiousness of another, the predilections of a third and anxiety not to offend. Always there would be colleagues to play up and elaborate; and (still better) colleagues to get angry and threaten action (sometimes playing up, and sometimes not). The experience has also been useful, since life has increasingly overtaken satiric fiction in British universities and Kent English has needed to learn a good deal of tolerance and good humour.

Moreover, like Falstaff, he is also the cause of jest in other men; notably the present incumbent of a Chair of Modern History in a Scottish university, whose opening gambit – a telephone call from the (mannish) headmistress of a girls' school, on the end of whose playing-fields Ian then lived, complaining that her girls were being embarrassed by the vision of a middle-aged gentleman undressing at an uncurtained window – is legendary. So is the letter on the paper of the Glasgow Newman Society, warning that the Bishop of Birmingham was so angry, because prominent Catholics attended the wedding of a radical priest who had left the Church, that he was threatening disciplinary action against all who had been there. The letter suggested that the proper propitiatory 'form' was an 'Act of submission' beginning 'Humbly prostrate before your Grace . . .' The jest depended once more on character perception, the calculation of the relative proportion, in Ian, of a sense of the absurd and a Roman duty of obedience. He thought it ridiculous . . . but, even better than hoped for, was worried enough to go off to consult the (also Catholic) perpetrator, as to what he should do! His 'revenge' bided its time, was the most elaborate of all, and gave its victim great pleasure: a correspondence involving him with 'Murdo Glowrie', Secretary of the Cultural Division of the Scottish National Party – who wrote to offer congratulations to the newly appointed incumbent of the Scottish History Chair and to point out the acute interest felt by the Party in how History was taught in Scotland. An invitation was issued, to a formal dinner and discussion in the society's rooms, followed by a correspondence of several letters and phone calls from a delightful Scots lady-secretary, until 'Mr Glowrie' called the victim out of the History Examiners dinner to present him formally with 'the Glowrie papers'.

Hyphenation of 'Brave'?
A friend writes: 'It is impossible for a well person to imagine what Ian has gone through since his illness'. (After an operation to remove a benign brain tumour, his right hand, walk, speech, concentration and memory remain affected.) Maybe the least said about the effect of the last three on a critic and teacher, the better? Yet that would not be brave – and perhaps there are one or two Gregorian ways to register, by grousing, a refusal to mope? The worst thing about the medical profession (he says) is that everyone you see is an expert in a piece of you, and one cannot abide being talked at piecemeal. Since he pictures Hell as an institution, he cannot be kept in the hospital, working improvingly, but is for ever ringing up friends, demanding to be taken out for dinner, risking what he refers to as 'my dome'. And the worst thing of all (he says) is that it is more difficult to time one's jokes . . .

Preferences
A Gregor-like game of 'spot the reason': there remain these three, Arnold, Eliot and Leavis, and the centre of the three is Arnold.

GLIMPSES OF 'GREGOR'

Both Hardy and Lawrence but preferably Hardy. Both Jane Austen and the Brontës but preferably Jane Austen. Both Dickens and Thackeray but preferably Dickens. Both Joyce and Woolf but preferably Woolf. In Golding, *Lord of the Flies* and *Rites of Passage* rather than *The Inheritors* and *Darkness Visible*. No science fiction, of any kind whatsoever!

Pictures on a literary man's (several) walls: two Turner landscapes, very sunny ones. Several Impressionists. 'The Empress Dowager on the beach' and 'Epsom Downs'. A Victorian narrative picture, 'The Letter', and next to it the Grimshaw which was the cover of *The Woman in White*. A Lowry. One Magritte. Three Hoppers. A picture by a Newcastle painter of a scene in a pub. And – a friend muses, 'certainly his most advanced picture' – a large print of Matisse's late 'Négresse' (thought to 'represent' Josephine Baker), a marvellous economy of lines and patches of colour, animatedly dancing, wearing the merest suggestion of a fringe.

In terms of critical pedigree he is by Leavis, out of Middleton Murry, of whose writings he owns almost all, having begun to collect them at school. The enthusiasm for literature, and for Murry, was stoked by Mother Noel, when the sixth form of St Cuthbert's Grammar School was amalgamated during the war with the neighbouring convent. (One runs one's eye across the Murry shelf in 143 Old Dover Road: *The Evolution of an Intellectual, The Problem of Style, Countries of the Mind, To the Unknown God, The Life of Jesus, God, Keats and Shakespeare, Son of Woman,* (D. H. Lawrence)). Then, Leavis. Impossible now for younger colleagues to imagine how *Scrutiny* changed the whole conception of studying and of teaching English, into a work worth giving a lifetime to. Ian writes one of the first critical essays on Leavis in 1952 – and gets a twelve page letter from Cambridge in reply. Thirteen years later he writes again, under the rubric 'The Critics Who Made Us', contending that reading Leavis was an experience analogous to reading literature itself. 'In Leavis we have someone who found in literature a registration of experience so intense, so precise, that he was able to write of it as if it constituted not a mediation of life, but life itself. Hence the singular nature of his criticism, and its disturbing appeal.' But he can never be a 'Leavisite'. His devotion to Arnold suggests one reason, his response to the Eliot of the *Quartets* another, his collection of Penguin New Writing a third, signalling a lifetime's engagement with the 'new'.

Hedonism

This is a humanist (Oscar Wilde) and a secular discipline, to fill available rifts with ore. To attend an academic conference with Ian is also to have the journeys meticulously planned, for 'Pleasure' – places, hotels, restaurants, cathedrals, galleries, battlefields – consciously scripted and beginning to be dramatized, even at best mythologized, almost in the acting-out. Experience becomes layered, occasion enhanced by alertness to what is available. ('Is it in the book?' he will cry, confronting the hostelry of life – in constant search to match the real with the imagined, and to make experience sufficiently artful. But – as with seminars – the need to plan conceals some nervousness about the unplanned as uncontrollable. What about hotels in Poland, or when the 'Michelin' restaurant is full?)

When art meets life, the pleasures of recognition become extraordinarily infectious: the deconstructive proliferation of Flaubertian parrots in Rouen, 'guided' by a Fernandel-like concierge who already knows his Julian Barnes; the delighted murmur of ah-huhs and yeses as he checks that 'It's *all* here' in the new *Galerie des Impressionistes*; the sparkle when (oh non-mechanical man) he asks, 'What's *that*?' in Proust's bedroom, and finds that it actually is the magic lantern.

And life keeps acting up for him, spontaneous and endless source of 'story'. A WEA class is hilariously mixed up with the annual meeting of 'Guide Dogs for the Blind'. Hitchhiking over the Pennines produces a lorry loaded with dog corpses. The door to the cockpit of a small aircraft (he had discovered a new way of getting to Swansea) swings open and a map falls at his feet, with a red line marking the route. The door is pulled closed from the pilot's side. (He is wearing tennis shoes.) The map remains with the passenger.

'Pleasure' does, however, have geographical limits: nowhere where the temperature exceeds eighty degrees Fahrenheit; not the Far East (nor the Middle East come to that); certainly not the Third World (though he once went to Jamaica . . . in the Blue Mountains, there you feel free). Taking a term in Chicago, he puts up at a Club where mainly Anglophiles are to be found. To go too far 'abroad' is to fall ill and hear the doctor murmuring above your sickbed, 'Give me your roubles' . . . (actually, it was 'Give me your troubles').

Graveyards

The zest for touring graveyards is a puzzle to friends, but many have endured it. Two he dragged, one freezing day, round Père Lachaise – to find that the Epstein statue on Oscar Wilde's grave had been emasculated. Another he took across Los Angeles to the original that Waugh worked up in *The Loved One*, only to discover after miles of freeway and some time searching, that this was The Wrong One. Yet another he persuaded to look for Conrad's grave in Canterbury, on interview day for posts in the unbuilt university. A hot summer's afternoon, absolute peace, no sign of human life. At last, a clink. Do they still call them 'sextons'? (What a strange word!) Can you tell us, please, where Joseph Conrad is buried? 'Oo?' Joseph Conrad, the novelist? 'You family?' Alas, not. 'Ave you got the plot number, then?' Alas, no. 'Oi'll 'ave to look in me book . . .' Too late, when almost through the Cs, it dawns that he should be looking under K. In the nick of time, inspiration by Catholic intellectual . . . Is there a Catholic section in the cemetery? 'Why on earth didn' you say so before . . .' And there it is. Immediate Gregor riddle. The epitaph is from Spenser: 'Sleep after toil, port after stormy seas / Ease after war, death after life does greatly please.' Was this Korzeniowski irony, knowing it comes from the Cave of Despair, or was it chosen by the family from one of those selections provided by undertakers, as an epitaph suitable for a seafaring man? Bet proffered. Not accepted.

The Common Pursuit

It comes back to this in the end, since he manifestly believes and lives it. He wrote one book, *The Moral and the Story*, with Brian Nicholas. He wrote another, *William Golding, A Critical Study*, with Mark Kinkead-Weekes. He brought a third about, by persuading fifteen Kent colleagues to write papers, discuss them over a year, and then publish them with an interleaved commentary, by one another, as a teaching book entitled *Reading the Victorian Novel: Detail into Form*. He was the original begetter of a fourth, being the moving spirit behind the Kent Interdisciplinary

Topic on 'Exploring Reality', which brought together literary criticism, theology, science, and philosophy, and which has recently produced a collection of essays. His first Kent Topic, 'Education and the Idea of Culture', though perhaps the most productive of all, was never alas written up. It did, however, produce, from the late Provost of Trinity College Dublin, the historian Leland Lyons, the public tribute that it was the most stimulating and rewarding teaching experience of his life – and the dedication to Ian of his book *Culture and Anarchy in Ireland*.

Added to which he has, simply, an extraordinary talent for friendship. Most readers of this book will know his criticism, especially of Hardy and Golding – these are offered as glimpses of the man behind the pen. One friend writes: 'I suspect that most people's friendship with Ian is unlike their other friendships.' So it is.

He is interviewed for a job in those bad old days when jobs were as few as they are now. It goes rather stickily; the chairman shuffles his mound of papers, then suddenly asks when the thesis is likely to be finished? The candidate explains, with some embarrassment, that he has held a doctorate for two years. 'Oh,' says the Chairman worriedly, 'You must be *Doctor* Parker, then.' Not so . . . This is 'Gregor'.

ACKNOWLEDGEMENTS

These glimpses have been compiled and written by Mark Kinkead-Weekes, with the aid and/or encouragement of: Malcolm Andrews, Stephen Bann, Shirley Barlow, Peter Brown, Julian Coles, Chris Collard, Sandy Cunningham, David Ellis, Steve Fender, Bob Freedman, Bob Gibson, Jim Gibson, Malcolm Gregor, David Harkness, Andrew Hook, Stuart Hutchinson, Mike Irwin, Frank Kermode, Maurice Larkin, Bob Lee, Graham Martin, Andrew Rutherford, Lewis Ryder, Martin Scofield, Alf Smyth, Peter Walsh, Dick Watson. (Most, predictably, teach English and American literature – but the list includes three whose field is Classics, one in Cultural Studies, three in History, one in French, one in Biology and one in Physics – and that too is typical of Ian Gregor's Kent.) None should be held responsible for what has been done with their contributions!

15 Ian Gregor: A Bibliography

Compiled by Louis James

Publications

Books

The Moral and the Story (London, Faber and Faber, 1962) – with Brian Nicholas.
William Golding: A Critical Study (London, Faber and Faber, 1967) – with Mark Kinkead-Weekes; revised edn, with new chapter, 'The Later Golding', pp. 161–292 (London, Faber and Faber, 1984).
The Great Web: The Form of Hardy's Major Fiction (London, Faber and Faber, 1974; paperback edn, 1982).

Collections of Essays Edited

Imagined Worlds: Essays on Some English Novels and Novelists in Memory of John Butt (London, Methuen, 1968) – with Maynard Mack.
The Brontës, Twentieth Century Views Series (Prentice Hall, Englewood Cliffs, New Jersey, 1970).
The Prose for God: Religious and Anti-Religious Aspects of the Imaginative Literature (London, Sheed and Ward, 1974) – with Walter Stein.
Reading the Victorian Novel: Detail into Form (London, Vision Press, 1980).

Editions

Matthew Arnold, 'Culture and Anarchy'. A scholarly edition, edited with an Introduction, Textual Apparatus and Notes by Ian Gregor (Indianapolis and New York, Bobbs-Merrill, 1971).

William Golding, *Lord of the Flies* (London, Faber and Faber, 1962) – with Mark Kinkead-Weekes.
Byron: A Selection (London, Chatto and Windus, 1963) – with Andrew Rutherford.
William Golding, *The Inheritors* (London, Faber and Faber, 1964) – with Mark Kinkead-Weekes.
Thomas Hardy, *The Mayor of Casterbridge*, New Wessex Edition (London, Macmillan, 1974) – with Bryn Caless.
Thomas Hardy, *The Woodlanders* (Harmondsworth, Penguin Books, 1981) – with James Gibson.

Contributions to Books

Jude the Obscure, in *Imagined Worlds*, pp. 237–56.
'Introduction' to *The Brontës*, pp. 1–7.

'Criticism as an Individual Activity: the Approach through Reading', in Malcolm Bradbury and David Palmer (eds.), *Contemporary Criticism. Stratford-upon-Avon Studies, no. 12* (London, Edward Arnold, 1970), pp. 195–214.
'T. S. Eliot and Matthew Arnold', in Graham Martin (ed.), *Eliot in Perspective* (London, Macmillan, 1970), pp. 267–78.
'*Jude the Obscure*: an End and a Beginning', in *The Prose for God*, pp. 63–85.
'Introduction', in Thomas Hardy, *The Mayor of Casterbridge*, pp. 11–26.
'Either Side of Wessex', in Lance St John Butler (ed.), *Thomas Hardy after Fifty Years* (London, Macmillan, 1977), pp. 104–115 – with Michael Irwin.
'Spaces: *To the Lighthouse*', in Louis L. Martz and Aubrey Williams (eds.), *The Author and His Work: Essays on a Problem in Criticism (in Honour of Maynard Mack)* (New Haven, Yale University Press, 1978), pp. 375–89.
'Introduction' and 'Reading a Story: Sequence, Pace and Recollection', in *Reading the Victorian Novel*, pp. 9–13, 92–110.
'Introduction', in Thomas Hardy, *The Woodlanders*, pp. 11–29.
'Liberal Education: An Outworn Ideal?', in F. S. L. Lyons and Nicholas Phillipson (eds.), *Universities, Society and the Future* (Edinburgh University Press, 1983), pp. 145–59.
'Newman's *Idea of a University*: A Text for Today', in T. R. Wright (ed.), *John Henry Newman: A Man for his Time* (Newcastle upon Tyne, Grevatt and Grevatt, 1983), pp. 16–28.
'Your Story or Your Life? Reflections on Thomas Hardy's Autobiography', in Norman Page (ed.), *The Thomas Hardy Annual, no. 2* (London, Macmillan, 1984), pp. 157–70 – with Michael Irwin.
'Virginia Woolf and Her Readers', in Eric Warner (ed.), *Virginia Woolf: A Centenary Perspective* (London, Macmillan, 1984), pp. 41–55.
'Contrary Imaginings: Hardy and Religion', in David Jasper (ed.), *Interpretations of Belief* (London, Macmillan, 1986), pp. 202–24.
'He Wondered: The Religious Imagination of William Golding', in John Carey (ed.), *William Golding, the Man and His Books* (London, Faber and Faber, 1986), pp. 84–100.

Articles

'The Criticism of F. R. Leavis', *Dublin Review*, Autumn 1952, pp. 56–63.
'Matthew Arnold and T. S. Eliot as Critics', *Dublin Review*, Autumn 1954, pp. 394–404.
'New Bearings in the "Catholic" Novel', *Blackfriars*, January 1954, pp. 24–6.
'The Greene Baize Door', *Blackfriars*, September 1955, pp. 302–10.
'The Last Augustan: George Crabbe', *Dublin Review*, Summer 1956, pp. 37–50.
'Graham Greene and La Critique', *Catholicisme Anglaise* (a Symposium), 1958, pp. 117–129.
'"The Fox": A Caveat', *Essays in Criticism*, January 1959, pp. 10–21.
'Culture and Society: A Controversy', *Essays in Criticism*, October 1959, pp. 425–30.
'The Strange Case of William Golding and His Critics', *The Twentieth Century*, February 1960, pp. 115–25 – with Mark Kinkead-Weekes; reprinted in W. Nelson (ed.), *William Golding's 'The Lord of the Flies': A Source Book* (New York, Odyssey Press, 1963).

'C. P. Snow: The Two Cultures Debate', *Dublin Review*, Summer 1961, pp. 62–72.
'The National Theatre: A London Letter', *Hudson Review*, Summer 1964, pp. 243–50.
'Towards a Christian Literary Criticism', *The Month*, April 1965, pp. 239–50.
'What Kind of Fiction Did Hardy Write?' *Essays in Criticism*, June 1966, pp. 290–308.
'Comedy and Oscar Wilde', *Sewanee Review*, July 1966, pp. 501–21.
'Hardy's World', *E. L. H., a Journal of Literary History*, June 1971, pp. 274–93.
'A Sort of Fiction? Graham Greene's Autobiography', *New Blackfriars*, March 1972, pp. 120–26.
'English, Leavis and the Social Order', *Twentieth Century Studies*, September 1973, pp. 22–31.
'Does Criticism Date?', *Literature and History*, Spring 1977, pp. 96–104.
'Lawrence and Joyce: A Critical Comparison', in C. T. Watts (ed.), *The English Novel: Questions in Literature* (London, Sussex Books, 1976), pp. 133–52 – with Mark Kinkead-Weekes.
'Graham Greene', *ibid.*, pp. 153–71 – with David Lodge.
'Thomas Hardy', *ibid.*, pp. 95–110 – with David Lodge.
'The Later Golding', *Twentieth Century Literature*, Summer 1982, pp. 109–29 – with Mark Kinkead-Weekes.
'Voices: Reading Virginia Woolf', *Sewanee Review*, Fall 1980, pp. 572–90.
'Critics Who Made Us: F. R. Leavis and *The Great Tradition*', *Sewanee Review*, Summer 1985, pp. 434–46.

Broadcasts

'Matthew Arnold and "Culture"', BBC Third Programme, January 1957.
'*Lady Chatterley's Lover*', BBC Third Programme, November 1960.
'The Victorian Social Critics', BBC, Open University, September 1971.
'Hardy's Novels', BBC, Open University, September 1981.

Tapes

For Ealing Tapes:
The Mayor of Casterbridge (with Michael Irwin, Judi Dench, Michael Williams).
Far from the Madding Crowd (with Michael Irwin).
Tess of the d'Urbervilles (with Michael Irwin).
Poems: Thomas Hardy (with Michael Irwin).
Poems: John Keats (with Michael Irwin).
Poems: T. S. Eliot (with Robert Kiely).
Lord of the Flies (with Hubert Richards, Damian Lundy).
For Audio Learning:
The Mayor of Casterbridge (with Michael Irwin).
Hardy and the Past (with Michael Irwin).
For Sussex Tapes:
Approaches to the 20th Century Novel: D. H. Lawrence's 'Odour of Crysanthemums'; James Joyce's 'The Dead' (with Mark Kinkead-Weekes).
Hardy (with David Lodge).
Graham Greene (with David Lodge).

Index

Adams, Henry, 7
Adorno, T. W., 33, 44–6
Amis, Kingsley: 155–66; *Jake's Thing*, 163–4; *Lucky Jim*, 156–65; *Take a Girl Like You*, 164
Amis, Martin: 165; *London Fields*, 165; *Money*, 185
Ariosto, Ludovico: *Orlando Furioso*, 187
Arnold, Matthew: 27–9, 35–6, 42, 47–64, 236, 241, 248, 249; *Culture and Anarchy*, 110; 'Empedocles on Etna', 52, 55; *Friendship's Garland*, 62, 63; 'Religious Isolation. To the Same Friend', 54; 'Self-Dependence', 53; 'Sohrab and Rustum', 55; 'The Strayed Reveller', 52, 53; 'The World and the Quietist', 54; 'To a Republican Friend, 1848', 55
Auden, W. H., 22

Ballantyne, R. M.: *The Coral Island*, 164
Barthes, Roland, 18, 216, 217, 234
Baudelaire, Charles, 229
Beckett, Samuel: 167, 168; *Endgame*, 171, 174–5, 180; *Waiting for Godot*, 167, 168, 171
Bellini, Giovanni, 151
Benjamin, Walter, 19, 40–1
Bennett, Arnold, 12, 14, 195
Bhagavad-Gita, 54
Blast, 7, 20
Bradbury, Malcolm: *The History Man*, 160
Brontë, Charlotte: *Villette*, 105; *The Professor*, 105
Browning, Elizabeth: 56; 'Aurora Leigh', 56

Camus, Albert: 225; *L'Etranger*, 225; *La Chute*, 225
Carlyle, Thomas, 48, 50
Cézanne, Paul, 227
Clough, Arthur Hugh: 47–64; 'The Bothie of Tober-na-Vuolich', 51, 52, 58
Coleridge, Samuel: 29, 86; 'Dejection: An Ode', 86
Conrad, Joseph: 6, 62, 121–36, 251; *Heart of Darkness*, 124; *The Inheritors*, 8; *Nostromo*, 121–36; *Romance*, 8; *The Secret Agent*, 109, 112; *Under Western Eyes*, 12
Crivelli, 151

Dante: 61; 'Inferno', 61
Darwin, Charles: *The Origin of Species*, 62
Defoe, Daniel, 189
Dickens, Charles: 109, 245; *Bleak House*, 106
Disraeli, Benjamin: *Coningsby*, 106
Donne, John, 82, 210, 211
Dostoevsky, Fyodor: 221, 223; *The Idiot*, 144
Douglas, Norman, 12

Eliot, George: 82, 93; *Daniel Deronda*, 191; *Middlemarch*, 137, 190; *Romola*, 105; *Scenes of Clerical Life*, 191
Eliot, T. S.: 5, 6, 20, 35–8, 180, 236, 248, 249; 'The Love Song of J. Alfred Prufrock', 38, 173–4; *Prufrock and other Verse*, 5; 'The Waste Land', 5, 20, 56
English Review, The, 9–14
Essays and Reviews, 62

Fielding, Henry: 185, 190, 195; *Amelia*, 105; *The History of Tom Jones*, 190; *Joseph Andrews*, 185, 190
Firdusi, Abdul: 55; *Shah Nama*, 55
Flaubert, Gustave, 103, 218–21, 226, 228
Ford, Ford Madox: 1–26; *Fifth Queen*, 9; *The Good Soldier*, 3, 14, 15, 16, 21; *It Was the Nightingale*, 21, 22; *Joseph Conrad: A Personal Rembrance*, 9; *Last Post*, 21; *A Man Could Stand Up*, 21; *No More Parades*, 21; *Parade's End*, 10, 19, 21, 22, 24; *Return to Yesterday*, 11; *Some Do Not...*, 21; *Thus to Revisit* 5, 10
Forster, E. M.: 12; *Howard's End*, 10; *A Passage to India*, 5
Fowles, John: 163; *The Aristos*, 165; *The Magus*, 163
Froude, James Anthony, 57

Galsworthy, John, 12
Gaskell, Elizabeth: *Cranford*, 204; *North and South*, 106

256

INDEX

Girard, René, 216–35
Gissing, George: *Demos*, 106; *The Nether World*, 106
Goethe, Johann, 50, 231
Golding, William: 155; *Lord of the Flies*, 164
Greene, Graham, 157, 246
Gregor, Ian, 1, 40, 81, 139, 145, 147, 148, 149, 152, 163, 236–55

H.D., 12, 232–4
Hardy, Thomas: 10, 12, 82–102, 137–54, 195, 246, 249, 253–5; *Jude the Obscure*, 144; *A Pair of Blue Eyes*, 105; *The Return of the Native*, 96, 138, 149–51; *Tess of the d'Urbervilles*, 144–52; *Wessex Poems*, 93; 'After A Romantic Day', 99; 'Afterwards', 95–7, 212–13; 'Ah, Are You Digging On My Grave?', 89; 'At A Seaside Town in 1869', 82–5, 87; 'An August Midnight', 90–1; 'Before And After Summer', 100–1; 'Birds at Winter Nightfall', 92; 'Castle Boterel', 99; 'The Darkling Thrush', 92–3; 'The Division', 100; 'The Haunter', 97–9; 'The House of Silence', 94–5; 'The Impercipient', 93; 'In Her Precincts', 100; 'Lyonesse', 99; 'Overlooking the River Stour', 86, 100; 'A Poet', 95; 'Proud Songsters', 95; 'Self-Unconscious', 85–8, 89, 99; 'The Self-Unseeing', 88–9; 'Shelley's Skylark', 91–2; 'A Sunday Morning Tragedy', 10; 'A Sign-Seeker', 93–4; 'Transformations', 95
Hartley, L. P., 157
Herbert, George, 82, 93
Homer: *The Iliad*, 56
Hopkins, Gerard Manley: 205–7, 211–12; 'Duns Scotus's Oxford', 205
Hulme, T. E., 6

Jackson, H: *The Eighteen Nineties*, 2
James, Henry: 4, 6, 12, 30, 35, 41–4, 82, 103–120, 137–8; *The Ambassadors*, 105; *The Bostonians*, 106, 107, 111; *The Golden Bowl*, 43, 103, 105, 106; *Hawthorne*, 111; 'The Next Time', 30; *The Portrait of a Lady*, 43, 103, 105, 106; *The Princess Casamassima*, 103, 104–19; *Roderick Hudson*, 103, 106; *What Maisie Knew*, 19; *The Wings of a Dove* 43, 103, 105, 106
Jonson, Ben: *The Magnetic Lady*, 242
Joyce, James: 6, 21, 146, 185, 190–2; *Dubliners*, 191; *Finnegans Wake*, 24, 191, 192; *A Portrait of the Artist as a Young Man*, 31, 146, 191; *Ulysses*, 5, 191, 192

Kafka, Franz: *The Trial*, 5
Keats, John, 229
Kermode, Frank: 12, 15, 18, 241–2; *Essays on fiction: 1971–1982*, 15

Kierkegaard, Søren, 33, 34

Lawrence, D. H.: 4, 5, 6, 12, 13, 82, 86, 137–54, 249; *Fantasia of the Unconscious*, 138; *Lady Chatterley's Lover*, 5; *Psychoanalysis and the Unconscious*, 138; *Twilight in Italy*, 138, 152; *The White Peacock*, 13
Lewis, Percy Wyndham: 5, 6–8, 13, 20; *Blasting and Bombardiering*, 7
Lodge, David: 148, 165, 185–202; *Changing Places*, 188, 196, 197; *Ginger, You're Barmy*, 201; *How Far Can You Go?*, 245; *Nice Work*, 197, 198; *Small World*, 185–202

Mallarmé, Stephane, 144
Malory, Thomas, 189
Mann, Thomas: 39, 40; *The Magic Mountain*, 5
Marcuse, Herbert, 44
Marinetti, 7
Marx, Karl: *Das Kapital*, 62
Maupassant, Guy de, 103
Melville, Robert, 142
Melville, Herman: *The Confidence-Man*, 105
Milton, John: *Paradise Lost*, 149
Mozart: *The Marriage of Figaro*, 45
Murdoch, Iris: 155–66; *The Black Prince*, 162, 164; *The Philosopher's Pupil*, 164; *Under the Net*, 156–62

Nietzsche, Friedrich, 32–3, 39, 40
North American Review, 54

Osborne, John, 168

Pater, Walter: 27–46, 217, 229, 230–3; *Studies in the History of the Renaissance*, 27, 28; 'The Chant of the Celestial Sailors, 231
Picasso, Pablo: 9; *Les Demoiselles d'Avignon*, 9
Pinter, Harold: 167–84; *The Birthday Party*, 172, 181, 194; *The Caretaker*, 167–73, 179, 180, 183; *The Dumb Waiter* 181; *The Hothouse*, 181; *Landscape*, 167; *No Man's Land*, 167, 171–83; *Old Times*, 167, 180; *One for the Road*, 181; *Silence*, 167
Plato, 203
Pope, Alexander, 210
Pound, Ezra: 4, 5, 6, 7, 8, 11, 12, 13, 14, 20, 21, 232; *Cantos*, 216; *Hugh Selwyn Mauberley*, 5, 20
Powell, Anthony, 157
Proust, Marcel: 21, 22, 89, 180, 221–8, 230, 250; *A la recherche du temps perdu*, 5, 167, 226, 227; *Jean Santeuil*, 226

Ransom, John Crowe, 203, 208
Rembrandt, 147, 150
Richardson, Samuel, 189, 190

INDEX

Rimbaud, Arthur: 'Le loup criait', 214
Ruskin, John: 27, 137, 138, 143; *Modern Painters*, 137

Sartre, Jean-Paul: 218–23, 226; *The Family Idiot*, 219
Schiller, Johann, 216
Scott, Sir Walter: *The Heart of Midlothian*, 190
Sellar, William Young, 57, 58
Shakespeare, William, 29, 187
Shaw, George Bernard, 6, 12
Shelley, Percy Bysshe, 91–2, 229
Smith, Alexander: 54; 'Life Drama', 54
Spencer, Herbert, 150
Spenser, Edmund: 29; *The Faerie Queen*, 187
Stendhal, 221, 224
Stevenson, Robert Louis: *The Strange Case of Dr Jekyll and Mr Hyde*, 85
Swinburne, Algernon Charles: 229, 230; *Atalanta in Calydon*, 230; 'Sonnet', 234; 'The Triumph of Time', 230

Tennyson, Alfred, Lord: 204–6; 'The Eagle', 204, 211; 'Enoch Arden', 205; 'Locksley Hall', 205; 'The Lotos-Eaters', 205, 211
Thackeray, William Makepeace: 249; *Vanity Fair*, 190
Tolstoi, Leo: 12

Transatlantic Review, 21
Turgenev, Ivan Sergeevich: *Virgin Soil*, 109
Turner, Joseph Mallord William, 138–54

Valéry, Paul, 209

Waugh, Evelyn: 24, 157; *Brideshead Revisited*, 163; *Sword of Honour*, 24
Wells, H. G.: 41; *The New Machiavelli*, 12; *Tono-Bungay*, 12, 106
Wesker, Arnold, 168
Wilde, Oscar: 27–46, 65–81, 251; *The Ballad of Reading Gaol*, 66; *An Ideal Husband*, 72; *The Importance of Being Earnest*, 65–7, 69, 74–80; *Lady Windermere's Fan*, 69; *The Picture of Dorian Gray*, 28, 85; *The Soul of Man*, 68–9, 70, 73, 80, 81; *A Woman of No Importance*, 66, 69
Woolf, Virginia, 9, 249
Wordsworth, William: 36, 49–51, 203–4, 206–8; 'An Evening Walk', 206; 'Peele Castle', 143; 'Phantom of Delight', 61; 'The Prelude', 50; 'Tintern Abbey', 49

Yeats, W. B.: 6, 29, 31–2, 36, 37, 38, 39
The Yellow Book, 104

Zola, Emile, 103